SUSTAINABILITY FOR
THE REST OF US

Sustainability for the Rest of Us

Your No-Bullshit, Five-Point Plan for Saving the Planet

JOHN PABON

Usually, books have a dedication in the front. Screw that. This book is dedicated to you, the reader, because you've picked this up and taken the step of saving our planet. Thank you for caring enough about our shared future to want to do something constructive to make it a better one for us all. There's a stiff drink waiting for you when you're done reading!

CONTENTS

| i |

Your Survival Guide for the Anthropocene

To most of you, the words within this book are going to seem like the ramblings of a mad man.

And you know what? I *am* mad!

I'm mad we've let it come to this.

Honestly. Do you ever feel that the world has gone completely insane?

No matter where you look, it seems like humanity is on an inevitable collision course, a very rapid path towards becoming completely obsolete.

Behind door number one is the rise of hyper-nationalism, unseen since the Second World War. Instead of reaching across borders to form a more global society, countries are starting to close themselves off from the rest of the world. Xenophobia and a sense of "us versus them" are now driving political discourse in many places. Some scholars point to a backlash against globalization as the reason for this rise.[1] In more developed, western nations like the United States, France, the UK, and Italy, we are seeing extremist parties—with related political views and proposed policies—rear their ugly heads. Bitter rivalries between states, such as those of India and Pakistan, Iran and Saudi Arabia, or the Koreas threaten stability in those regions. A growing global dominance by China is fueling a sense of pride among the populous and contributing to rising nationalist fervor there. In the background, as it has been since 1945, is the threat of nuclear annihilation. Whereas we once thought this danger would come at the hands of embattled superpowers, it's not certain in our current times just who might be in a position to press the proverbial red button.

Open door number two and you'll find greed, corruption, and covert lawlessness by the privileged and ultra-wealthy members of society. It doesn't matter which country you come from, the story's the same. The more money you have, the more power you wield. For those at the top of the pyramid, cash is king. They seem to be able to buy their way out of any problem with no more than a slap on the wrist. Sure, this behavior's been the same since the beginning of time. In today's democratized society, though, you'd assume it to be a relic of the past. The terrible case against billionaire Jeffrey Epstein is a great example of how far wealth and corruption can stretch.[2] Heinous allegations of pedophilia and sex trafficking were met with a *well that's how those guys get around* attitude. A sickening abuse of power, but unfortunately par for the course.

Next, you peer hesitantly at door number three. After seeing the other two, are you sure you want to open it?

Okay, here goes.

Contestants choosing door number three have won themselves a planet almost devoid of life, complete with acidic oceans, poisoned air, and probably countless cockroaches ready to take their rightful place at the top of the food chain. You won't need to bring a map with you to this planet; everything's changed. The places you used to put on your bucket list are probably now sitting underwater: New York, Shanghai, Rio. If you're lucky, you can hire a boat tour to take you around the spire of the old Empire State Building, but I hear it gets busy this time of year. Emaciated, disease-ridden beings might greet you along the way. Don't worry! Catching the once-eradicated ailments afflicting these folks, things like smallpox, polio, and measles, is a step up from getting caught in some of the wild weather the planet's been having. We long for the days where a category 23 hurricane was the worst it got.

Yet while all this may seem like a stretch, I'd guess that the scientific community would back up a good part of the story. From human-made climate change to widespread extinction, worsening severe weather patterns to the reemergence of once eradicated diseases, we've entered an era that will certainly be one for the record books. What's worse is that we're wholly unprepared to deal with it all. Just look at the current Covid-19 pandemic and how bungled responses have been. Right now, it's not looking like students of the future—in their cute little spacesuits and shiny helmets—are going to have a very good impression of us today. To paraphrase a line from one of my favorite movies, it's like we're taking crazy pills here.[3]

Ironically, just a few years ago, things seemed so much more hopeful.

Early one April morning on the outskirts of Paris, we find ourselves inside a beautiful white marquee. Hundreds of people clad in bespoke suits and colorful pashminas are celebrating like its New Year's Eve. Why? They're hailing the passage of the 2015 Paris Accord, history's most ambitious attempt at curbing climate change and the destruction of planet Earth.[4] For months in the lead up to this meeting of minds, talking heads the world over were hailing this as the critical moment where humankind would wrest back control of our future from the hands of environmental degradation, corporate pollution, and global ambivalence. We put so much hope into what this successful Paris meeting would mean. For many, it was our last chance to try and make things right.

The international community *did* come together to make things right. Those delegates had great reason to celebrate, too. In all my time working at the United Nations, it was a rare day when you had consensus on much of anything. A simple majority vote was hard enough to get. At the Paris meeting, you not only had a majority of countries voting in favor of the Agreement but also significant compromise. Through negotiation, hard work, and perhaps even enhanced by a magical alignment of the stars, delegates from 195 countries reached a consensus. What's more, it signaled a clear agreement among all governments towards the importance of climate change and an urgent need to do things differently. It was a massive leap of faith for many nations, especially those in the developing world. In the end, collective humanity won out over individual national interests. It was a rare decisive victory for the United Nations and Earth-loving humans alike.

Fast forward to today and I bet those delegates aren't celebrating anymore.

In such a short space of time, we've seen the legitimacy of the Paris Accord called into question by a massive shift not in the Earth's climate but the *geopolitical* climate. As previously noted, the rise of nationalism in Europe, Asia, Australia, and the United States is calling into question the long-held direction of globalization. Countries are now pulling out of the Accord, the most notable being the US under President Trump. Others, like Brazil, led by President Bolsinaro, are set to follow suit. This was unthinkable only a few years ago when delegates lauded their monumental win. In Australia, a land we often associate with being one of the greenest on Earth, loosened governmental policies now threaten endangered species, local communities, and even the Great Barrier Reef. What's worse, accounting firm PriceWaterhouse Coopers has found zero countries are doing enough to meet their targets as outlined in the Paris Accord.[5] This means that although delegates that night in Paris were happy with what the Agreement set out to achieve, convincing the rank and file back home to take action was proving much harder to accomplish.

Even with a majority of countries still aligned with our shared responsibility for a more sustainable future, it doesn't seem like it's enough. The performance of those people at the highest levels of society, who are entrusted with taking care of us and future generations, would get them fired from any other job. They've failed us, and it's not because they didn't have the vision. They've failed us because they didn't dare to turn their vision into reality. The Paris Agreement, the last great hope for saving humanity from environmental destruction, now seems to be going up in smoke.

And this is just the tip of the iceberg. We're exposed to so many negative messages in any given day that it's no wonder many have lost hope for a brighter future. Research in *The Journal of Applied Public Economics* found this is the first generation in human history where children are worse off than their parents.[6] Pretty startling stuff, which is even more jarring when you look holistically at our place in the human story.

If you're reading this book, it could be assumed that you are part of a society that is by far the wealthiest, most learned, and most interconnected in human history.

A little over one hundred years ago, immigrants from all over Europe crowded ships bound for New York Harbor. All were fleeing different things—war, famine, persecution—but the commonality among them all was hope for a brighter future. The "new world," with streets lined with gold, would offer opportunities beyond their wildest dreams. While in transit, these immigrants heard stories of the great families of American history undergoing the same dangerous journey: the Carnegies, Rockefellers, and Morgans. These families were also immigrants who went from rags to riches in the most American way possible. Although these people, and others like them, received most of the headlines, they were far from the norm in the US at the time. In 1910, a decade after the rapid economic growth of the Gilded Age, the average American worker could expect to bring home about $750 per year. Adjusted for inflation, this would equal a little over $20,000 today.[7] Remember, though, most immigrants weren't making nearly this much. Those immigrants, if they were able to make it past inspection on Ellis Island, would probably end up in crowded, rat-infested tenements in the Lower East Side. They were likely to spend their days in a hot, cramped, and dangerous warehouse, operating machines that could quickly turn into torture devices for misplaced limbs. If they did injure themselves, it was more than likely to be game over. They could attempt to rely on the charity of others, yet given how stretched most budgets were during this era, it was probably the end of their American dream.

However, their modern-day decedents now pay top dollar for the same apartments (of course, they've been gentrified to include a boutique café downstairs, rooftop swimming pool, and floor-to-ceiling windows with exposure to great natural light). If they go to an actual work site at all, it's highly likely to be an open-plan office with ergonomic chairs. They pop downstairs for lunch, hammer through a few more e-mails, and head home before the sun goes down. These folks are likely to earn four times more than their counterparts did in early 1900s New York, with an exponentially lower risk of losing an arm to the grinding jaws of a machine.[8]

Seventy years ago, and much further east, two decades of war had decimated Chinese society. As caskets returned from the front, younger and younger boys had to take up arms to fill the gaps. Like many other cultures, women were left at home during times of war. Little efforts were made for education when there was war going on all around you. By the end of the Chinese Civil War, and the founding of The People's Republic in 1949, only 20 percent of people in the Middle Kingdom could read. Through policy changes and a focus on education, the Communist Party was able to raise the average literacy rate to an astonishing 97 percent of the population today. On average, 86.3 percent of humans today can read and write. While there is still a lot of improvement to be had, especially in other countries of the developing world and for women, humankind is more educated than ever before.[9]

Now, in our post-millennial culture, our social systems have been radically changed by mobile technology. In only a few decades, we've gone from having to plan nights with friends a week in advance to direct communication with them via the smartphone in our pocket. Technology has done more to change the fabric of human society than probably any other advancement we've mustered our brainpower to create. We've also achieved this in such a short period of time and continue to make exponential technological advancements every day. We hold access to more information in the palm of our hand than past kings and presidents would ever have had at their disposal. You can talk to someone on the other side of the world as if they were in the same room as you. From coastal megacities to isolated mountain villages and everywhere in between, our everyday worlds are connected to a vast resource the planet has never known. As of 2019, 53 percent of the world had access to the internet, and along with it all the information, opportunity, and advancement one can imagine.[10]

But, what do we do with all of it?

Watch cat videos.

You have to ask yourself the obvious question: if we are so much more advanced compared to our ancestors, then why have we done such a bad job of taking care of things? Sure, immigrants sitting in those New York tenements didn't get to watch hilarious videos of kids doing stupid things. But you know what? They also didn't have to worry about the Earth ending on their watch. Mao's soldiers may have had to keep guard against the Japanese, but not for rising sea levels. Even with our access to technology, we're tuning out at the exact time we should be tuning in. Why are we sticking our heads in the sand as if nothing is going on?

I'm writing these pages from a cute café in Shanghai's Former French Concession. Right now, a girl is sitting at a table opposite, angling for a perfect selfie while trying not to spill her ice cream. Phones are on display all around me, taking pictures of little tarts and baked goods. While accordion music plays on the speakers above, few can hear it with their headphones on. With a room of nearly 30 people, there are only two people actually talking to each other. The rest, including myself, are buried in some form of technology (credit to the one boy I witness reading a physical book … the future looks bright for you!). We've tuned out from each other and we've tuned out from the rest of the world. In a time where we are overburdened in our everyday lives, all most of us want is to escape to a technological safe place we can make our own.

So, then, how have we come to this impasse?

It's certainly not because we don't care. There are people all over the world doing their part to save humanity.

It's also not because we don't know. We're inundated with news from around the world twenty-four hours a day.

It's not because we can't. For goodness sake, we've put a monkey into space.

It's because we're overwhelmed, desensitized, apathetic, and scared.

Another lesser-known statistic about the modern world can help to start explaining why. Humans today consume more information in a single day than our 15th-century forbearers did their entire lifetime.[11] From vast amounts of print, billboard, and online advertisements through to news, views, and yes cute cat videos, it's nearly impossible to not be impacted by all this information. While we may assume this is now part and parcel of our modern world, I'd like you to take a second and ask your brain how it feels about all this. Just over a century separates us from the invention of electricity, yet we're now asking our brains to adapt to what would normally take millennia. We're simply not built for all this and the result is pretty clear.

Perhaps it's because we are so overwhelmed and desensitized that many have also become apathetic. Saving the planet is no longer my problem. Now, I put the burden on someone else to solve it. This is especially true in more developed countries which by and large experience the impacts of climate change far less than those in the developing world. Sure, we see maps of what we perceive to be a far-off future New York City being swallowed up by rising tides. But, what about those places we've already lost to increasing sea levels? What about large swaths of the Maldives, Bangladesh, and the Solomon Islands? We think we're doing our part by purchasing a consciously made pair of jeans, never questioning how we're able to have clothes cheaper and more abundantly than ever before. Oh, and let's not forget about trash. Do you honestly think your local landfill can take it all? Places like China, Indonesia, and India have been your dumping ground for years. Only now are they starting to fight back, forcing leaders in the west to finally come to grips with an issue punted off like a candy wrapper.

Admit it. You're scared too. When you're scared, what do you do? You stick with what you know, what's comfortable, and what's familiar. It's a new type of rat race. We perpetuate an endless cycle of similar actions to keep us from thinking about all the scary things going on around us.

Let's run through a typical morning.

You wake up to the sound of birds outside your window as the sun gently hits your face. After a quick stretch, you get up and roll out your yoga mat for a few vinyasas. Your last namaste leads into a gentle meditation session where you place your intentions forward for the universe to answer. Smiling, you head to the kitchen for a fresh cup of coffee to energize your mind before sitting down for an hour of personal creative time. The dog gently taps your leg, letting you know they need to go out for their morning walk. Gently strolling down the tree-lined streets of your town you greet each person by name and truly take the time to hear how they are. Once home, you pack your bag and hop on your bike, headed for work. There's nothing quite like the feeling of peace and calm in the morning as the wind flows through your hair. Another amazing day is upon you, one where you can truly show the world all the things you have planned.

Oh, wait. You're not an Instagram influencer? Sorry about that. Let's try again.

It's the sound of the garbage truck which wakes you a good half an hour before your alarm is set to go off. Frazzled and blurry-eyed you grab your phone to check the weather, your e-mail, social media accounts, and maybe a bit of news. That post you put up before bed didn't get half as many likes or comments you wanted it to. What's more, every headline on the news sites seems to show some kind of tragedy, death, or despair. Your massive golden retriever jumps on top of your stomach, a sure sign he's likely peed somewhere in the house overnight. You wanted to get some stretching in this morning, but you put it off until tomorrow. A quick jog around the block with the dog and you're in the shower, your morning schedule already running late. You toss on whatever's not wrinkled, race to the subway, miss the train, and wait for the next one. By then the platform is heavily crowded with an army of mobile phone zombies, ignorant of your very existence. After an arduous journey of pushing, prodding, and stepping on toes you reach your final stop. It's another ten-minute walk to work, and you end up sneaking in just before the boss gets there. Another morning whizzes by, most of it on autopilot, and all of it spent two steps behind.

Both are pretty extreme examples of what a typical morning can entail. I'd hope most of you reading this fall somewhere in the middle. It's highly probable that you do not have the life of an influencer, nor are you so disorganized. Yet even though you may be somewhere in between, this still isn't particularly great, is it? You might have time to work out or meditate in the morning a couple of times a week. Perhaps you do have a job that lets you make your chosen contribution to the world. If you're lucky, your dog never pees inside. Regardless, how often do you actually take the time to mindfully go about your day? This isn't a metaphysical book about mindfulness, of course, but it's an important question nonetheless. You can only go about on autopilot because you instinctively know your routine. You've become trapped in the dreaded rat race.

Now if that includes trying to do your part to save the planet, excellent!

But, does it?

If you're on autopilot all the time, there's very little opportunity to inject new actions into that routine. Life becomes just an endurance challenge to try and make it from task to task. Add into that this very human instinct to keep up with the proverbial Jones's (have you ever wondered who they actually are?) and those things the most distant from you become those you care about the least. With the hustle and bustle of daily life—work, family, that all-important cocktail hour with colleagues—there's little time left to care too much about anything else.

And that's where we return to the purpose of our story…saving the planet.

It all seems so overwhelming, doesn't it? The fate of the planet, its nearly 10 billion people, not to mention countless other non-human beings, and your responsibility for it. Your singular action is what is going to make the difference between leaving a world for our children to live and play in or the inevitable hellscape where they have to hide underground. I'm going to tell you right here and right now: what you do won't make a bit of difference in the long run. It might make you feel good today, or save a turtle tomorrow, but this idea that you can be the change you want to see in this world is nonsense.

I'm also here to tell you, right here and right now: even though your individual actions will make little difference, humankind is much stronger when we work together. That's the step change I hope this book leaves you with. It's time to take a more sensible view of saving the planet, rather than this radical view of individualized progress propagated for decades. This view will force you to place a critical eye on the things you've held as sacred for so long. It will also require a change to the saints and idols we've come to admire. In short, to save the planet we need a drastically different, no-bullshit approach because as the adage goes, to do the same thing over and over expecting a different result is the definition of insanity.

Right now, we *are* all insane. Every. Single. One. of us.

"But, John, I'm already on the front lines of climate change." Great, but there's more to saving the planet than keeping our temperatures stable.

"Hey. I give my money to some of the best charities there are." Awesome, and keep it up. I'm here to tell you, though, there's a better way to support these groups.

"Ugh. Not another book talking about how we're all doomed. I've heard it all before." I highly doubt you've heard my take on things which, you may say, is a little unorthodox. Some of the material in this book is putting me at risk of becoming a pariah, but obviously our status quo just isn't working.

With this book, I hope to change all of this insanity. I'll discuss how we've come to this point in our shared human history. I'll also show you real-world, contemporary examples demonstrating the good, the bad, and the ugly of saving the planet. You'll get a fair dose of something I particularly enjoy doing: naming and shaming those responsible for the mess we're in today. People have become well too scared of offending, and that's a bad thing. If we keep pussyfooting around things and mollycoddling those who would aim to destroy us all, we're not going to get anywhere useful. This book will also arm you with some of the key ways you can truly make a difference. I mean... a real difference. Not a recycle-your-cans difference. A holy-shit-I've-saved-the-world difference.

In that respect, I've not produced a book with a million different tips and tricks, most of which you're probably not likely to do. I've opted instead for a concise, five-point plan to help make a better future. Everyone, regardless of how committed you are to the cause, will be doing a whole lot of good just by putting these points into practice as part of your everyday lifestyle. Some are conceptual, like having a full understanding of what sustainability is all about. Others are practical, like learning how to prioritize the precious time, resources, and talent you give. All are critical if we want to stop being so apathetic, get off our lazy asses, and solve this pesky issue of saving the world.

Before we go any further, a quick note on terminology to keep us all on the same page. If you haven't realized already, there are a lot of terms used when talking about saving the world. For example, sustainability is typically the umbrella term for anything related to saving the world or humanity. That could include environmental-ism, human rights, worker rights, supply chain, governance, trans-parency, to name a few. Basically, anything good will probably be rolled up into "sustainability" somehow. Environmentalism and ecology usually deal specifically with the Earth and its natural re-sources such as trees, water, and air. Corporate social responsibility (CSR), has to do with a company's actions concerning sustainabil-ity. The public sector is the government. The private sector is the corporate world. Non-governmental organizations (NGOs), non-profit organizations (NPOs), and government-organized non-gov-ernmental organizations (GONGOs) (phew) are all organizations you'd probably best associate with charities. I'll do my best to keep the jargon to a minimum and make sure you can figure things out by context. I mean, this isn't Thoreau. If you're still confused, there's always Google (which you're probably using right now to figure out who Thoreau is).

So, how about a little preview of what's to come? In the next chapter, The Sustainability Industrial Complex, I explain some of the history, actors, and ideas that have influenced modern-day sus-tainability. The goal is to give you a solid foundation for, and shared understanding of, points in the rest of the book. Then, we move into your no-bullshit, five-point plan. Point #1, Know What You're Talking About, explores a lot of the terminology and concepts as-sociated with sustainability. It also dispels the myths we often hold so dear. Point #2, You Can Do Anything (But You Can't Do Every-thing), encourages you to focus your time and energy when it comes to saving the Earth. Don't Be a Dick, point #3, talks about how to take back control from those energy vampires doing the world a disservice. In point #4 we discuss pragmatic altruism, the most important piece of this entire book. As you'll hear me say over and over, passion without pragmatism is just complaining. Finally, point #5 will serve as the swift kick in the ass you need to get up and get working.

One final note on how to read this book. As an avid reader myself, I know there are a million different ways people digest information. That's why I've tried to create something that each reader, no matter what their style, can become engrossed in. You can read it from front to back. You can read each chapter independently in whatever order you want. You can read one chapter and none of the others. As long as you don't start with dnE ehT and continue to read each letter backward, things should make sense.

Now, let's get to work.

| ii |

The Sustainability Industrial Complex

B efore trying to make sense of what action we need to take in helping save the planet, it's important we understand just how we've arrived here in the first place. I have mentioned the apathy people in today's society feel about any number of issues, not least around sustainability and the environment. We got here because we're inundated with information from the second we open our eyes in the morning to the final moment we close them at night. Instead of tuning in, we're all suffering from burnout and therefore tune out.

The work of saving the world is no different. For years we've been trying to get people to take action, but our message is increasingly falling on deaf ears. Sure, some are with us. But there are plenty of folks out there who don't exactly embrace the cause. You've got your polluting factories, meat-eating carnivores, cosmetic companies who test on animals. Then there are the lobbying groups, chief executives, and politicians who consistently place profit over planet. Let's not forget countries like China, India, and the United States, which combined make up nearly 50 percent of all greenhouse gas emissions.[1] From jets spewing fuel all through the atmosphere, to oil tankers spilling their contents into the oceans, to those pesky climbers leaving their shit behind (literally) while summitting Everest, everyone and everything seems to be going in the opposite direction of progress. The question is, why?

While I could point out any number of culprits, I know exactly where to start.

I blame the environmentalists.

How the Greenies Have Ruined Everything

I told you some sacred views about saving the planet were going to be challenged, didn't I? Well, I might as well rip the bandage off right away, then, with the patron saint of the environmental movement. Let's take a look at the proverbial greenie.

You know the type.

Go to any farmer's market or summer festival and they'll be there. You'll likely smell them before they come fully into view. Sliding towards you in their khaki green three-quarter pants, filthy toes sticking out from their sandals, they look like they just woke up from a forty-year slumber. Perhaps they have a wrist full of beads, a bindi on their forehead, or a hula hoop around their waist (be careful as they're known to fling fire around when the setting's right). You'll notice the tell-tale sign of their tribe, dreadlocks. On a Rastafarian these are sacred, representative of adherence to ancient Biblical command.[2] On a greenie, these could be viewed as a major biohazard. For those of you who don't know, there's only one real way to get that dark, matted look from your long strands of hair: you don't wash it. Well, at least not with anything that's going to do any good. So, the next time you see someone with big dreads, just remember how it got that way.

There's an old saying: you never get a second chance to make a first impression. When it comes to finding a poster child for a movement, we couldn't have done worse than a greenie.

That's because, except for a small segment of the population, your quintessential environmentalist isn't relatable enough to entice supporters or followers. And, it shows. Since the start of the environmental movement some fifty years ago, people have generally ostracized greenies from mainstream society. They're referred to by all manner of defamatory names and seen through a very particular lens: lazy, dirty, and weird. Think about that for a second. Who in their right mind would want to be associated with that? Except for the very committed, few would willingly set themselves so far outside societal norms. We're all altruists and bleeding hearts when we're young. But, how is a fifty-year-old in tattered jeans supposed to make a living?

While what they do, day in and day out, is worthy of high praise, it isn't very practical from a marketing perspective. By forming what could be seen as an exclusive (and smelly) cliché, they've turned environmentalism into something only societal fringe-dwellers care about. Instead of placing environmentalism front and center as part of international dialogue, the greenies have continued to push issues like climate change, animal welfare, and human rights further and further out of the light. They seem to almost relish their exclusivity, as if it's a badge of honor to be part of a group seen by many as a nuisance. The further they push themselves away, the harder it is to bring supporters into the fold.

But their unconventional appearance isn't the only reason greenies have ruined everything.

Take a look at their tactics.

For being a group promoting peace and harmony among all the Earth's creatures, they sure are a violent bunch. Greenpeace, probably the most well-known environmental group the world over, is notorious for being less than civil with their disobedience. Violent disturbances of the peace are pretty much their strategic go-to. They've intentionally rammed Japanese whaling ships, hijacked Russian oil rigs, and damaged UNESCO heritage sites in the name of protecting the environment.[3] The modern-day Extinction Rebellion, with their work in shutting down cities around the world, is another example of extremist environmentalism. In the end, all this has done for these groups has been to get them into trouble with the law. So now, not only are those pesky environmentalist people framed largely as weirdos, they're also criminals to boot.

I can hear you already, screaming yourself hoarse into the pages of this book. But John! How are we going to get people to listen if we don't make a bunch of noise? Fair point. To disrupt, you've got to be disruptive. Apple wasn't Apple until they turned computers into works of art. Tesla wasn't Tesla until they showed us just how far electric energy could change our lives. Netflix, by personalizing the movie-watching experience, brought the traditional entertainment industry to its knees. All of these companies, and countless others, disrupted their industries by taking a non-conventional look at "this is how we've always done things" behavior.

However, there are certainly more productive ways to disrupt. Getting one's message across doesn't require attacking others, ruining property, or getting yourself locked up behind bars. We've got to be more creative than that. Unfortunately, the image of the angry environmentalist is already engrained in the publics' psyche. It's too late to change what has been seared into peoples' minds about those saving the planet. That's why we need a reset on what it means to be an altruist, a do-gooder, a modern-day greenie, which I'll delve into later in the book.

One final way greenies have really messed things up for us, aside from their appearance and tactics, is in their lack of social awareness and realism. While they aren't the only ones guilty of this cardinal sin (I'm looking at you, too, academics), greenies have been the paramount contributors to an absolutely unattainable world vision.

To prove this, let's do a little experiment.

I'm going to guess since you spent your hard-earned money on this book you do care a bit (hopefully more than a bit) about the Earth, the future of humanity, or even the dog in that commercial with the sad background music. Now, I don't care where you're reading this. Raise your hand high up in the air if you'd be willing to give up your smartphone.

My guess is your hand is still down.

Ok. Shoot that arm into the sky if you could live without your car.

Maybe a few of you might be looking silly right now with your arm up in a crowd, especially if you live in a place with a good public transit system.

How about air travel? Would you forego that bucket list destination you've been saving for?

Now, if you're like most people you may have considered putting your hand up. But in all reality, you didn't did you?

Wait … one last one.

Put your hand up if you'd be willing to go off the grid.

Wow! I felt that all the way over here. It's almost like you shoved your hand deep inside your pocket to make sure nobody else could grab it. There's no way in hell you'd be caught dead trying to go off the grid, amirite? We're at the height of human civilization, with all the technology and modern conveniences that come with being lucky enough to live today. Throwing all of that away to live as a subsistence farmer on a mountain top—no cell phone, running water, or electricity—seems like one of the most foolish ideas ever. Right?

Well, this is the future true greenies would have for you if they got their way. Sure, the upside of this scenario is that we have the opportunity to restore the Earth to its former glory. The truth, though, is that it just isn't realistic. Going off the grid means upending everything we've created over the past two centuries. Some of you are probably saying this is what must be done, regardless of how hard it might be. Think logically. Are the majority of people really going to go so far and work so hard? Of course not.

Imagine the implications of that proposal. All private-sector corporations would have to essentially shut down (or become farming cooperatives if they didn't want to shutter their doors). People would have to be self-sustaining: building their own homes; making their own food; bartering if they could not. Life expectancy would drop steeply as we would no longer produce modern medicines. Global connectivity would be a thing of the past.

If this is the goal, greenies are going to be constantly disappointed because it just ain't happening.

Even if this example is a bit extreme, and maybe they aren't all coming for your smartphones, it doesn't matter. That's because public perception may not match up with the truth. After their unorthodox appearance and violent tactics, who knows what this exclusive group has in mind? Instead of digging into the details, many would simply lump all of us altruists into the same bunch.

Greenies have set the foundation for the modern movement to save the planet. Yet, through their appearance, antics, and lack of pragmatism in their approaches, we have come to discount all the work they do and ostracize them from the rest of us. This then translates into how people view those who work towards saving the planet: we're an indecipherable, unrelatable, exclusive rag-tag operation that gets angry when we don't get our way. No wonder so few people want to sign up to support. The poster children for the movement do very little to resonate with, or be relatable to, most people. Until recently, most saw being green as some dirty little secret you had to keep to yourself. It was almost as if supporting a sustainable planet was embarrassing. Why? Because the people out and proud about it definitely should have been on the radio rather than television. They're an embarrassment that's forced sustainability into the shadows.

As you'll soon understand, this environmental stereotype permeated throughout the critical formational years of environmentalism and took it off in a direction nobody intended. Many are still grappling with this misdirection today, which can help explain why society is in the mess it's in.

How We've Really Messed Up Sustainability

Things could have been so different. I'm convinced we wouldn't even need to be having these in-depth discussions, conferences, and books about saving the planet because we already would have been well on our way. We would certainly not have had to grapple with issues like whether we were headed for a 2-degree or 4-degree rise in global temperatures. But, let's be very clear here. That ship's sailed. Instead of spending our time building out a future fit for all, we've wasted over three decades continuing to do things that don't make a bit of difference. We've totally screwed up sustainability, and refuse to acknowledge the overt reasons why. What's worse, since many do not recognize the mistakes being made it's difficult to change the trajectory in a more positive way.

As far as I see it, we've messed up the idea of sustainability in two major ways. Greenies are primarily responsible for setting the tone, but perpetuating these mistakes is on all of us.

When greenies started to do their work in the mid-1970s they had first-mover advantage. For readers with a background in business, that's a very advantageous position to be in. Nobody else was doing all that much to save the world, so the environmentalists stepped in and filled the void. As with any good business venture, environmental activists started to carve out their niche. It wasn't long before they procreated and filled the Earth. They held a monopoly on doing good.

In the beginning, things were going great for environmentalists and their causes. This period of the 1970s saw the passage of regulations catalyzing environmental protection in many parts of the world. These regulations cleaned up waterways, stopped us from littering as much, and made recycling a household practice. Animals that were once at risk for extinction now grew in numbers. We identified a problem with aerosol sprays and the damage they were doing to the precious ozone layer. Then, we solved the problem. All of this was thanks to those early environmental pioneers.

Because they were doing so much, other critical actors started to believe that they didn't need to do anything at all. Governments, particularly those in developed countries, began to rely entirely on environmental, non-governmental, and charity groups to do their work for them. This is actually supposed to be the job of the government. With all of that extra cash, the powers that be were now able to spend even more on military toys and their own fat-cat bonuses. It seemed like the perfect solution. Of course, governments still monitored whether or not businesses were staying in line with environmental regulations. They also busied themselves passing new and complex policy rules and regulations. In reality, though, they weren't pulling nearly their fair share.

Over time, the formalization of this relationship led to unforeseen negative consequences. Take financial budgets as an example. While a lot of people think corporate or governmental budgets are projections of expected expenditure over the course of the following year, the reality is a bit different. Budgets are usually set based on historical precedence. For example, how does one put together line items for a 2020 budget? Look back at how much was spent in 2019, or 2018, or 2017. Did a certain department spend all the money allocated to them, or did they go over or under? If they went over, someone probably gets fired and the budget stays the same. However, if they underspend, then you're likely to see that line item decrease the following year. If they aren't spending the money, why should we allocate it to them?

As governments began to rely on the cause-centric world to do their work, line items for related areas started to decrease. Then the next year they decreased some more. On and on until there was little money left to be allocated to anything.

While all of this was going on, the global issues we were trying to tackle took an extreme turn. Climate change and the threat of mass human extinction were no longer problems environmentalists could handle on their own. People turned back to their governments to take care of the problems at hand. While this worked in a few places, many governments had lost capacity, resources, and willingness to help. Yet, we continued to place our hope in their hands.

We've seen time and again, however, that governments just aren't up to the challenge. Like petty schoolchildren, they hold onto ancient grudges that have no place in today's society. My favorite comes from some of the hard-headed leaders of the developing world. Many believe that the industrialization of the western world, with its grotesque consequences on the environment, gives developing countries carte blanche to do the same today. Never mind how inane and selfish this "you got yours and now I'm gonna' get mine" idea is. It fails to take account of all the positive economic impact employing modern, clean, green technology can have. These advancements can help expedite not just development, but sustainable development. By sticking to outmoded, polluting practices, these countries are essentially shooting themselves in the foot and taking us all down with them.

If you thought that was petty, just wait. Instead of focusing on solving climate change, delegates to the United Nations often fight over critical things like the placement of a comma. Talk about losing the forest for the trees! Even worse is the lack of transparency and goodwill on the part of governments just to act in good faith. If they can't even manage this, the most basic tenet of diplomacy (to "come to the table"), it's clear we can't trust governments to do their job to save us.

So, if organizations like Greenpeace don't have the ability to solve today's pressing issues, and governments lack the willingness to do so, who are we supposed to turn to for help?

This brings me to the first point on how we've messed up sustainability. Far too long we have been focusing our reliance on the public sector to do the lion's share of the work. In reality, though, we've been approaching the wrong audience. Instead of fighting and vilifying them, we should be turning to and working with the private sector to save the world.

Why?

Because the private sector—major businesses—has the capital, access, and capacity of scale governments, non-profits, and most private citizens simply do not.

Think about the private sector and its impact on our daily lives. There is nowhere you go and nothing you do as a modern consumer outside the realm of the private sector. They provide goods for you. They feed you. They employ you. And you love them for it.

Since they are part and parcel of our daily lives, private sector companies have grown to overshadow some national economies.

Business Insider ran a fun little column back in 2018 listing which companies were bigger than entire countries.[4] You had those on the smaller end of the scale, like Spotify outpacing the entire GDP of Mauritania or Netflix that of Malta. Then you had the big boys. In 2017, Apple's revenues outpaced Portugal's GDP. German automobile maker, Volkswagen, was on par with the GDP of Chile in 2016. Of course, sitting at the top of the list was Walmart, which would be the 24th largest country in the world, and 6th largest in the Eurozone, based on GDP.

If these companies, and countless others, are the size of entire nations then can't they also have just as big an impact? Given how they operate, without burdensome bureaucracy and red tape, I'd argue they could actually get more done if put to the task. Being able to get the results we want, though, takes a receptive audience. That brings me to the second way we've really been messing up sustainability. Not only have we been approaching the wrong audience, but we've also been approaching them in the wrong way.

Put yourself in the corner office for a minute. You're taking a second for yourself after a hectic morning of meetings. The office door is closed, and you've walked over to the clear glass window overlooking a beautiful park. You try and enjoy the view, but there's a nagging in your head. Those budgets aren't going to approve themselves. Behind you are a pile of papers on your desk, waiting for your signature. The red light on the phone keeps flashing, a clear sign of messages waiting for you. Your laptop makes an incessant ding, ding, ding, as more and more e-mails flood your inbox. Then, your marketing vice president comes in suddenly to add something else to your to-do list.

This time it's a new program some external consultant is recommending. They want the business to enlist volunteers to work with a local charity feeding the homeless. It's a big problem in your city, so a team of volunteers would make a big difference. The charity doesn't really have any money, though, so it'll be up to your business to front the cash and the people. To make things more difficult, volunteering has to be done during normal working hours. That means you're going to be down a hundred staff when there are so many other things to be done. Without hesitation, you kill the idea and warn your VP never to bring something like this to you again. It's a waste of company talent, time, and resources. The idea should have been vetted better before coming to you.

For too long we've approached business with an altruistic imperative for adopting sustainability. On the surface, feeding the homeless is a worthy cause and something most people would be happy to volunteer for. At a business level, though, it doesn't make much sense. That's because a business doesn't care about altruistic pursuits. What do businesses care about most? That's right: the bottom line.

Now imagine the scenario tweaked ever so slightly. The marketing vice president again comes into your office, but this time the narrative is different. An external consulting firm has asked for your business to partner with a local charity to help the homeless population in your community. The charity's asked for monetary assistance in setting up a program to provide community members with training on job search, resume writing, and interview skills. Your staff will provide the training, which is also a great opportunity to upskill them on interpersonal communication. Who knows? Maybe you'll even find a few new staff members from among the participants as well. The charity's public relations arm has also been able to garner a bit of press from this. In addition, the mayor's office will help subsidize the cost of the project as part of a city grant program.

Now, things start to make a little more sense. In the sustainability world, this is what we call strategic philanthropy: charity which not only helps populations in need but also has a direct and correlated positive impact on a business. Whereas the first scenario was what game theorists might call zero-sum, one party wins while the other gets very little, this other approach is a true win-win. The charity gets help from a cashed-up organization with lots of volunteers, while the company gets to engage important stakeholders beneficial to their business. This then becomes the basis for these programs. The feel-good stuff is an added benefit.

In order to work with the private sector, we need to speak in the language of business—the only language they understand.

Machiavelli Walks into a Bar...

Early morning in the beginning of July. The city is already steaming. Shanghai in the summertime isn't for the faint of heart. There's nothing quite like it when it comes to stifling, all-encompassing heat that rips open the pores and boils the blood. The city only gets up to about 85 or 90 degrees, not bad for a summer's day. On paper. Then you have to add to that nearly 100 percent humidity, heat bouncing off the city's miles of asphalt or coming from its millions of cars, and the near-constant cloud cover that traps all of that in. Then there are the people. Nearly 30 million people call Shanghai home, making it the most populous city on Earth. Crossing busy streets, getting in and out of the metro, and up or down endless skyscrapers without fainting takes a certain kind of finesse. I like to call it the Shanghai Walk: it's slow, methodical, with limbs held away from the torso, and likely covered in lots of baby powder.

As the city begins to wake, an army of green-vested, gray-haired volunteers take up their posts. They fan out across all parts of Shanghai reporting for duty. Their posting, though, is a most unusual place. Sure, it's the frontlines of a war that's being waged but it isn't on some bombed-out intersection or in a rubble-filled trench. No, their posting is much worse. They steady themselves for a day spent next to one of Shanghai's filthy, smelly, rodent-infested dumpsters. With all they've been through in life, you'd figure these folks would not want to be spending their golden years cleaning up trash. But, for them it's about so much more than that. It's about the future.

These volunteers are helping city residents understand Shanghai's new garbage-sorting regulations. The first of their kind on the mainland, the city government had worked hard over the preceding six months of 2019 to educate tens of millions on how to separate not just glass from plastic, but wet waste from dry, hazardous from non-lethal, and pork from chicken. No, seriously. Pork from chicken (for those of you interested, pork bones are dry waste while chicken bones are wet...I have no idea why).

Overnight, Shanghai's waste sorting went from an underground, black market industry with opaque transparency to near German levels of perfection. Until the new regulations came online, entrepreneurial individuals would take it upon themselves to help sort, separate, and recycle the city's waste. It was an industry and a big one at that. To get a sense of just how enormous this task was, you have to understand the recycling game in China.

Long before the rest of the city files into gleaming skyscrapers, a procession assembles. Their mission is driven less by civic duty and more by market demand. Although ill equipped, armed often only with the strength of their hands, people break the quiet of dawn with their rallying call. "Recycle your old fridges, old televisions, air con-di-tion-ers, and microwave ooooovvvvvvveeeeennnnnsssssss!" This pierces the gentle morning strains of birds and tai chi music. Invisible to the rest of the world, these are the scavengers keeping places like Shanghai above ground. Before formal recycling programs, like those launched in Shanghai in July 2019, this job fell to an entrepreneurial cadre able to turn people's trash into treasure.

During the frenzied peak of first-tier city development in the late 1990s and early 2000s, lumbering carts hauling Babelesque structures were common sights. Their composition—piles of metal, wood, and other "junk"—teetered back and forth. Clipping a telephone line would send the whole thing tumbling to the ground. These were mobile monuments of the human desire to advance. The lives of those at the helm are not ones of luxury. Many members of the community would consider them a nuisance. Sit on any Shanghai street corner long enough and you're likely to see one of these carts leading a parade of honking Maserati's, Lamborghinis, and BMWs. They toil from morning to night, often earning no more than $15 per day. These were the pickers, recyclers, and trash separators which made up the informal recycling sector across China.

But even informal is a bit of a misnomer. These pickers were part of a well-oiled machine that included weigh-stations, collection outposts, and consolidation centers in each city. In Shanghai, for example, plastic, paper, wood, metal, and Styrofoam waste would make their way from apartment buildings all the way through to far-off trading centers on the outskirts of town. Private companies would then take the goods and sell them on to the highest bidder, which sometimes included the Shanghai Government itself.[5]

So, preparing for and launching Shanghai's new garbage-sorting regulations wasn't going to be an easy task. It would require breaking down an entire industry while simultaneously building up previously unfamiliar knowledge and behaviors. To be successful, it was going to take much more than just a couple of fliers and the goodwill of the people. Luckily, when China wants something done, they don't do anything in half measures.

These elderly volunteers manning the bins were just one of the fail-safes to keep the program going. While they were tasked with answering questions and helping people sort, they were also making sure people did what they were supposed to. Flout the regulation and you get a ding against your national social credit score. These cute little grannies were actually vigilant monitors. Now I hear you saying, well they can't be everywhere all the time, right? You're right. So, what do you do when the monitors are taking a lunch break or afternoon nap? Lock the bins. That's right, Shanghai locked up all of its garbage bins so people could literally not throw away their rubbish except during mandated trash hours. That way the green-vested army was always there to watch, help, and report.

Anywhere else in the world and there would be a simple solution to that: dump your trash where you please. It's not like this is Japan, where there's a long history of public cleanliness. If you've ever been to a big Japanese city, like Tokyo, then you probably know what I mean. These cities have one strange thing missing from the streetscape: public trash cans. Yet, they also have another thing missing: litter. The Japanese will go as far as to put their trash inside their purses or backpacks to take home with them. The idea of littering on the side of the road is unthinkable. When you see an old lady putting a bag of dog poop in her purse, instead of leaving it behind, you know you've done something right as a society.

In China, people are still prone to throwing trash anywhere they please. At the beginning, I wasn't the most optimistic about the new program's potential for success. I assumed people would just stick to their normal behaviors, especially since there was little incentive to change. I was so wrong. I started to notice this in my residential complex, a series of twelve 30-story buildings housing at least 5,000 people. First, they came for the public bins. The can where I would throw my dog's dirty-business bags had now been removed, leaving behind a patch of dead grass. I wasn't about to throw it on the ground, so I took the extra walk to the back of the complex to throw it into one of the approved central bins.

Then, building management came for the bins on each floor. Stepping out to the designated rubbish area on my floor one evening, a sign greeted me in lieu of a trash can. All residents were requested to separate their garbage and bring it to the central trash receptacles at the back of the complex. Ugh. Yet, instead of dumping my trash right there and then, I took the elevator downstairs to do my civic duty.

These excursions became a mass exodus of residents, out on their nightly waste constitutionals. Bags, boxes, and cans in hand, everyone was doing the exact same dance. Nobody, at least to my knowledge, was willing to break social protocol and just dump at will. Even with the anonymity that a massive housing complex affords, there was still a sense of community. As part of the culture of this community, one had to follow the norms, even if the risk of ostracism was next to none. I'd guess my complex wasn't the only one where this dramatic routine played out nightly.

While this waste-reduction program did have its fair share of anticipated wrinkles to iron out, by and large it was a resounding success. It was so successful, other municipal governments quickly began to adopt similar programs. At the time of this writing, over a dozen cities are now successfully sorting and separating, making the management of waste in China much easier than ever before. It's not just a success for China, though. While China may not have nearly the same amount of waste produced per capita as, say, the United States, they're no drop in the bucket either. On average, Chinese produce 228 million tons of municipal waste each year.[6] The country is home to the world's largest waste incinerators, recycling plants, and management systems. With these new regulations coming online each week, the system can hum with the efficiency it was always meant to. A big win for a greener planet.

However, many people still seem to reject how these types of governmental strategies can innovate and solve some of the world's biggest environmental problems. At least that's my takeaway from reading a not-so-silent segment on social media platforms. About a month into these new Shanghai waste-sorting regulations, I put up a post on LinkedIn talking about the program. Instead of praising its speed, efficiency, and scope, one commentator felt we should be pushing an idea of eco-democracy (his words, not mine), not eco-authoritarianism. He labeled the Shanghai plan as draconian and out-of-date with what modern environmentalism should be.

Wait a sec.

Modern environmentalism? Isn't that the same broken system which, for over forty years, has done little to prevent our increasingly steady march towards extinction? The system with good intentions and early wins, but one coopted by private interests and greed? This system which I've been talking about and like to refer to as the Sustainability Industrial Complex?

Perhaps this individual just doesn't realize how far off track and bastardized environmentalism has become. While there is certainly so much to celebrate, there is also a lot that can do with an overhaul. Going back to the start of the modern environmental movement, looking at its history and evolution, will likely reveal where we need to make those changes.

A Not-So-Silent Spring: The Early Years

While the nucleus of environmentalism and the conservation movement began in the middle of the eighteenth century—primarily as a response to the negative effects of the Industrial Revolution—things started to ramp up following World War Two. Propelling the need for ecological balance into the limelight was the publication of two highly influential novels on conservation: Aldo

Leopold's *A Sand County Almanac* in 1949 and *Silent Spring* by Rachel Carson in 1962.[7]

A collection of essays rather than a single novel, Leopold's work is considered one of the foundations of the modern ecological movement. *A Sand County Almanac* is beautiful in its simplicity and accessibility. In it, Leopold promotes what he terms a land ethic. He calls for a responsible relationship with the land humans inhabit. Rather than getting bogged down in convoluted messaging, the author is clear in what he means. "A thing is right when it tends to preserve the integrity, stability, and beauty of the biotic community. It is wrong when it tends otherwise."[8]

Often cited as the catalyst for the modern environmental conservation movement, Rachel Carson's *Silent Spring* focused on the unintended negative impacts of DDT and other pesticides on the environment. Her argument was that the effect of these chemicals was never limited just to their intended targets. She elucidated the links between pesticides and deadly diseases, like cancer, while also excoriating the chemical industry for malfeasance. *Silent Spring* was wildly successful, selling over 2 million copies in a number of languages. Scholar Patricia Hynes notes "...Silent Spring altered the balance of power in the world. No one since would be able to sell pollution as the necessary underside of progress so easily or uncritically."[9]

Hynes was right. Around the world, people embraced this need for a new way forward. It was during this period, in the late 1960s and early 1970s, where we saw the formation of frameworks, organizations, and events still tied to the movement today. We can link the creation of the Environmental Protection Agency (EPA) in the United States to Carson's work as an author and activist. Grassroots organizations that would come to dominate the conservation narrative also started to emerge. These included, among others, the Environmental Defense Fund, Greenpeace, and the National Resources Defense Council. Globally, groups like The Club of Rome, the World Conservation Union, and the United Nations Environment Programme brought issues to the international stage. Of course, we also had the first Earth Day on April 22, 1970.

National governments passed a treasure trove of environmental and conservation measures in the late 1960s and early 1970s. Unfortunately, many of these came about a little too late. The 1968 grounding of the SS Torrey Canyon along the western coast of the UK dumped 36 million gallons of crude oil into the sea. Although it is known to this day as the worst oil spill in UK history, it brought about the first International Convention on Civil Liability for Oil Pollution Damage.[10] Up until that time, nobody was legally responsible for disasters like this. In fact, during the spill itself, the UK undersecretary responsible for handling the disaster said the Government clearly "... has no responsibility in law for what has happened."[11] Today, it would be political suicide to ignore an environmental issue of the scale of the SS Torrey Canyon.

Overall, these early days of the movement proved to be strong support against a clear-and-present danger. The threat of nuclear war, use of damaging pesticides like DDT, and major environmental disasters all made the issues much more tangible. You had the eco-activists, like James "The Fox" Phillips, going out of their way to make life hell for corporations stupid enough to flout environmental law. Grassroots organizations took their message to the public, increasing awareness and buy-in. Even politicians were onside. Earth Day was founded by a group of American Senators, including John F. Kerry and Gaylord Nelson. It certainly looked as if we were all working in tandem and collaboratively to ensure a brighter future.

Then, we were made to wade through the muck of the 1980s.

The Privatization of Sustainability

Synonymous with greed, indulgence, and questionable fashion choices, the 1980s were a time of big business getting bigger. In the developed world, it was the era of pure capitalism. Up until the end of the decade, small businesses still employed about a third of American workers. A *New York Times* analysis notes that small businesses accounted for many more jobs overall than large corporations.[12] Then, the mergers began. It was during the late 1980s and the early 1990s where a large number of business conglomerates began to form. From KKR purchasing Nabisco for a cool US$68 billion in today's dollar to Vodafone buying out Mannesman for US$304 billion, corporations were becoming larger and more powerful than ever.[13]

This hasn't stopped, either. Think about what your local neighborhood shopping strip looked like a couple of decades ago. Remember the old mom-and-pop shop where you could buy a hammer, electrical tape, and a pack of gum? Now, it's probably a big-box home improvement store. How about the local grocery store replaced by a Walmart or Wholefoods? We continue to see a consolidation across industry. To put things into perspective, today just 10 brands own the majority of consumer packaged goods and most media is controlled by only 6 companies.[14] Although we think as consumers we have a choice in how we spend our money, in reality that choice is likely an illusion.

Whether it was this increasingly complicated web of conglomeration, confusing bureaucracy, or sleight of hand, over the course of the two decades between 1980 and the year 2000, corporations seemed to think they were invincible. Their new levels of leverage, coupled with consumers' inability to vote with their wallets, began to result in greed and hubris of biblical proportions. A favorite example is the 1998 Cendant Corporation accounting incident, one of the largest financial scandals of the 1990s.[15] The company was found to have reported US$500 million in false profits, costing shareholders a whopping US$19 billion. That a corporation would think they could get away with this as if it were a simple accounting error shows just how indomitable they thought they were.

This mindset didn't just apply to financial behavior, either. The corporate world's involvement in sustainability was just as unsavory. Consider the example of ExxonMobil. Formed in 1999 by the merger of Exxon and Mobil, the 2019 Fortune 500 places the American oil and gas giant as the second-largest US corporation by revenue. Given its size, ExxonMobil has immense lobbying power and influence. On paper, they purport to use this for the good of humanity. The reality, though, isn't as altruistic.

Lucky for us, we now have the privilege of hindsight and a ton of informative documents released by the Union of Concerned Scientists (UCS).[16] These reveal just how far the oil giant has gone to steep itself in the language of sustainability while actively working against building a more sustainable future. On the surface, corporate executives say nice things like the "…risk of climate change is real and it warrants action. Ninety percent of emissions come from the consumption of fossil fuels."[17] This makes you feel as if Exxon is doing the best it can to decrease its negative impact on the Earth. That is until you witness what they were doing behind the scenes.

The Union's documents highlight how Exxon executives in the 1980s fully understood the negative impact companies in their industry had on the climate. Rather than take this knowledge and do something positive, the company continued to publicly deny any links between fossil fuels and climate change for decades. Even more covertly, they funded influential groups that actively discounted the science of climate change. All the while, Exxon publicly called for greater efforts to be made to curb climate change and environmental degradation.

> One 1998 memo by the American Petroleum Institute, an in-
> dustry group that is bankrolled by ExxonMobil and other oil
> and natural gas companies, laid out a strategy to get the public
> to 'realize' the 'uncertainties of climate change.' It would target
> high school science teachers, conduct a media campaign, and
> distribute 'information kits' that included peer-reviewed papers
> emphasizing 'uncertainty' in climate science.[18]

When this information finally came to light, the public was out-
raged and pressured ExxonMobil to change its evil ways. Unfortunately, when you're a multi-bajillion dollar corporation, screams
from the peons below are hard to hear from the top of your office
tower. Sure, they did change a bit of what they were doing. On the
surface at least. In 2008, the company publicly stated it would no
longer support climate-denial groups.[19] Great! Except they are still
part of the American Legislative Exchange Council (ALEC), a group
that lobbies US senators and representatives to block action on environmental issues. Not exactly the kind of company you want to
keep if you're serious about sustainable practices.

Exxon wasn't the only group saying one thing and doing another. This period was also one where those do-good grassroots organizations began to grow up. In so doing, the likes of Greenpeace,
the World Wildlife Fund, and the Nature Conservancy started to
emulate their private-sector peers. They shed off the dead weight of
the non-profit world, embracing operational models, spreadsheets,
and business suits in their place. While in many ways this helped
to legitimize their work practices—taking them from fringe activists
to players at the big boy's table—it also restricted the action necessary to make a genuine impact. As Sunil Babu Pant of *The Guardian*

notes concerning the professionalization of non-profits, "…efficient doesn't necessarily mean effective."[20]

Remember when Exxon gave some big money to those climate-denial groups? Well, it's safe to say those groups were probably quite beholden to the interests, whims, and orders of Exxon. That's the same thing going on with the professionalization of NGOs. To get there, they've had to gather funding from donors and other stakeholders. These folks aren't giving their hard-earned money because they're altruistic. Importantly, they want to be able to dictate the direction these groups are moving towards. It might be a small thing, like which events the group speaks at. Or, it could be something bigger, like the causes it puts on its agenda. Eventually, the NGO is doing what the donor wants and not necessarily what they originally intended to do. In essence, they've traded effectiveness for efficiency.

With all the action happening in the corporate and NGO world, political actors began to take a step back. While they would retain oversight, they weren't very interested in getting into the day-to-day running of the business. Essentially, they were outsourcing their responsibility. Now, the foxes were able to freely patrol the henhouse. They became the Sustainability Industrial Complex.

It took a lot of missteps, but the powers-that-be began to realize this wasn't the best model to follow. Enter the United Nations as it prepared to celebrate the 10th anniversary of the Rio Earth Summit. Officials began to note just how little governments had done to uphold their end of the bargain over the past several decades, so were looking for ways to encourage the now-obligatory public-private partnerships. The UN wanted governments and corporations to work together for a brighter future. There was talk of "Type-II Partnerships" that would meet seven criteria, including being voluntary and based on shared responsibility, international in scope, and having clear objectives, targets, and timeframes while also maintaining transparency.[21] Basically, the UN was creating accountable partnerships to try and get the hard work of sustainable development done.

Unfortunately, it only fast-tracked the privatization of sustainability. An excellent piece by the UN watchdog Global Policy Forum sums up the idea of privatization perfectly. They state that the "...Type-II approach is essentially the privatization of implementation. The job of ensuring sustainable development will be outsourced to various NGO and corporate actors, while governments look on approvingly and compare verbiage."[22]

All of these unfortunate mistakes were on full display with the creation of the Millennium Declaration and its associated Millennium Development Goals (MDG). While drafted and passed by the United Nations, the documents were reflections of donors' vested interests. The Goals were a set of eight simple targets—such as eradicating extreme poverty, halting the spread of HIV/AIDS, and promoting gender equality to name a few—all to be completed by 2015. Nearly all UN member states, and an additional 23 international organizations, signed on to support the Goals.

Yet, by their deadline it wasn't really clear how much had been achieved. There was a lot of good that came from having these Goals, but the Goals were more a tool for powerful blocs and donors to focus direction on what *they* considered the most important issues, not necessarily what the most important issues were. For example, Fehling, Nelson, and Venkatapuram note the main creators of the framework were the United States, Europe, and Japan. By the time of their approval, only 22 percent of the world's national parliaments had even seen the Goals. In another example of vested interests driving creation, "a small number of UN members influenced the initial rejection of a reproductive health goal...the 'unholy alliance' of the Vatican and conservative Islamic states made the goal disappear from the original MDG list."[23]

As a result of this not-to-open process, the MDGs ended up being focused on efficiency over effectiveness. These were key performance indicators (KPIs) to meet. They weren't human-centric issues to address. Michael Hobbes of *The Huffington Post* examines Goal 2, Achieve Universal Primary Education, in his criticism of the MDGs. The Goals measured this target by the number of kids attending school, not necessarily the quality of their education.

> *In many cases the rapid expansion of schools aimed to grant an increasing number of students access to primary schools had in many cases a deteriorating effect on the learning quality, first and foremost due to teacher shortages, resulting in single teacher schools with one teacher responsible for one multigrade classroom, or the hiring of so called para-teachers with considerable less educational qualification as regular teachers. ... 130 million children completed primary education but without being able to read or write.[24]*

The Pressure Mounts: Sustainability Today

Fortunately, we've done a good job over the past few years at course correcting from some of our big mistakes. Since 2010, there's been a palpable shift in the way we are approaching the topic of sustainability. Not only is it more mainstream than in previous years, but also more collaborative between individuals, companies, and governments. Perhaps it's because, like our 1960s predecessors, we're beginning to experience the impact of climate change first hand. Maybe the monumental Paris Agreement set the foundation for a galvanized fight. Or, as I'd like to think, it's just that people want to live in a cleaner world and leave an even better one for their children. Really, though, it doesn't matter which straw broke the camel's back. All that matters is that we're finally taking some kind of action.

We first started to see this shift coming from the private sector. Yes, those same organizations which caused many of our current woes were the ones who also started the post-modern environmental movement. Instead of hiding behind corporate jargon and processes, you started to see large multinational companies coming forward in efforts to be more transparent. They basically gave a big *mea culpa* to the public, resetting their starting point for a new way forward.

This move towards transparency initially came in the form of corporate reporting. Between 2011 and 2014, there was a four-fold increase in the number of corporate sustainability reports. During the same period the S&P 500, widely considered to be the best indicator of US stock performance, saw corporate reporting increase from 20 percent of members to 81 percent.[25] Today, corporate sustainability reporting and high levels of transparency are table stakes. Don't expect anyone to throw you a parade for putting out your first corporate social responsibility report in 2020. Although the impact of sustainability reports has slowly diluted over time, the early examples were truly part of setting a benchmark from which to improve. These pioneers all put their necks on the line by being more open and honest with what was previously going on behind closed doors. In doing so, they hoped to show just how good they were while also galvanizing support from the public. As we'll see a bit later, these moves were not made solely out of altruism. There are certainly business imperatives that these early adopters recognized, especially when it came to saving the planet. Over the past decade, more and more companies have realized this as well. In short, doing good for the planet just makes business sense. If you're interested in learning how, keep reading this book.

There's also been mounting pressure from the public to hold companies, governments, and NGOs accountable for their actions. One cannot deny the impact of sustainability ambassadors like Greta Thunberg and the Extinction Rebellion at putting the issue of climate change front and center in the public eye. I mean, they shut down entire cities when they march. They've even encouraged people to skip work and school to force action. You'll see pretty quickly (if you haven't already) that I take issue with their approach. But we certainly can't say that today people aren't aware.

While the Greta's of the world are resorting to tried-and-true measures to get their message out, others are taking a different approach. Interestingly, and to probably even greater effect, many have started to use the power of the ballot box and their wallets to do the talking.

One telling example of this was the 2019 European Parliamentary elections. Held at a time when the impact of Brexit was still looming, and nationalist movements from South America, to Japan, to Europe on the rise, people earnestly watched (and likely worried) about what the results would be. While results didn't go exactly to plan—there is now more division than ever across the political spectrum, with higher numbers of far-left and far-right members of parliament—the big winner was the environment. That's because Green parties across member countries had significant gains.[26] The UK Green party doubled its voting share (remember, they were still technically in the EU at the time of the elections). Germany's Greens came in second with nearly a quarter of the country's total votes. The Greens are even recognized now by the more dominant parties of the EU Parliament. The European People's Party, which holds the most seats in Parliament, expressed an interest to partner with the Greens in developing its next 5-year agenda. Citizens were voting to save the world.

We're seeing people do the same thing at the shops. When it comes to sustainable purchase behaviors, consumers are taking a fringe consideration and making it part of their buyer journey. Media conglomerate and market research giant A.C. Nielsen has followed trends in sustainable consumer behavior for several years. In their most recent report, they show a full 81 percent of consumers say it's extremely or very important for companies to implement programs to improve the environment. Consumers in the developing world, those most at risk from climate change, are also the most favorable to sustainable products. India tops the charts with 97 percent of consumers citing the importance of corporate environmental protection.[27]

That's all well and good for a survey, you're probably thinking to yourself, *but what actually happens when people have to spend their own money? Do they care as much about sustainability then?*

The answer is: it's improving, but is still largely dependent on product cost. Overall, people's awareness of products that are organic, natural, or eco-friendly is at the highest point it's ever been. Nielsen's report notes 66 percent of consumers said they were willing to pay more for sustainable goods. When you drill down to millennials, that number jumps to 73 percent However, ultimately it comes down to what the product is. Paying more for an electric car may be a bit of a stretch for some people. Paying more for coffee or produce, though, seems to resonate. That's because people are willing to pay a premium for products that go in or on their bodies.

In response, companies are ramping up their research and development processes to meet consumer demand. Rather, they're trying to ramp up their processes. Consumer perception of sustainability is changing faster than these mega-companies can keep up with. The CDP, formerly The Carbon Disclosure Project, ranked some of the world's biggest food, beverage, and cosmetic brands in terms of how ready they are to respond to consumer needs for sustainability. Coming out on top were Nestle, Unilever, and L'Oréal. Further down the list were Kraft Heinz and Estee Lauder. Instead of changing their behaviors accordingly, many are resorting to buying up smaller ethical brands. Unfortunately, this is only window dressing to what consumers are actually asking for. CDP's research notes more than half of the brands in their top-10 ranking "…have failed to deliver low-carbon innovations in the last 10 years." Pressure by consumers isn't going anywhere. As such, corporations are going to have to "…up their game or risk falling foul of changing consumer demands."[28]

Paradoxically, technology is also playing a key role here. For a glimpse of the future, take a look at China.

This technological drive in China is coming from places most people have never heard of. To the uninitiated, Silicon Valley might seem like the center of the technological universe. Those of us in Asia, though, know the real heavy hitters are in places like Hangzhou and Shenzhen. These cities are where the world's largest technology companies, like Alibaba and Tencent, are based. China is also home to more internet users than any other country in the world. According to China Internet Watch, the country has 904 million current internet users, more than the entire population of Europe.[29] Like much of the world, technology has entirely changed the make-up of Chinese society, providing access to products, services, and ideas unimaginable only a decade ago. The difference, though, is in the scope of this impact. China makes up over half of all global internet purchases, nearly triple that of the United States.[30] Today in China, if it's not online it doesn't exist. People buy clothes, food, cars, and even private islands, online. Physical cash is now obsolete in most places.

In speaking with Cater Zhou, a social entrepreneur and founder of Hi-In, an online job search and counseling company based in

Shanghai, he noted technology's centrality and evolving role in society. "It's part of who we are as a people now. You don't leave home without your phone." Companies, products, campaigns, and ideas are starting to see diminishing returns as they try to compete in this increasingly saturated space. Technology is no longer a guarantee of success. Savvy products must address more than just the latest fad. "Being a cool tech company isn't enough anymore," Zhou says. "Now, you have to be cool and do good."

Technology companies are responding to this demand through the lens of social belonging and environmental wellbeing. A movement towards using tech for good is following the country's exponential rise in information technology in three key ways. Firstly, alongside air quality monitoring apps are real-time data trackers for factory emissions, wastewater and effluent discharge, and individual carbon footprints. Secondly, the Chinese Government is capitalizing on technology in its efforts to green the country's manufacturing sector and with it, global supply chains. Finally, technology is also addressing a number of other issues indirectly linked to protecting China's environment such as food security, food waste, fitness, and healthy lifestyles.

Technology was certainly part of the vanguard in China's fight for the environment. Early on, the Beijing-based nonprofit Institute of Environment and Public Affairs (IPE), led by world-renowned environmentalist Ma Jun, began providing real-time tracking of China's factories.[31] IPE monitors air and water pollutants by province and factory using an aggregate of governmental and factory audit records, environmental quality indicators, and factory-level emissions data. It has been instrumental in strengthening environmental and governance reporting, while pressuring national and local government officials to address the issue of pollution. In fact, the Chinese Central Government and Environmental Protection Bureau use IPE data to deal with polluting factories.

Then came the air quality trackers. These seemed to, overnight, turn everyone into a meteorologist and brought terms like PM2.5 into everyday conversation. The sharing economy is also jumping on the tech-for-environment bandwagon. Mobike, one of China's homegrown bike-sharing success stories, tracks how much carbon a rider offsets while cruising around. This is a fun way to educate and inform its estimated 200 million registered users, all while reducing the environmental impact of the individual commuter.[32]

On an even larger scale, the Chinese Government is doubling down on technology to green its manufacturing sector. Long seen as the world's factory, China is evolving towards a more service-oriented, import-driven economy. To spur this, President Xi Jinping has called for a "robot revolution."[33] He intends to automate the country's factories, thus improving efficiencies across the entire global supply chain. Southern Guangdong Province, across the Pearl River estuary from Hong Kong, is the center of the country's manufacturing industry. It's home to the likes of giants Foxconn and Huawei, as well as supplier factories for Walmart, Target, and most other global retailers. Guangdong is also where the local government has invested $150 billion over three years to subsidize the purchase of industrial robotics.[34] In so doing, factories will reduce waste, improve energy usage, and better comply with China's strict environmental regulations. Officials are also hoping automation will help encourage the movement of blue-collar workers into more service-oriented, white-collar jobs.

Lastly, technology is being used to indirectly address several environmental issues. Food safety and provenance are a critical concern for China's consumers. Numerous food-related scares, including the notable melamine scandal of 2008,[35] mean shoppers now want to know exactly where their products are coming from. Way back in 2014, grocery chain Metro Supermarkets China created the mobile app, Star Farms,[36] where shoppers can scan a particular produce item in-store to learn about every step of the product's lifecycle, from planting, to harvest, to delivery, including who handled the product at which stage. With such levels of transparency, there is little room for unscrupulous environmental practices.

The Chinese restaurant industry is also developing applications to monitor and reduce food waste, which is a huge problem in the country, with consumers throwing out 17-18 million tons of food per year. While this pales in comparison to the 60 million tons of food Americans waste each year, it's still enough to feed 30 million people.[37] Such stronger monitoring mechanisms will reduce the strain on food security and the agricultural supply chain, especially as 370 million more Chinese enter the middle class over the next decade.[38]

A country which is now recognized as evoking constant iteration and innovation, China is already on to the next frontier—exploring even newer ways to capitalize on technology for good. Bolun Li, founder of social change startup Diinsider, told me data shows an uptick in the development of online programs and apps to address gaps in the educational system. Environmental concerns are also turning from air pollution to resource and waste management problems as described earlier in relation to Shanghai's waste-disposal process. About a quarter of the requests for funding coming in to Diinsider involve local-level solutions to environmental issues. This is testament to the power of technology to inform and provide transparency for the everyday Chinese citizen.

Yann Boquillod, Director of global air quality monitoring application IQAir Air Visual, notes technology is: "…bringing innovative ways to solve environmental problems [beyond just China]. A number of startups have jumped onto the opportunity to bring solutions that will help to solve not only China's concerns, but also some of the world's environmental problems." In our conversation, however, Boquillod cautions that "while new technologies enable new solutions, the government still needs to develop policies that will favor the implementation of those environmental solutions." Technological private players and the public sector will have to form a symbiotic relationship to make this effective. It doesn't matter how much data gets collected if there is no willingness on the part of government to do anything constructive with that data. In the same respect, a government that wants to use technology for positive change can only do so if tech companies give such information freely and with the same intent in mind. That applies as much in China as it does everywhere else in the world.

How far have we come in such a short amount of time? Earlier, I gave the example of the MDGs and how pressure from the donor community basically derailed what was meant to be a globally impactful project. Well, when they expired in 2015 the United Nations devised something else to replace them: the Sustainable Development Goals (SDG). While the names are nearly identical, the approach and the potential impact couldn't be more different.

Rather than allow their development to occur in secret by a select group of people with little knowledge of the issues, the SDGs came about through a highly collaborative process. In fact, the UN recognized the problematic "donor-recipient" relationship which prevented the full implementation of the MDGs. To overcome this, the development process for the SDGs favored input from all countries. The three-year Post-2015 Development Agenda, which led to the creation of the SDGs, included opinions from 193 member countries. International, regional, and national meetings incorporated input from close to one million civil society, private, and public sector actors. All of this resulted in the 17 goals of the SDGs.[39]

The consultative practice isn't the only thing separating the SDGs from the MDGs. The 2015 Goals are much more comprehensive, branching out from issues related primarily to poverty and towards more holistic global issues. These are also supposed to be applicable in the context of every country, versus repeating the Rwanda debacle. In the same vein, the SDGs focus on quality over quantity. Instead of just putting kids through school, for example, the new Goals focus on learning achievements. Collaboration, rather than patronage, is a principle message. Holistically addressing the issues facing all of us, instead of a select number of countries, aims to make even bigger progress than the MDGs. In this way, the Goals are more sustainable over time. If done correctly, continuous improvement will last far beyond their 2030 end date and result in a virtuous cycle for our shared future.

While the SDGs are definitely a big step in the right direction, don't get complacent. Even with all these positive changes, we're still having to fight against the Sustainability Industrial Complex. Like any good bureaucracy, pharmaceutical company, or military force, their purpose is to keep themselves in business. It's going to take more than a few good moves to win this chess match. That's why it is more important than ever to become informed, aware, and armed for the fight. Just by picking up this book, you're taking a critical step in making that a reality.

| iii |

Point #1: Know What You're Talking About

You can barely feel your nose anymore after nearly an hour outside in the crisp, early spring evening. The sea breeze whips across your face as you take breath after breath of fresh sea air. Although it's late, the unusually bright moon lights up the distance. The ocean in front of you is still, broken only by the wake created from the hulking ship under your feet. A couple takes a romantic stroll behind you while a few kids, up well past their bedtime, scurry by in a game of tag.

Suddenly, a horrific scream from up above wakes you from your trance. "Iceberg, straight ahead!" Within the minute you feel the great power of the ship try and turn course to avoid a head-on collision. Screeching and lurching, it's no small task to pull hundreds of tons in one direction or another. Yet, the captain seems able and, after all, this is the greatest ship ever created. You feel several bumps, almost like a snare drum rat-a-tat-tatting. Then the massive, gleaming iceberg comes into view. It passes on your side, dropping small chunks of ice on the deck as it does. Passengers, unaware of the calamity about to befall them, even kick the ice around like footballs. It's all just another piece for them to add to their story of Titanic. Something to tell family and friends when they dock in New York.

Today we know only too well the fated story of that ship and the horrific events to follow. On that April night, nearly 2,000 people lost their lives through a series of unfortunate, but largely preventable, circumstances. We've read about the lack of lifeboats, reduced in both number and capacity for a focus on aesthetics rather than safety. The monumental hubris of passengers and crew riding aboard the "unsinkable" ship meant too little was done too late. Socio-economic protocols even played a disastrous role as those in lower-class cabins were made to wait below deck while the upper class, in their tuxedos and pearls, evacuated first.

What we don't often hear about are the myriad other events going on around *Titanic* that night. James Cameron's 1997 blockbuster missed a lot of these details. Certainly, *Titanic* was not the only ocean liner in the area. No less than 28 other ships were in communication with *Titanic* that night, meaning they were within range and likely could have lent help. Yet only one ship, Carpathia, was able to finally get to *Titanic* and bring on board what would become some of her only survivors. If there were at least 27 other ships in the area, how on Earth did they not come to the rescue?

Morse code.

That's right. The series of dots and dashes which we now attribute to international shipping played a critical, but detrimental role, in solidifying the fate of thousands that evening. In 1912, when *Titanic* sailed, most considered the British Marconi System the gold standard in the industry. That didn't mean it was without rivals. Chief among these was German group Telefunken. The rivalry between Marconi and Telefunken was so bitter, radio operators held a gentleman's agreement preventing them from passing messages between the two systems.[1]

As a British ship, Marconi of course held primary position on *Titanic*. Creators spared no expense in equipping the ship with the most advanced instruments of the day. Radio operators were top of their game. It was a technological marvel. Yet, the use of wireless transmission aboard ships was still quite novel. Rather than a robust safety and communication system, most passengers used transmissions to send short messages to friends shoreside. It sounds like a lot of work for a couple of quick *wish you were here* notes.

Confusion immediately set in when *Titanic's* radio operators finally employed wireless transmission to try and call for help. Ships within range questioned how a liner like *Titanic* would actually be sinking. Their confusion only heightened when *Titanic*, using the Marconi system, sent through conflicting distress signals. Four years before the night of the infamous sinking, international shipping convention adopted the Morse Code signal of dot-dot-dot-dash-dash-dot-dot-dot—SOS—as the call for distress on the high seas. *Titanic*, though, was using the outdated Marconi code CQD ("all stations, distress") to signal trouble. Most listeners assumed it was all a big mistake.

With an SOS, all other radio ship transmissions were required to cease until the emergency was over to free up communication lines. In using CQD, however, ships continued jamming the airwaves. This translated into crossed signals and even more confusion. In those precious minutes between *Titanic's* first signal for help, and it's eventual sinking to the bottom of the Atlantic, this spelled all the difference. Just think of how many more people could have been saved if those 28 ships were all using the same system instead of letting pride and rivalry get in the way. It feels a senseless waste of life to me.

So why a tandem onto a century-old event? Because in the modern-day struggle to save our ship—Mother Earth—we're repeating the same mistakes as those *Titanic* wireless operators. While we may have a shared goal, we aren't sharing the approach to that goal. It's important, critical actually, to be on the same page if we're trying to achieve anything meaningful. When we're not, we step on toes, confuse ourselves, and confound those on the outside. That also means we're wasting precious resources and capacity, likely duplicating efforts in the process. It's pretty evident that up until today we've not done a good job at being on the same page. The result? A lack of traction, action, and getting others to join the cause.

To show just how much of an issue this is, take a minute and close your eyes.

Imagine what a perfectly sustainable world looks like.

Got it?

Great!

Now, I'm sure you had images tinted in greens and blues as far as the eye could see. Lush jungles, idyllic fields, and azure skies hum with the sounds of wild animals, birds, and insects. The oceans crash onto shore while the wind whips through your hair. People are likely riding their bicycles, obviously because cars were now obsolete in cities purpose-built to blend into the natural environment. Clothes are sustainably sourced, free of dyes and chemicals. Everyone looks extremely healthy because, well, they are.

Pretty easy, right? Most of us have a fairly shared understanding of what a sustainable world looks like. After all, that's our ultimate goal.

Now, take another minute and try to define the word sustainability.

Go on...

Do you have it yet?

How about corporate responsibility? Global warming? Ethical?

While it may have been easy for you to come up with some sort of definition, if you were to ask your neighbor I bet they'd have a different take. That's because these terms, the mechanisms meant to get us to our goal, are nebulous and iterative—constantly evolving. They mean different things to different people in different places. If you were to ask 10 people to define sustainability, you're likely to get just as many unique answers. That's not a good thing if we are to focus on a collective approach to saving the planet.

Having a shared understanding of the mechanisms behind our work is just as important as having a shared understanding of what we're trying to achieve. The problem is that we have been defining and using terminology in different ways for a very long time. That's because it's not just about the etymological meaning, but the varying linguistic, social, and culturally specific interpretations of these concepts. On the surface, we think we're speaking the same language when we're really coming from totally different planets. And just so you know, on some of these planets the definitions are really out of this world.

So, if we're going to reach our goal then we all need to get on the same page. It's time to forget about your allegiance to the Marconi system or Morse Code, SOS or CQD. I want to start with a fresh slate, free of any loaded terms and preconceived notions about what something is supposed to mean. Can you do that for me? Please?

Pretty please?

Well, at least try your best then. But I've got to say that if you want to be part of that proverbial change in the world, you're going to have to link hands with all the people in it. A common understanding is only going to fast track that. So, before we even start to attack saving the planet, we better get straight on what it is we're all supposed to be talking about.

A Crash Course

Class pay attention!

What follows are some of the most widely used terms in the field. They're thrown about quite frequently, usually to varying degrees of correctness. While the definitions I propose might be different from those you believe in, trust that they are the most popular versions. Basically, stop being an outlier and join the fold. This covers everything from sustainability to CSR, environmentalism to ESG.

Sustainability

> *Sustainable development is development that meets the needs of the present without compromising the ability of future generations to meet their own needs.*
>
> *-UN World Commission on Environment and Development[2]*

Out of everything we'll talk about, sustainability seems to be the most confusing term. That's probably because it serves as an umbrella term for many of the topic areas in the cause-centric world. It's multifaceted and prone to different definitions. Even in my day-to-day, I use the word sustainability interchangeably with several other terms. It's a great catch-all, but that can lead to confusion.

To get over that confusion, let's break the term down into its individual parts. Traditionally, sustainability consists of three distinct pillars: environment; society; and, economy. Some people toss in culture as another pillar, which is fine. Because each pillar is so broad, it can consist of any number of issues. Environment can include ecology, water stewardship, air pollution, environmentalism, and on and on. The societal pillar is chiefly concerned with human rights, but also corporate responsibility and community affairs. Economy deals with matters like the private sector, supply chains, and sustainable finance. I could continue for pages, but I won't. Just understand that everything related to saving the world sits under the term sustainability.

Depending on where you live, your understanding of the field, and your line of work, sustainability may have a very specific context. In China, which in many respects is just starting on its national sustainability journey, the word is most often referenced to mean corporate responsibility. For countries of the European Union, sustainability has to do with regulation and governance. Left-leaning places like Melbourne or San Francisco would use sustainability interchangeably with environmentalism. Confusing? I know. Yet all of these would be correct.

Now the aim of this exercise isn't to make things more confusing for you. It's to show the need to qualify what you're saying when you talk to people. As a general life rule, this is probably a good thing to remember. In the sustainability world, being clear with your words ensures you're collaborating with the right people in the right way.

Corporate Social Responsibility (CSR)

> *Corporate social responsibility (CSR) is a self-regulating business model that helps a company be socially accountable — to itself, its stakeholders, and the public. By practicing corporate social responsibility, also called corporate citizenship, companies can be conscious of the kind of impact they are having on all aspects of society including economic, social, and environmental. To engage in CSR means that, in the normal course of business, a company is operating in ways that enhance society and the environment, instead of contributing negatively to them.*
>
> *-Investopedia[3]*

When you hear CSR, what do you think of? If you're like most people, it's either charity work or a long, boring corporate report. CSR is probably the most widely used term within the field of sustainability but is also the one most coopted and misused. As we'll see, corporations have taken this term and had their way with it. They've twisted and beaten it into submission. Instead of being a term for good, it's now all too often a term used to position an irresponsible corporation as a responsible one. But, more on that later.

When a corporation is socially responsible, they will contribute positively to the building of a sustainable world. That might take the form of a socially conscious business model, like the café that donates all its proceeds to the homeless. For larger corporations, it might mean having a strong environmental mandate, refined labor practices, or a culture of volunteerism. All of this is typically measured in those lengthy, dull corporate responsibility reports. That's because a modern corporation cannot exist without at least claiming to be responsible. CSR programs have become a critical ingredient to modern business success.

At this stage in the game, any company without some sort of CSR program is dead in the water. Most companies have something in place. Because everyone is now claiming to be socially responsible, they've managed to dilute the term. What's the phrase? A rotten apple spoils the whole bunch? In the world of CSR, this couldn't be truer. CSR is meant to be a means of keeping companies accountable for their actions, whether good or bad. Now, CSR has become a label to try and gloss over the negative impact a company might have on the world. It's often used as much for accountability as it is for window dressing.

Because it has become such a loaded term, I tend to stay away from using CSR. If I do, it's usually related to what I'd term the early stages of sustainability: charity; philanthropy; and, community engagement. It no longer relates to the more strategic sustainability work of board governance, supply chains and logistics, or human rights. Some, though, will still equate CSR with sustainability. I guess you could swap these two pretty easily, as long as you're clear about what you mean. Again, definitions matter.

Environmentalism

1. *a theory that views environment rather than heredity as the important factor in the development and especially the cultural and intellectual development of an individual or group*

2. *advocacy of the preservation, restoration, or improvement of the natural environment especially: the movement to control pollution*

-Merriam-Webster Dictionary[4]

I think we all have some idea of what environmentalism means. Some people study this in university, risk their lives high in the trees of the Amazon, and painstakingly categorize seeds in the frozen Scandinavian north. The environmentalists have been the vanguard in the battle to save the world. They are the greenies, the eco-warriors, and the Prius-driving neighbor all doing their part.

Let's be clear, though. Environmentalism isn't the only aspect of sustainability. It sits under the umbrella of sustainability but is not the umbrella itself. Some people confuse this. There is so much more to saving the world than just hugging the trees. While the environmentalists may be the loudest bunch, they certainly aren't the only ones putting in the work.

ESG

ESG means using Environmental, Social and Governance factors to evaluate companies and countries on how far advanced they are with sustainability. Once enough data has been acquired on these three metrics, they can be integrated into the investment process when deciding what equities or bonds to buy.

-Robeco[5]

The acronym ESG is most often associated with the private sector and is a close cousin to CSR. Both are ways of benchmarking and evaluating corporate performance relative to building a sustainable future. ESG, though, is quite specific. In it, we're looking at environmental, social, and governance metrics.

The environmental aspects of ESG have to do with the negative or positive impact a company has on the Earth. This could be through its air or water emissions if it's a factory, green building record if it's an architecture firm, or carbon offsets if it's an executive jet-setting around the world.

Social aspects of ESG relate to the way a company treats its workers and stakeholders in the local community. Are all labor rights and employment protections in place? Do workers receive training or education, and are they offered opportunities to grow? Is the company a good corporate citizen and do they act responsibly towards their local communities? Do they support the local economy or, like Walmart and Starbucks, aim to put mom-and-pop shops out of business?

Lastly, governance involves how a business monitors itself. Good governance models allow for transparency and the full disclosure of information. Even better models tie executive and board remuneration to ESG KPIs. This term has nothing to do with politics unless you're talking about the frustrating internal politics of an organization.

You'll see ESG indicators in corporate responsibility reports, materiality analyses, and financial statements. Investors especially love ESG as a way to value companies they may or may not invest in. Major multinational organizations use it as a key factor in deciding which factories and suppliers to work with since supplier audits generally include this information. If you're a factory in Dhaka and you get a bad ESG audit, good luck getting any company in the

United States or Europe to work with you. That's why this little acronym is so important to the field of sustainability.

Carrying Capacity

> *Carrying capacity refers to the number of individuals who can be supported in a given area within natural resource limits, and without degrading the natural social, cultural and economic environment for present and future generations.*

> *-GDRC[6]*

Everything, including the Earth, has its limits. Carrying capacity is the measure of what these limits are. Intelligent humans will try and live within these means. Unfortunately, sometimes we're not the brightest species.

Where this plays out the most is in the food space. Everyone needs food to eat, but as we know there are a lot of people around the world who lack proper nutrition. With the United Nations estimating the world population to increase to 10 billion people by 2050,[7] the question becomes how we keep everyone fed. There are already too many people, which means we are over capacity with the amount of food we can provide.

Sustainable Development Goals

The Sustainable Development Goals (SDGs), also known as the Global Goals, were adopted by all United Nations Member States in 2015 as a universal call to action to end poverty, protect the planet and ensure that all people enjoy peace and prosperity by 2030.

-The United Nations Development Programme[8]

Many of you might remember the Millennium Development Goals (MDGs). These targets were meant to solve a slew of humanity's problems by the year 2015. Well, the year came and went but the problems remain. That's why the UN came up with the Sustainable Development Goals (SDG) to replace the MDGs. If the authors are to be believed, these new goal sets are now more streamlined and easier to understand. They also bring together the public and private sectors towards realizing these targets.

The 17 SDGs cover everything from the environment to poverty, food security to collaboration. They are broken down into fairly easy-to-understand metrics, which many organizations have taken to heart. Most major corporations now use the SDGs as their roadmap for a sustainable future, and for how they lay out ESG targets. With about ten years to go until the 2030 deadline for the SDGs, it's going to take a laser focus and strong will to make sure we all succeed.

Two Degrees Celsius

You'll often hear scientists and politicians talk about the two-degree threshold. For many, this is the point of no return. If humanity increases the global average temperature by more than this, we're certain to face calamity and a permanent change to our way of life. We'll enter a tipping point which we won't be able to reverse. Keeping things to an optimal 1.5-degree increase will still see long-term negative impacts on the environment but to a manageable degree. This was the aim at Paris in 2015, codified into the Agreement signed by all but two nations.

Unfortunately, scientists now believe we are on a trajectory to break the two-degree mark.[9] In 2019, French scientists ran projections showing between a six- and seven-degree increase by 2100. The United Nations Intergovernmental Panel on Climate Change, the international body tasked with handling this stuff, has said there's a 95 percent chance we'll pass two degrees by 2100. The term itself should make you shudder because it seems the tipping point isn't that far off.

International Protocols

There are a few important international meetings you have to remember when you're talking about sustainability as well. You've got your Montreal, Rio, Kyoto, Copenhagen, and Paris. Arguably, the most important of these was the 2015 Paris meeting which led to the landmark Paris Agreement. But as discussed earlier in this book, this was just a culmination of nearly two decades of work in the climate space. A quick breakdown should help make sense of things.[10]

Montreal (1987). The Montreal Protocol, which is still in effect today, was the signature agreement to combat the growing hole in the ozone layer over the Antarctic. Montreal put restrictions on aerosol products (like your favorite hairspray) and other man-made airborne contaminants.

Rio (1992). This meeting established the United Nations Framework Convention (UNFCCC) on Climate Change. The UNFCCC is tasked with keeping all nations on track to reduce greenhouse gas emissions and mitigate humanity's negative impact on the climate.

Kyoto (1998). Pushed mostly by President Clinton, the Kyoto Protocol was the embryo of an international emission trading scheme. Unfortunately, the Protocol never got traction with the US or other developed nations.

Copenhagen (2009). This was supposed to be a historical highlight for the UN but ended up as one of its biggest diplomatic blunders. Delegates were meant to pass a protocol that set out a strategy for the UNFCCC but squabbling between developed and developing nations meant very little actually happened. This led to the need for the 2015 meeting in Paris.

Paris (2015). The most well-known of the UN climate protocols, the Paris Agreement was a hard-fought win for environmentalists the world over. From the Center for Climate and Energy Solutions:

> ...the agreement represents a hybrid of the 'top-down' Kyoto approach and the 'bottom-up' approach of the Copenhagen and Cancun agreements. It establishes common binding procedural commitments for all countries, but leaves it to each to decide its nonbinding 'nationally determined contribution' (NDC). The agreement establishes an enhanced transparency framework to track countries' actions, and calls on countries to strengthen their NDCs every five years.[11]

I think that's a pretty good primer on some of the major terms you'll encounter. Having this shared understanding of the basics is going to make your life—and saving the planet—so much easier. This is especially true as we now try to navigate the trickier obstacles which lie ahead of us. These include many of the false narratives you often hear when talking about saving the planet. Some of these you might not even know are false. Messages have become muddled, making it difficult to decipher and tell the difference between reality and lies.

False Narratives

Now see. It's not your fault.

How the hell are you supposed to keep up with the latest trends when it comes to saving the world? First, it was the polar bears on the melting ice caps and the forests in need of a savior. Then, there was that group of friends who wanted you to give up eating meat every Monday. Now, you have to quickly finish your drink at the bar because if not that damned paper straw is going to disintegrate. Oh, don't even get me started on the wooden spoons splintering up your tongue. What's it going to be tomorrow? What cause *du jour* will people get behind and how are you going to know what it is when it happens? All you know is that if you don't keep up, you're at risk of social suicide. It's like the world's strangest dinner party. Grab the wrong utensil the wrong way and expect ridicule.

You haven't been able to keep up, not because of some fault in your character or through lack of trying. It's not just the speed at which things change that leads to confusion either. Today's causes are the fruit of baggage brought along from the half-century or so since the start of the environmental movement. Like the trauma we carry with us from relationship to relationship, the baggage in the sustainability world doesn't do us any favors. This weight is dragging behind us, slowing things down. It often points us in the wrong direction. We keep using what's useless, touting what's false, and supporting what should be knocked down and rebuilt anew.

Sustainability professionals, myself included, have tried hard to correct our course. Unfortunately, we've done a pretty crap job at it. I think a lot of that is because we've started to embrace these falsehoods as gospel ourselves. If you've got the people who are supposed to know what they're talking about regurgitating misinformation, what hope does the world have of making anything better?

So, I guess now's as good a time as any to start to clear some of this up then, right? It's like having to define common terms. Except these are larger themes with lots of little moving pieces. I'm talking about the old "climate change is a hoax" mantra, myths about recycling and ethics, as well as where we're getting the most bang for our buck to save the world. Let's take a look at some of the biggest fallacies when it comes to building a more sustainable future and, hopefully, convince you to change your mind.

Climate change is a hoax

I can't believe I actually have to write this, but here goes.

If you're not American, this section is optional. If you're from the US (especially if you're a prominent politician on the red side of the aisle) please read on. That's because it seems like my native land is the only place left in the developed world still questioning the validity of climate change. I mean... come on. Climate change is not a hoax. It's not a secret agenda hatched up by Chinese scientists to upset the global balance of power. Nobody is sitting in a lab fudging figures to make it seem like the average temperature of the Earth is rising. George Soros is not a criminal mastermind. Those television news segments and documentaries by Leonardo Di Caprio are not expensive red herrings meant to throw people off the scent.

At this stage, it's not even a majority of scientists who believe climate change is real. Today we have nearly unanimous agreement, sitting at 97 percent and growing, on the matter by the scientific community. Academies of science from 80 different countries agree and endorse this consensus. There are 18 scientific groups in the United States as well.Hell, even a group called Skeptical Scientists believes climate change is real.[12] They debate the actual consensus but agree the percentage is more than 90 percent. When the skeptics join the majority, it's probably time for those in the minority to reconsider their position.

If that's not enough, how about your own place in the *Guinness Book of World Records?* Yes, you're in there. That's because over the past decade humanity has had the hottest summers on record. The National Geographic Society notes the five years between 2014 and 2018 were the hottest ever recorded. We're talking 1 to 2 degrees centigrade hotter than average. Of course, you also have the outliers like Australia, which clocked temperatures of 49 degrees (120 F) during their most recent heatwave.The numbers continue to go up, too. Average temperatures have been rising steadily since 1998, with each year hotter than the one before.[13]

"Well, John, if temperatures are rising why was last winter so much colder than normal? My aunt in Wisconsin had to shovel her driveway three times a week!"

We tend to use the terms *global warming* and *climate change* interchangeably, but this is incorrect. Global warming is just one aspect of climate change and deals with rises in global temperatures due, primarily but not exclusively, to greenhouse gas emissions. Climate change, on the other hand, is
all-encompassing. It includes other aspects of the weather, like pre-

cipitation and wind patterns, all of which are changing right before our eyes. Your aunt having to wake up early more times than last year to dig her car out is another example of climate change. It's exactly what it sounds like: the climate, changing.

We also often confuse differences between climate and weather. Climate is long-term and global. Weather is short-term and localized. Just because your corner of the world may have had a blizzard this year doesn't mean the whole Earth is cooling down. But, sadly, only an American would think a hailstorm in Dallas is indicative of what's going on in the rest of the world.

If you are reading this and still on the fence about the validity of climate change, I want to applaud you for at least picking up my book. I'm sure by this point, though, you're a little surprised at the content. Wasn't what you were going for? Well, you already spent the money so you should just continue reading.

Trash sorting is going to save us all

The next biggest fallacy, after denying climate change in total, may come as a bit of a shock. It involves all those beautifully colored bins we chuck our trash into. That is after spending hours separating it all.

I'm from southern California. Sorting my trash into separate buckets is part of my DNA. It's been part of our way of life since the early 1980s, well before the rest of the world embraced the practice. Today, trash sorting is fairly universal in the developed world. Even China's gotten on the bandwagon with it. Of course, there are varying levels of adoption. On one end you have the newbies who are just starting on their trash-sorting journey. On the other are the Germans. Seriously. If you're ever in Berlin, just watch the fanaticism with which they separate their waste. It's quite a sight.

Have you ever stopped to think about why we engage in this pretty arduous practice at all? Sure, we know it's supposed to help with recycling somewhere down the supply chain. But the whole thing is pretty much out of sight, out of mind. You separate. The trash collector comes and dumps the bins into their noisy, smelly truck. Then off it goes down the street. Bye-bye waste and hello green future!

Unfortunately, this isn't exactly the truth.

That's because your household waste only makes up a very small part of all waste headed to the landfill. For the US, estimates put household waste between 3 and 10 percent of the total. That means that no matter how much recycling you do (mind you, Americans have the lowest recycling rates in the developed world), there's still upwards of 97 percent of trash coming from other places. Most of that is industrial waste.[14] Collectors are essentially taking all the bins and throwing them together into the same dump. All that effort you put in! How dare they? Well, that's because most of the downstream recycling is handled by private companies. The collection itself is usually done at the municipal level, but once it leaves that trash truck all bets are off.

As we've seen, private companies are primarily motivated by profit. The trash trade is no different. As a multinational business, it's alive and well. The privatization of the trash trade really got its start in the 1980s with the advent of neoliberal economic ways of thinking. Deregulation and the opening of borders started to result in trash—much of it toxic—finding its way to the global south. In 1989, the United Nations passed the Basel Convention to try to curb the dumping of hazardous waste and create more environmentally friendly practices.[15] Private companies, seen as more cost-efficient, cleaner, and safer than their public-sector counterparts, began to grow in number. They also grew in value. One of the world's largest waste management companies, Veolia, had 2019 revenues of approximately US$30 billion. This places it on the Fortune 500 list...for collecting trash.[16]

The typical process goes something like this. Once the private trash collection company gets hold of that smelly gold, they take what they can and then sell it off to the highest bidder. Normally, those with cash come from the developing world, typically from China or Indonesia. Your trash (or at least the profitable part of your trash) is then shipped across the Pacific to be handled in places without human, labor, or environmental protections. Children and old women sift through the waste to break things down into even smaller parts. The conditions are brutal, pay low, and reward non-existent. We've just offset one problem and created another.

Now developing countries are fighting back. Recently, both China and Indonesia passed regulations refusing the acceptance of foreign waste. This has had a knock-on effect, with at least ten other countries passing similar acts. Trash now has nowhere to go. Back in the US, local communities have had to figure out what to do with all their newfound recycling. Without the capacity to handle it, many have decided to shutter recycling programs altogether. Curious if this has happened in your community, too.

Not only is your trash hardly making a dent in waste and pollution, but all our work may be causing more of a headache than you realize. Most communities ask us to separate items into paper, plastic, metal, and waste. A lot of trash, though, is a combination of different materials. If we don't break things down into their components, then private recycling companies are loathed to do anything with it. In some cases, mixed materials cannot even be properly sorted by the massive machines these companies use. So, it might end up in the wrong pile or thrown in with all the waste. This might explain why 91 percent of all plastics ever thrown away have ended up in the landfill instead of repurposed into something else.[17]

The best analogy I've read on the futility of recycling sums things up well. Stated by *Matt Wilkins*, "Recycling plastic is to saving the Earth what hammering a nail is to halting a falling skyscraper."[18] In short, it's a lot of effort for very little return.

The biggest threat to our future

What's the biggest threat to creating a more sustainable future? Is it the polluting greenhouse gas emissions from the developing world? How about the massive bergs of plastic littering our oceans? Or could it be the agriculture sector and its impact on air, water, and soil?

Do you have your answer?

Actually, none of those answers are correct.

While these are all problems working against us, they pale in comparison to the number one threat to saving the world. If everyone just did this one simple task, we'd be in a much better position. All it takes is a bit of will power, planning, and lots of condoms.

That's because the biggest threat to the planet is *us*. To be specific, more of us.

Remember when we talked about carrying capacity. Well, the Earth is pretty much holding as many humans as it can. We're at full capacity. I mean, like, no room at the inn full. We have to understand just how many of us there are now. While it's taken for granted that crowded cities are part of modern life, this wasn't always the case. Up until the last century, we were quite a limited group of animals. From time immemorial, the human population stayed well below half a billion people. In 1700, though, things started to change. Then, there were about 600 million humans worldwide. By 1900, we doubled this to 1.65 billion. For the next century, we would add a billion people almost every couple of decades. Today we stand at 7.7 billion strong, an exponential increase from our stone-age days. As we mentioned earlier, experts expect this number to grow, topping 10 billion by 2050.[19]

However, if we look at carrying capacity just through the lens of food, we've not significantly increased our amount of arable land or expanded the size of the Earth. We haven't found any extra-terrestrial planets to colonize, or new technologies to feed us (except cricket protein, which I'm never going to get on board with). Like spoiled teenagers, we keep raiding the fridge without concern of where the food is going to come from. As Agent Smith so subtlety put it in *The Matrix*,

I'd like to share a revelation that I've had during my time here. It came to me when I tried to classify your species and I realized that you're not actually mammals. Every mammal on this planet instinctively develops a natural equilibrium with the surrounding environment but you humans do not. You move to an area and you multiply and multiply until every natural resource is consumed and the only way you can survive is to spread to another area. There is another organism on this planet that follows the same pattern. Do you know what it is? A virus. Human beings are a disease, a cancer of this planet.[20]

I do find that to be a little harsh, but it sure gets the point across!

That's why the biggest thing you can do to save the planet is to have fewer children. I'm not advocating for you to have no children. Why don't we just start with one fewer per person? Take a look at what kind of difference that can make.

According to IOP Science, having one fewer child will reduce annual personal emissions by an average of 58.6 tons of CO_2 if you live in the developed world.[21] Compare this to living without a car, which only reduces your emissions by 2.4 tons. How about going on a trendy plant-based diet? That will only reduce your emissions by a measly 0.8 tons a year. It gets worse. Recycling, which we all hold dear, reduces annual emissions by less than 0.1 tons. That means having one less child is exponentially more impactful than most of the things we're doing today to combat climate change.

Oh, I hear you already. You're screaming about China's one-child policy and all the unintended consequences it unleashed. Maybe you're railing against me because I've called into question a woman's right to choose. Calm down, everyone. Nobody is starting a modern-day eugenics program here. I'm simply advocating that it makes sense to reduce how many of us there are. Fewer humans means fewer cows to raise, slaughter, and transport for hungry mouths to feed. It means fewer cars on the road and planes in the sky. It means a greater carrying capacity for a planet already stretched to its limit. Not everyone is going to get on board with this idea, but for those of us who can and are willing, it should be our duty.

If you truly want to sacrifice for the greater good, now's the time to do it.

Eco-friendly behaviors

Damn it feels good to be an eco-gangster.

You've popped in a fully biodegradable coffee pod, jumped into your ethically sourced jeans, and drove to work in your electric car. Basically, you've helped save the Earth and all before lunch. If only everyone was just like you, we'd all be in a better place.

Hold on a minute.

We rarely question the everyday behaviors we've adopted as environmentally friendly in modern society. Taking things at face value, we trust our pods, jeans, and cars are as environmentally sound as the packaging says they are. I mean, how could I show my face at work if I wasn't carrying my reusable mug? People would start talking!

It's probably a good thing that they'd talk because at least then you'd be starting a conversation. Today's eco-friendly behaviors are often just smokescreens to divert attention away from some very unsavory practices happening underneath. It's not as if you're supposed to know that. Companies do a great job of hiding it. As an educated environmentalist now, though, you've got to be held to a higher standard. Like recycling, that new standard involves you critically questioning your everyday actions and commonly held beliefs.

Take your ethically sourced jeans for example. Regardless of whether you purchased them at a fast-fashion behemoth or some boutique shop in Soho, the process of getting them from factory to showroom floor was likely less than ethical. Denim, by nature, is particularly harmful to the environment because of its typical production methods. First off, it uses a ton of water. To be more specific, 57 tons of water for a single pair of jeans. The processing and dyes in many cases run off into waterways near factories. It's estimated 70 percent of Asia's waterways are polluted by the textile industry.[22] Add in toxic chemicals, labor issues, and agriculture depletion, and your favorite pair of sustainable jeans now has a very dirty backside.

As consumers, it's impossible to change the way companies run their businesses. We have very little say or sway to fix fast fashions' labor practices or international logistics. What we *do* have power over, however, is where and how we spend our money. If you want to go full eco-warrior with a product, consider buying a pre-loved version. Better yet, don't buy anything at all. Remember, it's *reduce* first, then *reuse*, and finally *recycle*. If you're not willing to wear someone else's used clothes, at least acknowledge that you perhaps aren't as environmentally friendly as you think. The sooner we stop kidding ourselves, the sooner we can all move forward.

While the number of truly ethical companies is growing by the minute, it's up to all of us to make sure we know who those companies are. While ignorance may be bliss, it does nothing to help the environment. The false narrative which allows us to live in an ignorance where truths are ignored is something we all need to combat.

West is best

President Trump (hopefully, former President Trump by the time you read this) hasn't accomplished much while in office. Well, at least not much we could regard as positive. He's aggravated long-standing American allies, rolled back equal protections for minorities, fumbled a pandemic, incited near civil war, and brought the economy to its knees. All of this is nicely wrapped up with an impeachment bow. In short, not the best record imaginable. Nixon must be livid he's had his crown taken away.

There has, however, been one big positive to come out of his term in office. Believe it or not, the Trump administration has inadvertently created a more sustainable future for us all. Of course, we know he dismantled domestic environmental protections and tried to pull the US out of the Paris Agreement. Trump has left America in what is technically defined as a shit sandwich. Halfway across the world, though, a very different group of leaders were more than willing to take what Trump was offering up on a silver platter.

From their highly secure gated community within view of the Forbidden City, Chinese Party cadres were probably skipping around and high fiving each other as reporters called the 2016 election. While they understood Trump as a businessman, something highly regarded in the Middle Kingdom, they also realized just how big of an opportunity was on offer. For years, Beijing had been looking for a way to gain legitimacy on the world stage as it began its pursuit of global reputation building. Now, that time had come.

Little did they know, though, just how much of a windfall they'd be getting. Over just a few short years, Trump was able to destroy the ethical and moral leadership that the United States wielded since the golden post World War Two era. He created a power vacuum—one which China was more than happy to fill. While Beijing couldn't pick up every piece from Trump's broken America, they certainly homed in on one piece in particular—the environment.

Coincidentally, this also happened to be the biggest issue facing humanity (including the 1.6 billion people who call China home). Where Trump dropped the ball, Beijing was right there to do an *alley-oop* straight into the basket. Nothing but net. China is now, without a doubt, the world's leader in sustainable investment. Beijing has invested close of US$400 billion on domestic green technologies since 2017, more than twice that of the entire European Union, and an additional US$250 billion on global projects. China created the world's first taxonomy on sustainable investment, which is now the global gold standard in impact investment. Public transportation in numerous cities, like the southern megalopolis of Shenzhen, runs entirely on electric vehicles. China also has a long list of superlatives to add to its resume—the world's biggest electric vehicle market; the world's longest high-speed rail network; the world's largest solar and wind energy producer. The list goes on.[23]

China's big coming-out party, at least at a policy level, was at Davos in 2017. There, President Xi Jinping made a laudable address to the world's elite supporting globalization, international cooperation, and environmental stewardship. As Xi Jinping stated, "It is important to protect the environment while pursuing economic and social progress—to achieve harmony between man and nature, and harmony between man and society."[24] He also upheld the primacy of the Paris Agreement at a time when the US announced it was pulling out of the plan. Xi admonished the Trump administration in all but name. In this, he said what everyone else was thinking. They loved him for it.

This is quite the step change from just a few years ago when most considered China not only the world's factory but also its biggest polluter. While things certainly aren't perfect, China is now doing more than its fair share of creating a more sustainable future for us all. This was always the direction they were headed in, but Trump kicked this into overdrive. Now, it's time to look east for inspiration.

These are just the tip of the iceberg when it comes to false narratives that we face day in and day out. In some cases, like that of recycling, the ends justify the means. Sure, the narrative isn't exactly right, but it's great we've created a culture whereby recycling is just an expected part of everyday life. Others, like assuming the US and Europe hold all the knowledge on sustainability, are truly detrimental to progress. Ultimately, though, any false narrative is negative. That's because it takes our attention away from those critical things which we should focus on. Imagine the impact we could have if instead of worrying so much about recycling our cans, we helped to find a way to reduce their use in the first place. We've got to move away from these false narratives and speak truth to power. Only then will we be able to make the positive impact I know we so desperately desire.

Read Between the Lines

At this point, I hope you're familiar with some of the key terms you'll see floating around. Also, you're now armed against many of the false flags plaguing sustainability. But the fight is far from over. It's like a rabbit hole—the more you know, the more complicated things get. Now that you're well and truly into the sustainability twilight zone, you'll start to realize people, governments, and companies are not always so overt when they lie to you. Often things are much more subtle or tacit. So subtle, in fact, they sometimes even deceive the experts.

Unless you want to have the wool pulled over your eyes forever, it's time to leap into advanced territory. We're no longer in the 101 class anymore. Now, it's time for your MBA in sustainability marketing. You're going to need to develop a keen eye, an in-depth understanding, and a healthy bit of cynicism to pass. I know you've got it in you, so let's keep moving.

What you're going to learn in this section is how to understand what you read and hear when it comes to saving the Earth. Words should never be taken at face value. After all, they only tell part of a story. We're going to take you from being a passive observer to someone who can push for change. To get there, you're going to have to learn to read between the lines. Like a good journalist, it'll be your job to get to the true heart of a matter. Now's not the time to take prisoners or pussyfoot around the issues. In this game, you've got to be brave enough to name and shame.

That's because for too long some of the individuals, governments, and companies claiming to do the most are nowhere near walking their talk. They've put up beautiful window dressing to distract from all the horrific stuff happening inside their houses. These actors have treated all of us like fools. In so doing, they're holding back the progress they claim to support. All the while we've fallen into their trap by believing their lies and refusing to question their sincerity.

We could go on and on with how individuals and their charitable organizations are corrupt, or how governments are doing little to meet their international environmental commitments, but that's a little pedestrian. Instead, a good starting point when learning to read between the lines is the corporate sector. Corporate business tends to be the most vocal in their support of a more sustainable future. Of course, this is actualized in varying degrees. I'm in no way trying to say all corporate actors are bad. Later in this book, I'll explain how the private sector is best placed to have the most positive impact. For now, I'm speaking directly about those companies engaged in bald-faced lies.

Instead of trying to teach you critical reading skills (which, I assume, you have since you've made it this far in the book), I'm going to unpack a few corporate case studies to show you just what I'm talking about. Be forewarned. Once you're equipped with this knowledge, you'll start to question everything they tell you. But, isn't this exactly what we want? Criticality could be seen as an underused skill in today's society, where we are constantly walking on eggshells to avoid offending anyone. I'll tell you straight up—the world is burning so there's no time to cry over spilled milk. We must hold those in power to account, regardless of whether they sit on Capitol Hill or in the corner office.

The case studies that follow are great examples of subversion and deception. They encapsulate a critically important term that was skipped over in our definitions earlier—greenwashing. Investopedia does a good job at defining greenwashing when it says "…greenwashing is conveying a false impression that a company or its products are more environmentally sound than they really are."[25] It's a play on the term whitewashing, which is used when someone, or some company, is trying to put a good spin on something bad.

The same holds for greenwashing. Companies engaging in green-washing are just trying to put a good spin on their bad actions. Perhaps it's on the environmental sustainability of a product or service. Maybe it goes as far as to position a company as eco-friendly when, in reality, they aren't. No matter how it's used, greenwashing at its core is a lie.

One of the earliest examples of greenwashing is something we take for granted today. Think about the last time you stayed in a hotel somewhere. What did you do with your towels? If you're like most people, you hung them up to be reused. Why? Because that little card on the bathroom sink reminded you. These cards, which originated in the 1960s, tell us to save the Earth by reusing our towels. They often have some statistics talking about how much water we waste in the shower or how many people go without clean drinking water each year. You're encouraged to do your part by keeping towels out of the wash, thus saving millions of gallons of water in doing so.

On the surface, it seems like such a simple thing to do. Individual action making a huge positive impact. In many ways, this is certainly true. Laundry accounts for about 16 percent of a typical hotel's water use, second only to landscaping. Every 10 kilograms of laundry uses about 50 gallons of water.[26] Do the math and there's a lot of water to be saved. Now, scratch beneath the surface and you'll start to question the *why* behind these campaigns. By consumers saving water, the hotel is saving costs. The American Hotel and Lodging Association notes these programs can save a hotel up to 17 percent on associated costs.[27] That's a huge benefit to their bottom line. Think, too, about all the other ways these hotels could save the Earth if they truly cared. How about installing water-saving toilets or showerheads? How about sustainable landscaping or farm-to-table food products? How about not producing millions of little plastic bottles filled with soap and shampoo—usually parked right next to that plastic sign telling you to reuse your towels, mind you—opting instead for a single refillable container in the shower? Or, how about they stop wasting paper and plastic printing up the little placards telling us they care about the Earth? There's so much that can be done. Instead, hotels expect you, the customer, to do the heavy lifting.

Over the years, several other companies have been caught trying to pull a fake-out on consumers. Chevron's famous "The People Do" environmental campaign of the 1980s came at the same time the company was violating the US Clean Air and Clean Water Acts. In 2017, Walmart was made to pay $1 million to settle claims that its' environmentally friendly product descriptions misled consumers. Most notably, the 2015 Emissionsgate scandal embroiled German automaker Volkswagen. The company tried to refute negative claims against diesel fuel, announcing the launch of new technology to reduce emissions from their vehicles. Analysts found that VW intentionally programmed these emission controls to only work during government inspections. Federal agencies made Volkswagen pay $14.7 billion in restitution, while ex-CEO Martin Winterkorn was indicted on fraud and conspiracy in the United States.[28] Imagine what could have been done if they applied that technological know-how and innovative thinking to a good cause!

To try and combat greenwashing, while increasing transparency, stakeholders began to ask for corporate sustainability reporting. Early on, these reports worked to get under the hood of sustainability efforts. Eventually, though, the system became bloated, broken, and more a ticking-boxes exercise. Instead of providing the hard data readers needed to make an informed decision, reports became glossy magazines filled with pictures of smiling children. More space was spent talking about charity (usually in the form of forced employee volunteerism), messages from executives (usually templated from year to year), and corporate credentials (usually to sell more of their products).

Those reports that do provide information tend to either incite fear, given how long they are, or inundate readers with numbers. Water effluent performance, energy efficiency, worker empowerment programming, office recycling data, employee volunteerism, supplier audits, revenue, profit, emissions, numbers, numbers, numbers. Spreadsheets in landscape format, with tiny numbers bleeding together into a black blob on the page. Lists upon lists of performance indicators. In trying to be more transparent, these reports are doing the opposite. These tell readers a whole lot of nothing. Complicating matters are multiple global standards that make for messy reporting. In a recent McKinsey poll, nearly 70 percent of investors said there should only be one standard to avoid "inconsistency, incomparability, or lack of alignment."[29]

Further exacerbating the issue of greenwashing is the exponential growth of companies claiming to care about the Earth. Of course, some may have altruistic intentions. Most, though, are simply capitalizing on the green wave to keep their necks off the chopping block. In this day and age, a private-sector enterprise has little social capital if it doesn't talk about how sustainable it is. We've gone beyond the point where sustainability was considered "nice to have" for a company. Now, it's imperative.

To educate consumers on greenwashing, the US Federal Trade Commission has issued a series of guidelines on deceptive green marketing claims. These guidelines cover everything from environmental benefit claims to offsets, copy stating something is free-of or non-toxic, and what it means if something is renewable. They also lay out a few interesting examples of greenwashing to get consumers thinking critically:

A plastic package containing a new shower curtain is labeled 'recyclable.' It is not clear whether the package or the shower curtain is recyclable. In either case, the label is deceptive if any part of the package or its contents, other than minor components, cannot be recycled.

An area rug is labeled '50% more recycled content than before.' The manufacturer increased the recycled content from 2% to 3%. Although technically true, the message conveys the false impression that the rug contains a significant amount of recycled fiber.

A trash bag is labeled 'recyclable.' Trash bags are not ordinarily separated from other trash at the landfill or incinerator, so they are highly unlikely to be used again for any purpose. The claim is deceptive since it asserts an environmental benefit where no meaningful benefit exists.[30]

Unfortunately, few people read what's actually being said here. They take at face value the validity of green claims no matter how greenwashed they may be. That's what brings us here to try and read between the lines. As we're the ones on the frontline, it's up to us to become more educated and vigilant. Only then will everyone else follow suit and start to take a critical eye to claims being made.

Modern-day greenwashing comes in many forms. Firstly, you've got your blatantly false claims, like how Chevron continues to push how environmentally friendly it is. Then, there are misleading labels that do little to support their claims. Some companies swap out one good for one bad, like sweeping the child labor in Bangladesh under the rug because you've given to a children's charity in Zimbabwe. Irrelevant claims also pop up, whereby company X will say that their products don't have a certain chemical but fail to mention that the particular chemical is already banned by local regulation. They didn't do anything themselves. They're simply following the law. Last, but not least, are products doused in the color green, or with pictures of serene landscapes. Just because it looks environmentally friendly on the package doesn't mean it is. How dumb do they think we are?

This brings us to our case studies. What I'll do next is highlight the original claim from each company. Once you read each case study, take a second and try to think critically about how the claim could be a form of greenwashing. Then come back and read my analysis. These case studies are not intended to discount the work of some of these companies. They will spotlight ways, however, in which we can improve sustainability messaging to make sure all stakeholders are satisfied.

Zara

> *The fast-fashion giant pledged that by 2025, all of its eight brands will only use cotton, linen and polyester that's organic, sustainable or recycled, which is 90% of the raw materials it uses. CEO and executive chairman Pablo Isla said that renewable sources will power 80% of the energy consumed by the conglomerate's distribution centers, offices and stores. It also plans to transition to zero landfill waste.[31]*

Most scientific and United Nations estimates place our environmental tipping point to be occurring right now. We have, in essence, reached a potential point of no return. When a fast-fashion company like Zara makes target dates well into the future, then it calls into question their actual commitment to the cause. But, that's just the beginning.

This is an excellent example of swapping out one issue to distract from another. To see why that is, we have to dig into Zara's business model.

According to experts, the fast-fashion giant churns out nearly 500 new designs each week. That's close to 26,000 in a given year! Annually, Zara produces over 450 million pieces of clothing.[32]These don't just magically make their way from paper to peg. It takes a huge amount of resources. We've already mentioned the impact of jean production on the environment. Water, chemicals, and other contaminants are all major drags on sustainability. If it takes 57 tons of water to produce one pair of jeans, imagine how much water is used to produce 450 million pieces of clothing.

Getting these to the consumer cheap, cheap, cheap isn't an easy feat either. It's not as if the price of commodities has gone down over the past decade. No. To get those rock-bottom prices someone has to pay. Unfortunately, that someone is most likely the person who put their blood, sweat, and tears into your clothes. According to Refinery29, a single Inditex factory (Zara's parent company) in Tunisia pushes out 150 pieces an hour. To get there,

> ...each worker is timed (there is a woman with a stopwatch to make sure things are running smoothly), and it's called 'working to the minute,' which means it should take 38 minutes to finish one shirt; if it takes longer than that, the plant begins to lose money. ... Employees who perform well will earn a 45-euro bonus at the end of the year.[33]

I really hope that situation doesn't sit well with you, because it sure as hell doesn't with me.

For the company to claim it will push for more non-virgin, sustainable materials glosses over the other problems inherent in what makes it, well, Zara. It's a bait-and-switch tactic of global proportions. With information like this, it's hard not to see through the deception.

Starbucks

> *Starbucks will stop using disposable plastic straws by 2020, eliminating more than one billion straws a year, the retailer announced on Monday. Instead, Starbucks, which has more than 28,000 stores worldwide, will use recyclable, strawless lids on most of its iced drinks.*[34]

I first encountered these new straw-less lids at my local Xujiahui Starbucks in Shanghai, and immediately snapped a picture to post on my social media networks. What a step in the right direction for a company growing by thousands of stores a year in China. There really is no need for straws in your iced coffee so I saw eliminating them a great move.

See. They can even trick the best of us.

If you've yet to use one of these lids, it's essentially a grown-up version of a toddler's sippy cup. I'm constantly worried I'll spill or splash coffee all over my shirt since the hole cover tends to pop out of its socket. However, this was just a small price to pay for a more sustainable world. As I started to delve deeper into the science behind the lid, though, I found a lot of grumbling from my professional peers. Their studies have shown that the new lids actually use more plastic than the original lid and straw combination.[35] While it is apparently made of a better, more biodegradable type of plastic, it's still contributing to the over inundation of plastic to the environment.

At its core, the fight to eliminate plastic straw use is not only about plastic straws. It's about the total elimination of plastic, full stop. While Starbucks may have hit the mark when getting rid of straws, the company went off the rails in their interpretation of what this was really all about. For example, they could have spent their considerable R&D budget on devising a new, fully biodegradable paper cup. Instead, they wasted money and brainpower on something worse than the original problem.

Natural American Spirit Cigarettes

This group has made a number of claims, including:

> *We saved 280,000 paper hand towels in 2010 by installing hand dryers in our Santa Fe office.*

> *We saved 30,000 paper cups in 2010 by glazing ceramic mugs for ourselves and for our guests in Santa Fe.*

> *Our sales team's hybrid car fleet saved 312 barrels of oil in 2009.*

> *We have been 100% wind powered since 2008.*[36]

This should have been a pretty easy one. All you had to know was the industry—tobacco—to know that its claims of sustainability could hardly be truthful. For an industry with a pesky tendency to kill its customer base, talking about its hybrid car fleet is a little on the nose. I mean, how can you claim to support anything when you've been killing people with your product for generations?

Natural American Spirit Cigarettes had a bit of a heyday in the early 2000s. They were particularly popular among the hipster set because the company claimed it was a healthy, eco-friendly alternative to other cigarettes (as if there were such a thing!). They sat under parent company, Reynolds American, which is one of the largest tobacco manufacturers in the world. While they shut down their Santa Fe headquarters in 2018, the claims above are still useful as a case study.

What makes these claims so egregious is that they focus exclusively on the environmental efforts of the company while completely ignoring the human health tolls their products produce. Remember, sustainability isn't just about the environment. There are so many other elements involved in saving the world. Yet, the company decided to talk about their meager environmental efforts. Saving paper towels? Come on! While reducing paper use and vehicle emissions is great, Natural American certainly wasn't doing all it could. Being part of such a megacompany would surely mean they could do more than just purchase a few glazed mugs. You also have to question where, how, and what they mean by being 100 percent wind-powered in the running of their production.

Of course, these claims also have the predictable aim of glossing over the negative and environmental implications cigarettes have. According to the Campaign for Tobacco-Free Kids, "...cigarette smoke spews more than 7,000 chemicals into the environment, including hundreds that are toxic and at least 69 that cause cancer."[37] This doesn't even mention the number of cigarette butts thrown away when a smoker finishes their toxic snack. The Campaign notes that at least 5.6 trillion cigarettes are discarded every year. As cigarette butts are non-biodegradable, all the wind power in the world won't offset the industry's negative impact.

But hey, at least our guests have nice mugs to drink their coffee from!

To help you avoid the trappings some companies parade in front of you, check out Futerra's Selling Sustainability Report,[38] which outlines 10 basic rules to avoid greenwashing. These are just as useful for consumers wanting to decipher messaging as they are to sustainability pros trying to avoid a PR nightmare.

- **Fluffy language**: Words or terms with no clear meaning (e.g., "eco-friendly")
- **Green products vs. dirty company**: Efficient light bulbs made in a factory that pollutes rivers
- **Suggestive pictures**: Images that indicate an (unjustified) green impression (e.g., flowers blooming from exhaust pipes)
- **Irrelevant claims**: Emphasizing one tiny green attribute when everything else is un-green
- **Best in class**: Declaring you are slightly greener than the rest, even if the rest are pretty terrible
- **Just not credible**: "Eco-friendly" cigarettes, anyone? "Greening" a dangerous product doesn't make it safe.
- **Gobbledygook**: Jargon and information that only a scientist could check or understand
- Imaginary friends: A label that looks like a third-party endorsement...except it's made up
- **No proof**: It could be right, but where's the evidence?
- **Outright lying**: Totally fabricated claims or data

If your head is hurting now, don't worry. All of this will take a while to digest and sink in. The most important thing is that you're now a little bit more educated, aware, and awake. Even if you throw this book away now, just by reading this last chapter you are in a much stronger position to save the world.

That's because we've covered and dispelled some of the most hurtful baggage impeding progress. Through our crash course on important terminology, we have been able to come together and build a shared understanding of what it is we're all talking about. From there, we explored many of the false claims we've come to hold true. These included the need for recycling, which actions are having the biggest impact, and where to turn to for inspiration. Lastly, we covered a bit of marketing to teach you how to read between the lines. This is a critical skill that you're going to need to employ as we move along through the rest of our five-point plan.

| iv |

Point #2: You Can Do Anything (But You Can't Do Everything)

As a child of the '80s, television was pretty much everything. From weekly detective dramas and evening sitcoms to Saturday morning cartoons, Americans were spoilt for choice when it came to TV shows. Some might even say this was the golden age of television. By most accounts, it was certainly the most pervasive age for television. By 1986, 82 percent of American adults were watching TV, with the average household keeping the box on seven hours a day![1] At this stage, most Americans had at least one television in the house. Some, like mine, had many more. I remember having one in the living room (of course), but also in the bedroom, dining room, and kitchen. We'd watch TV while we were cooking, eating, resting, and nodding off to sleep. Even when we weren't watching it, we certainly weren't out of earshot. Whether people loved television because it offered an escape from their daily lives, or just as a bit of background noise while they did the housework, it was clear 1980's America was obsessed.

Television doesn't pay for itself, though. With all that TV watching came the inevitable commercial advertisements. Remember, this was a time before YouTube and the digital video recorder (DVR). You couldn't simply skip or fast forward through the content. Instead, you were forced to either watch them in their entirety or, if the energy moved you, get up and go to the kitchen or bathroom. Either way, you were still subjected to their droning, jingles, and catchphrases. I bet all the American '80's kids' reading this right now could finish the rest of these one-liners without missing a beat.

I've fallen and I ...

Only you can prevent ...

For only two dollars a day, less than the price of a ...

That last quote, made famous by the dozens of charity advertisements at the time, was a staple of morning cartoons, evening news, and Sunday football commercial breaks. For those who somehow managed to get to this point in their life without knowing what I'm talking about, American or not, I'll sum up the advert.

You've got a street scene. Unpaved roads kick up dust and give the image on the TV set a golden glow. The corrugated iron roofs of the slum housing reflect the sun's rays as the camera takes a close-up shot of two people. A child, covered in dirt, shoeless, and clothed in tattered rags sits perched on a white guy's knee. With perfectly pressed clothes, silver slicked-back hair, and a bearded smile, he implores you to take a long look at Maria, or Pemba, or (insert foreign-sounding name here).

She grew up on these streets, her parents killed long ago or perhaps off at the factory in some faraway town. Poor Maria has to fend for herself. These wretched conditions aren't fit for a dog, let alone a human. How could anyone watching think differently? But, there's a ray of hope. You, the television viewer, sitting comfortably in your suburban home thousands of miles away, can make a difference in this girl's life. That's because for only two dollars a day, less than the price of a cup of coffee, you can give Pemba what she needs to survive.

World Vision, one of the biggest humanitarian organizations utilizing TV advertising at the time, promised your money would go towards a number of different things that could make a difference, such as clothing or education. In essence, and in name, you would be virtually adopting a child. Once you donated, you'd receive a picture of your child in the mail, as well as a hand-written letter from them to you (how in the world did they learn English so fast?!?). At the other end of the world, your child would receive access to clean drinking water, sanitation, education, skills for future livelihood, nutrition, and health care.[2] Not bad for just a couple of bucks. Talk about armchair altruism!

As a total aside, World Vision has consistently come under fire for its misrepresentation of funding allocation. Case in point.

> In a 2008 report on famine in Ethiopia, reporter Andrew Geoghegan, from Australian TV programme Foreign Correspondent, visited his 14-year-old sponsor child. The girl has 'been part of a World Vision program all her life' yet says (in translated subtitle) 'Until recently, I didn't know I had a sponsor.' and when asked about her knowledge of World Vision sponsorship says, 'Last time they gave me this jacket and a pen.' Geoghegan was disconcerted to find that despite being 'told by World Vision that [the girl] was learning English at school and was improving...she speaks no English at all.[3]

In response, World Vision stated that they take a "community approach" in which the money is not directly provided to the family of the sponsored child. The organization argued that the "direct benefit" approach would result in jealousy among other community members without children and would not work.[4]

At best, this was a mischaracterization of where your money was going. It might even go far enough to be understood as false advertisement. Not only was the donor's money not going directly to the person they were told it was going to, but it didn't seem to be stretching very far at all. Giving Pemba two dollars is a whole lot different than giving her entire community two dollars. One is microfinance. The other is wasted investment.

Of course, World Vision wasn't the only one pushing this notion of easy charity. There were countless others at the time, including major names like Save the Children and UNICEF. They were using the power of television to reach into the homes of millions of Americans. What better way to educate, inform, and call to action than with the captive audience huddled around that ubiquitous box? On the surface, their work with child welfare was commendable and of the utmost importance (assuming everything was above board).

The problem, though, was in the execution. Once this campaign idea caught on, it spread like wildfire. I remember sitting through a five-minute commercial break and seeing three, four, five similar charity adverts. The names changed whilst the template and message remained the same. How was the general American armchair altruist going to tell the difference? In a time before the internet and fact-checkers, I suppose people just gave to whichever charity screamed the loudest. Unfortunately, they were all yelling at the top of their lungs.

Fast forward to today. You're not as likely to see these old-school television advertisements as you would have been thirty or forty years ago. What we do see now, however, are appeal campaigns that spring up after some disaster. With the Darfur crisis, you had

Matt Damon smashing a dollhouse in some sort of symbolic gesture around lost childhoods. When it was the Haitian earthquake of 2010, George Clooney and his celebrity friends ran phone banks to raise money. Most recently, a number of charities and relief organizations were happy to help you part with your money to combat Australia's horrific wildfires.[4] So, while you might not see as many commercials begging you to give to a poor child in the developing world, the pressure to do so via modern social media platforms and advertising is just as prominent.

It's this pressure that I want to explore.

What happens when the idea of giving changes from an act of charity to one of group peer pressure? What impact does this have on the psyche behind philanthropy and volunteerism? Beyond this, are we shooting ourselves in the foot by trying to do too much at once? Like the money intended for that poor girl in those dusty streets, are we stretching ourselves too thin by saying yes to everything?

The Power of No

We've all been there. As working adults, there is one thing all of us share regardless of age, gender, or location. I'll give you a scenario. Try and tell me you've never been through something similar.

It's Friday afternoon and you've been working hard all week. The only thing that's really helped to get you through the stress is the thought of your weekend plans away with friends at the beach. It'll be great to catch up with the guys, relax and hang out. Plans have been in the works for weeks, and you've only got a few more hours until it's time to clock off. Your overnight bag is sitting under your desk, and you're planning to change into your shorts in the bathroom. You watch the clock like a hawk.

Then, it happens.

Your boss, the one who signs your checks and holds the power of your promotion in their hands, walks by your desk nonchalantly. You let out an audible breath as they pass, but just a moment too soon. As you do, he takes a step back and is right in front of you. "Hey, Jim. You've been doing such a good job on your reports this week. We've got just a couple of others that came in this morning. Since this is your specialty, why don't you stay and work on them over the weekend?"

Noooooooooooo!!!!!!!!!

Well, at least that's what your brain is screaming. Before you know it, your mouth is saying something totally different. "Sure, boss. Happy to help out!"

Or maybe you haven't had the pleasure of joining the workforce yet. I bet you can still relate. Think about one of your most recent group assignments. If I remember my communication theory courses right, there are a few different actors in every group. You've got the leaders and the information gatherers. There's usually someone who will record what's going on. There are blockers who like to get in the way of progress or play devil's advocate. Of course, you also have connectors who like to make sure the group dynamics are always positive. Then, there's the playboy. This is the one person who just doesn't care at all about what's going on. They don't participate and might even try to derail what progress you have made. Even worse, they expect to take credit for work the rest of the team has done. Like a parasite, they latch on for dear life.

On paper, there seems a simple solution to this problem. Tell the person to pull their weight. Or, dob them in to the teacher if they refuse to do so. Yet, what did you actually say to this person when push came to shove? I'm guessing this playboy is either the campus jock, cool kid, or bully. To say anything would be social suicide. So, instead of speaking up you just let them keep messing around. Sure, you resented them for it. Hell, the whole group did. But none of you spoke up to say enough was enough. Instead, you just let things continue on.

Have you ever swiped right when you should have swiped left? Eaten that extra donut instead of having a salad? Had that last shot of tequila when you knew it was time to go home?

No matter what, we really have all been there.

That's right. You've said yes to something either at the time, or in hindsight, you realize you should have said no to. Against your own better judgment, you agreed when you should have denied. Now, you're kicking yourself for saying yes. But, it's too late. You're stuck in a situation of your own doing. It's that extra five pounds, killer hangover, or another late night in the office away from your family and friends. All of this, then, begs the question...

Why in the hell is it so hard for us to say no?

No is one of the first things we utter as children. I mean, after mamma and babba it's probably the third word we speak. Yet, from the moment "no" comes out of our mouths, it's given an almost taboo quality. Think about it.

No, spoken sternly by an authority figure indicates you've done something against the moral code.

No, spoken by someone on television could mean a tragedy has befallen them.

No, spoken by a loved one translates to rejection or disappointment.

It's as if the word is cursed. There is very little power in being the recipient of the word no. For those that have to say it, they are often the bearer of bad news. So, it makes sense that we hold "no" at arm's length and avoid it at all costs.

But what if we were able to take back the word and embrace the power that it offers?

In his hilarious and telling book, *Rejection Proof: How I Beat Fear and Became Invincible Through 100 Days of Rejection*, Jia Jiang purposely goes out and looks for people to tell him no.[5] He gets himself into all manner of predicaments which would make most of us electric red with embarrassment. His goal? Ask for things that nobody could ever say yes to and see what happens. He starts small, asking a total stranger if he could borrow $100. Ramping up over time, he asks for: a burger refill at his local fast food restaurant; a haircut at the dog groomers; to become a pizza delivery guy for a night; and, eventually, to interview President Obama. I won't spoil the book for you but suffice to say it's a great read.

Surprisingly, you'd expect all 100 attempts to go down in flames, right? Well, not so quick there. Sure, he wasn't able to do some of the things he asked. But he wasn't entirely unsuccessful either. That's because he learned something pretty much at the outset of his challenge—no doesn't have to mean no. No can actually be the beginning of a conversation that can eventually lead to yes. Like the old saying goes, when one door closes another one opens. That's exactly what Jia found out and it's the same thing I'm arguing for here. Just because you say no to something now, doesn't mean you're rejecting that thing, person, or role forever. You're taking back the power of no and becoming stronger in the process.

There is no shortage of books, magazine articles, and publications on the power of no. Many executive coaches have banked their entire careers around this. William Leith from *The Guardian* newspaper does a better job than most at summing up how no-obsessed we've become.

In 2002, the behavioural psychologist Daniel Kahneman won a Nobel prize for his work on saying no to your impulses; in 2017, Richard Thaler won another. Dozens of researchers and writers have picked up on the work done by Kahneman and his late colleague Amos Tversky. I have a whole shelf of their books. Of course, there's Kahneman's Thinking, Fast and Slow, and Thaler's Misbehaving. But also The Marshmallow Test by Walter Mischel, The Impulse Society by Paul Roberts, Irresistible by Adam Alter, Your Money and Your Brain by Jason Zweig, Wait by Frank Partnoy. And there's The Life-Changing Magic of Tidying Up by Marie Kondo, for those who have said yes too many times, and need to clear their clutter.

But even with all of this information seemingly at our fingertips, we still go back to the default, "Bartender, I'll have another please!"

As the late, great philosopher Charlie Brown says...argh!

Let's dive in for a second to explore the totally damaged system that is our brain. Put your goggles on because it might get pretty messy. On one side you have the limbic system, which psychologists and lay folk have called anything from the "feeling brain" to "monkey brain." Essentially, this is the part of the brain which is impulsive and tends to do whatever the hell it wants. From an evolutionary perspective, this reactionary brain helped us sense danger and escape from it without having to rationally consider why. Oh, and it's also responsible for stuff like the gorging you did last week at the buffet, or all those early morning walks of shame during college.

On the other end of the spectrum, you have the not-so-impulsive part of the brain which is known as the prefrontal cortex. Spiritualists might say this is where the soul resides; the part that makes us human. It's rational, logical, and loves to go through piles and piles of boring data before it makes up its mind. However, as we'll come to find out in the next section, your monkey brain tends to scream louder and react quicker, before your spirit brain even knows what's going on.

And that starts to explain why we'd impulsively say yes without thinking through the rational implications of the word. In our modern world, where we aren't having to face down the threat of a saber-toothed tiger jumping out at us from a tree, the closest thing is a boss asking us to stay late. It's the pressure that exacts a fight-or-flight response, an impulse which nine times out of ten will lead to a hearty "yes, please!"

At work, this isn't such a big deal. Really, the only one you're actually hurting is yourself, right? Sure, you've pissed off some friends you were supposed to hang out with. And, you missed out on a potentially good tan. At the end of the day, though, it's kind of no harm, no foul.

When it comes to saving the world, however, this predilection towards saying yes hasn't done us any favors. In fact, it's actually making things worse for everyone. It's just that we don't realize it.

Why Saying Yes is Killing the Planet

I haven't sat through commercial advertisements in a long, long time. So, I'm not really sure if World Vision or any other charities are still running those same commercials they had in the '80s. If they are, I can only imagine what they look like now. Today, instead of just the image of a poor child on some dusty street, they'd likely use some form of virtual reality. You could tour this girl's village, her home, and see how she lives her life. Sure, you don't have to actually go there to do anything. You'd still have to donate that cup of coffee equivalent each day. The charity organizations would really have you by the heartstrings, though. It would be impossible to say no.

Today, we're surrounded by advertising. Even if you can fast forward through an ad on television or skip one on YouTube, there's still no getting away. From billboards to product placement, Facebook adverts to those annoying banners that follow you around on the internet, we live in a hyper-advertised world. This is far worse than anything our parents experienced fifty years ago. For a marketer, it makes it next to impossible to cut through the proverbial noise. For a typical consumer, all this advertising disrupts the buyer purchase journey. But for us altruists, a hyper-advertised world makes it hard to prioritize.

That's because people like us can't turn a blind eye to the problems of the world. While these might not be shoved in our faces through traditional advertisements, our social media feeds are strewn with images, news bites, and calls to action. That's a problem. In the first section of this book, we talked about the importance of understanding what you're doing. Instead of blindly following a cause or trend, you have to gain a deep knowledge of the who, what, when, where, why, how, and impact of your actions. That helps us to filter out things which, although important, may not be a high priority on our lists.

Now, though, it seems everything is a critical high priority.

This has translated into many misbelieving all altruistic endeavors are equal. The easiest parallel I can think of to this comes from the theological world. For any Christian denomination, the notion of sin is central to their teachings. Yet worshippers tend to erroneously believe there are different levels of sin. In the Bible, though, all sin is supposed to be equal in the eyes of God. James chapter 2, verse 10 clearly states "…whoever keeps the whole law and yet stumbles in one point, he has become guilty of all."[8] That means murder is the same as lying is the same as checking out that hot guy playing soccer. There is no such thing as a Cardinal Sin because all sins are uniformly punishable. The Ten Commandments are just the first among equals. Supposedly, that means you may as well go out and kill that boss of yours instead of just bad-mouthing him. If you're going to hell anyway, why not go out in a blaze of glory? It's all the same.

It seems pretty silly, right? This idea that all sin is equal when obviously it's not? Murder is not the same as lying. Stealing is not the same as having naughty thoughts. This isn't a book about religion, and I'm not even a religious person, but you'd be hard-pressed to find even the most devout monk who would believe differently. Our interpretation of holy texts reflects this. Our laws reflect this. Our moral and ethical guidelines reflect this.

Yet when it comes to altruistic endeavors, like saving the polar bears, feeding the hungry, or ditching our straws, we sometimes place them all on the same pedestal. Sure, they can all be understood as morally and ethically righteous (sticking with the religious parlance, here). They are not, however, equal in terms of weight, importance, or criticality. To save God's green Earth, recycling your cans doesn't equal reforesting the Amazon. Buying a reusable coffee cup isn't the same as breaking up a modern slavery syndicate. Skipping school in protest doesn't match up with cleaning plastic from the oceans. Sure, they are all part of one big holistic system, but where are we going to get the biggest bang for our buck?

If we're going to save the world, we've got to learn how to prioritize. The most important question is, how?

When faced with a situation like this, pragmatic people will often use what's called the Eisenhower Decision Matrix. Named after the former US president, this matrix is a simple yet effective way of deciding the criticality of something. As Eisenhower often said, "...what is important is seldom urgent and what is urgent is seldom important."[9] This couldn't be more important than in today's world, where everything is operating at a very high frequency.

To move himself successfully through the Second World War, where he was Supreme Commander of the Allied Expeditionary Forces in Europe, Eisenhower had to prioritize his time. He would do so by putting things into four quadrants on a matrix: important and urgent; important, but not urgent; not important, but urgent; and not important, not urgent. In the most-critical first quadrant would go things like crises, deadlines, and persistent problems. Important, but not urgent, issues included relationships, planning, and recreational activities. Further down in importance were things like meetings. Then there were trivial things—time-wasters—relegated to the least-critical quadrant of the matrix.

Why do you need to prioritize the great things you're doing? All these things are important, right? You give to charity, volunteer at your local soup kitchen, read to children, recycle, bike to work, and sit on the board of a human right's group. The stuff you're doing is making a huge impact, too. You're a die-hard altruist with plenty of time to give, give, give.

Stop right there.

I'm going to tell you my favorite bit of advice. I don't know where I first saw this, or who originally told me it, but this piece of wisdom has really had a profound impact on my life. That's because, like many of you altruists out there, there are so many things I want to help out with. We have this pesky little habit of trying to save everyone and everything, taking it upon ourselves to be the saviors of the world. It doesn't matter if it's an animal crossing the street or a homeless person panhandling. Trees, polar bears, even aluminum cans are all equally worthy of saving.

In this, though, is an inherent problem. You're only one person! How can you expect to do everything and still have enough energy left for you?

That's why it's important to remember: you can do anything, but you can't do everything.

Read that again.

Now, read it a third time.

Good.

The world is an amazing place filled with so much opportunity. For those that have the desire and ability, there really isn't anything you can't do. That doesn't mean, though, that you have to do it all.

Much like embracing the power of no, as previously discussed, understanding the limits of what you put yourself forward for is important for self-preservation and happiness. That's because a couple of things happen if you try and do everything. First, you'll likely burn out before you get around to it all. We're not robots. Humans have this funny little habit of needing sleep because we're frail and get exhausted easily. Second, trying to do everything means you'll never be good at anything. Malcolm Gladwell, in his popular book *Outliers*, notes it takes around 10,000 hours of practice to become an expert at something.[10] It doesn't matter if it's flying a plane, being a doctor, or underwater basket weaving, there is a certain amount of time necessary to master things. If you're out there trying to do it all, you'll never work up those 10,000 hours. Lastly, exhaustion and frustration will eventually lead you to unhappiness. With this comes discontent and disillusionment. Nobody wants that, so why set yourself up for it?

Now, take this idea and apply it to the world of the altruist. Even when we understand and limit what it is we want to devote our time, effort, and money to, it's unlikely you'll have just one thing. That's when saying no becomes important. Sure, you can still do a couple of different things. But it's important to have that one thing which takes priority. You've got to have that one thing which you'll say no to everything else for.

So, what's your one thing?

This is going to be different for everyone. If we go back to the Eisenhower Decision Matrix, consider where you would place a lot of the issues that you're passionate about. Write them all down. Then plug them into the Matrix. I'm sure they all automatically went into the most critical quadrant, right?

Okay... let's do this again, but a little more critically. Take your list of passion points and think about the time needed to do them, your level of passion for them, and just what kind of impact they'll have in the short, medium, and long term.

Go on. I'll wait.

Done?

So where did you put everything? I'm sure that by looking at these issues through a different lens, you were able to spread them out a bit more. Perhaps it was the time factor, as some things are certainly important but not necessarily urgent. Maybe it was relevance, where you figured someone else had more mastery on an issue than you. No matter what your deciding factors were, this simple exercise can quickly demonstrate why some of those "critical" issues might not be as important as you think they are. Like a savvy business leader, you are now equipped to ration out your capacity in a more useful way.

For a lot of you, this is the point where you're probably thinking "but doesn't saying no to some of these things make me a bad person?"

NO!

Here's why.

It's not you against the world. I'll let you in on a little secret. You're not the only person in this world who cares. That's a good thing. That means there is an army out there ready to make a positive change on this world. While some have tried to statistically measure global altruism, including the 1981 *Self-Report Altruism Scale* by Rushton, Chrisjohn, and Fekken,[11] there are too many changing factors to give us a reliable statistical model. These factors include age, wealth, education, and proximity to issues.

Therefore, we need to be unscientific and do some math of our own. There are nearly 10 billion people on this Earth. Let's give a conservative estimate that 50 percent of them are altruists in one form or another. Some care more than others, but all of them actively do something good for this world. That could be as simple as recycling their cans or the extreme action of strapping themselves to the side of a whaling ship. So, that means there are five billion people just like you, looking to do good where they can. Again, some will do more, and some will do less. But all will do something. I'm going to guess, though, there are a lot more people than this who want to make a difference.

By these calculations, then, there are approximately five billion altruists in the world. Each of these people brings with them a unique worldview, passion, and set of skills. When you think about it, it's highly unlikely all five billion will care about the same issues in the same way. We all care about building a more sustainable, livable future. Yet this can take many forms. That means there's a ton of expertise to go around in a lot of different areas. Maybe it's recycling, or animal welfare, or the elderly. Some care about the air, water, or soil. Others, building social enterprises that can counterbalance economic greed. You, too, have your specialties and passion points. Your valuable contribution to this colorful quilt of altruism certainly doesn't go unnoticed.

What ends up happening, though, is many of us start to hone in on the same areas of doing good. We all want to save the animal on the verge of extinction. Most of us find ways to reduce our carbon footprint. Some even donate two dollars a day. But have you ever stopped to ask yourself if this is really where your expertise is best placed? Are you giving your expertise to the cause, or just going through the motions to tick a box? I fear we're missing out on a whole lot of expertise simply because everyone is prioritizing the same things. You might be a brilliant engineer. Your brain might hold the answer to weaning us off fossil fuels or solving world hunger. But you are more than content with separating your paper and plastic because you've come to believe that's also a critical issue worthy of your precious time.

This is pretty much what's happened in the world of sustainability. Instead of tapping into expertise, we have people half-assing their way to a better world. Worse still, they don't know that's what they're doing.

We put a lot of pressure on ourselves as altruists to do as much as possible. We're the warriors for change! If we're not going to do it, who is? Five billion other people, that's who. If we keep approaching this like solo operators, with nothing much to show in the way of progress, then we'll eventually become disillusioned or resentful with the whole thing. There's nothing sadder than a resentful altruist. When you're resentful, you don't do nearly as good a job as when you're passionate. You'll also find yourself tired of trying to help. After all, if you're the only one doing anything then what's the point? At best, you'll continue to act out of a sense of guilt or habit. That's not altruism. It's robotics.

What I would like to propose here is a different mindset. This is one where everyone focusses on what it is they care about and what they are good at. This is a mindset where everyone can say no to what they don't want to do, without guilt heaved on them from naysayers or those who would accuse you of heartlessness. Only then will we truly be able to tap into the expertise locked away within our tribe. Once this Pandora's Box is open, magical changes are bound to happen.

Getting (You) to Yes

I want to help you get over the hurdles in minimizing, and thus maximizing, what you're doing to save the world. Believe me. This idea of doing anything, but not everything, is something most people grapple with every day. I've struggled with it for over a decade, especially every time I see a starving dog in the street. My heart tells me to take it home and care for it. My pragmatic mind tells me I can't save every dog and that there are plenty of organizations already doing their part. It's tough turning my back, but I know that I have limited capacity that needs to be focused elsewhere.

In their best-selling 1981 book, *Getting to Yes*, Harvard professors Roger Fisher, Bruce Patton, and William L. Ury discuss the essential elements of a successful negotiation.[12] As a former negotiator myself, I would often turn to this book for inspiration and instruction. It doesn't require some United Nations resolution to break out their tactics, either. *Getting to Yes* can help you with everything from a pay raise to getting your kids into bed. Interestingly, it also works well in figuring out how to give structure to your altruism.

Getting to Yes introduces six tactics to keep in mind when negotiating. Here, I present them in a way that hopefully gets you to say yes to yourself and prioritize the time you give saving the world.

Tactic #1. Separate the people from the problem

In a negotiation setting, we can forget that those on the other side of the table are people too. They have emotions and interests vested in the process, as much as we do, yet we can sometimes treat them as mere chess pieces. Separating the problem that you're discussing from the people you're discussing it with is a critical element of negotiation.

This also holds true when trying to figure out how to help. The commercial minds behind those 1980's advertisements certainly banked on the idea most viewers couldn't separate the people from the problem. That's why they personalized things so much. It's a lot easier to say no to The Philippines than it is to say no to a poor Filipina child named Maria. Your job is to keep the people and the problem separate.

In fact, I'd rather you not think about the "people" element at all.

Look at the problem by itself and then look at it again within the grand scheme of things. Ask yourself if it's a pervasive problem that needs addressing, or is it something other people are already handling? Is it a localized issue or does it have global implications? The second you start to identify, personalize, or take that puppy home, the problem grows that much more important in your mind. Separating the people from the problem helps you to take a critical, impartial view of a situation. From here, you can decide whether it's worthy or necessary of your time.

Tactic #2. Focus on interests, not positions

You may have heard of a negotiator's "red line." These are the positions they will not budge on, no matter what. Usually, you'll find negotiations begin with each side laying out their positions. Not only does this start negotiations on a tense, negative footing, but it also sets the talks up for an impasse, especially when the red lines overlap.

Instead of worrying so much about positions, the authors recommend considering the why behind them. Getting to an understanding of why a certain position is so important can help you better grasp the intentions of the person sitting across from you. It also opens up the possibility of tradeoffs and a creative solution. They give the following example.

Two men [are] quarrelling in a library. One wants the window open and the other wants it closed. .... Enter the librarian. She asks one why he wants the window open: 'To get some fresh air [his interest]'. She asks the other why he wants it closed: 'To avoid a draft' [his interest]. After thinking a moment, she opens wide a window in the next room, bringing in fresh air without a draft.[13]

When it comes to your own red lines around saving the planet, it's important to ask yourself why you have them in the first place. Are these positions of your own, or did they evolve out of pressure from external groups? Do you hold them because you believe in them, or because you're afraid of going against the norm? When you start to look critically at these interests, instead of the positions you've come to hold onto, you'll have an easier time separating the wheat from the chaff.

Tactic #3. Learn to manage emotions

The number one rule in negotiating is to keep your cool at all times. There's nothing worse than seeing someone fly off the rails, pound the table, or throw something across the room. Once that happens, it's all over for them. The other side just got the upper hand and is likely to get everything they've come for.

Managing emotions—the art of diplomacy—is easier said than done. Much of negotiating is predicated on getting under your opponent's skin. Albeit done tactfully, if you can get them to "blink" then it's smooth sailing for you. On the same token, learning to manage your own emotions in highly charged situations can make or break your talks. If necessary, the authors say you can have structured times where each side expresses their emotions. Doing so in this manner can help move negotiations along.

Activists, as we've seen, are not good at managing their emotions. They wear their hearts on their sleeves. This tends to get them into trouble, most often because they act emotionally outside a structured confine. They'll scream during a city council meeting, disrupt train service, or attack world leaders. All this does is push them further to the fringe, giving the other side ammunition against them. If they were able to manage their emotions and civilly come to the table, I'd guess a lot more could have been done together.

Don't be like the activist. Manage your emotions.

Tactic #4. Express appreciation

We're all human at the end of the day and like to be appreciated. The same goes for heated negotiations. Appreciation and recognition are two of the most important factors in getting through an impasse. Making the other person know they are being heard and understood can go a long way in getting to yes. If you've ever been to a psychologist, you'll know how well this works. They'll often say phrases like "I understand what you're saying" or "thank you for being open and honest about this sensitive issue." This bit of recognition helps the patient open up and divulge even more information. The same holds true in negotiations.

When's the last time you've sat back and taken stock of all the good you're doing? When's the last time you've expressed some appreciation for yourself?

As altruists, we might find this idea kind of unpleasant. It seems counterintuitive to pat yourself on the back when there's so much more work to be done. But doing so is critically important in helping us stay energized and ready for the fight ahead. It's also a great way to see where we're adding value versus where we might be wasting our time. Reward yourself for a job well done, but then double down on where you're needed most.

Tactic #5. Put a positive spin on your message

In the business world, this is sometimes called a "shit sandwich." It's a piece of constructive criticism smooshed between two niceties. During negotiations, putting a positive spin on things has the effect of taking the person out of the message. Blaming someone for something will put their back up against the wall. They'll react with fight or flight (probably fight) and things will stall. Consider the all-too-often uttered phrase "...we just don't think you're pulling your weight around here."

Instead, think about how to turn this on its head. Perhaps "...we have pretty high standards around here and noticed you haven't been able to meet them. What can we do to get you there?" The heart of the message is the same—underperformance. The delivery, though, couldn't be more different.

When you're on the journey of minimizing (and, remember, thus maximizing!) your work for the world, people are likely to hound you. They'll hand you plenty of shit sandwiches. "Wow, I love what you're doing with those kids, but don't you think you should be helping out the elderly too?" "You've got plenty of money. How could you not give a few cents to that homeless guy?" "Your voice is beautiful. Would you mind being the emcee at my charity gala tonight?"

Your goal is to put a positive spin on your message. Explain to people how you are laser-focused on the particular areas you care about because you feel you're adding the most benefit to them. Talk about the many other great organizations already helping out X, Y, or Z cause. Going a step further, convince them they should minimize (and maximize!) too.

Tactic #6. Escape the cycle of action and reaction

Negotiation jujitsu. That's what the authors of *Getting to Yes* call a sometimes inescapable cycle of action, reaction, action, reaction. It's like trench warfare around the negotiating table. Someone takes a position. The other side counters with their position. They make a demand. You make a demand. This continues as each side digs in just a little bit deeper. Eventually, both sides are so entrenched they can't see the forest for the trees.

Instead, don't react. By doing so, you're no longer escalating the situation. Now, you've diffused it.

At no time in human history has it been more important to practice a bit of non-reactive negotiation jujitsu. With the rise of bots and internet trolls seeking attention by saying the most asinine things, the easiest way to stop them is to ignore them altogether. It's a reaction they want. Don't react.

I often face this when I speak to groups about China. My position continues to be that China is doing more for sustainability than most other countries. They are a leader in the field and a critical player in getting us to a better place. Of course, I'm met with commenters writing such lovely things as "bullshit," "fuck you commie," and "go to hell you traitor." Not only is it not worth my time to respond to some troll sitting in their mother's basement, but it accomplishes nothing. All that will happen is an escalation in the situation. Like trying to teach a parrot ancient Greek, it'll go nowhere, fast.

By being firmly committed to what it is you're passionate about, ignoring all other things, you'll break free from the cycle of action and reaction. Your tunnel vision will not only be your saving grace but also serve to push you to greater success. Instead of giving your money and time to every cause du jour, spreading yourself thin in the process, you now know what needs to be done. Like a red-belted grandmaster, you're ready to step onto the mat.

I know all of this may be a bit uncomfortable because it's asking you to go against your better nature. It's asking you to stop giving, doing, and helping. Really, though, all of this is freeing you up to do even more giving, doing, and helping in a way that will have a greater impact overall. Remember that you don't have to do everything. There is an army right alongside you, fighting our shared battle. With them at your side, pulling their own weight, you can say no to things without feeling bad about it. You can now devote your expertise and energy where it's best placed.

Take the time, today, to sit down and prioritize. Be introspective and honest with yourself in the process. Then, be vigilant in sticking to your guns. No matter what grief others might give you, you're now armed with everything you need for success. Not only can you breathe easy in that knowledge, but know those you are caring for are thankful too.

| v |

Point #3: Don't Be A Dick

You'd think this would be a pretty short chapter, right? As a general rule, "don't be a dick" is up there with wash your hands after you poop. No matter who you are or where you're from, you just know it instinctively. Don't be a dick is what helps societies function (although, yes, its opposite—be the biggest dick—has caused more than its fair share of problems).

But, alas! Even in the bastion that should be saving the planet, we have had folks breaking this simplest of tenets for years. You might be asking yourself, "how could someone be a dick if they're trying to do something good?" That's because, like the heart of a Shakespearean drama, not everyone's intentions are true.

To start, let me draw back the curtain on a seldom-seen world. This is the world of the altruist, namely those working in the non-governmental sector. These are the NGO do-gooders, the seeming face of the environmental campaign. If you live in any big city around the world, you'll probably know them best as those people in blue shirts you try to avoid while walking down the sidewalk. Sure, you'd love to help them save the children or restore the forests, but you've got to get to work! They wander around Fifth

Avenue or Oxford Circus with their clipboards, asking if you have just one minute of your time to help save the Earth. Like the best Olympic bobsledder, you duck and weave to keep out of earshot. Surely, the person behind you will donate, right? Yeah... you're probably right because, as history has shown, there's a sucker born every minute.

What? These people are hustling every day to make the world a better place. How could you say they're doing anything but good? Yeah, I'm sure these kids got up and put on their very brightest smiles to change the world. Their purposes were pure. Unfortunately, non-governmental organizations are businesses like any other. And like any business, the higher you go up the food chain the less altruistic things become. No matter what business someone is running, there is always KPI #1: keep the business alive.

For the world's large NGOs, things are the same. The mission of the organization might be different from your typical Fortune 500, but the purpose is similar. To stay in business, NGOs have developed to become just as cutthroat as their private-sector siblings. In fact, out of all the people, businesses, and organizations doing their part to make the world a better place, NGOs are probably the worst of the bunch. Those of us in the sustainability space have known for years just how much they are wolves dressed in sheep's' clothing.

To show you how, let's go back to that example of the campaigners on the streets. When I first moved to New York City in the winter of 2004 for grad school, I had all intentions of changing the world and making my mark on the City. Like just about every young person who moves there, though, I was wholly and entirely unprepared. I had my acceptance letter to the City University of New York (CUNY) Grad Center and an e-mail from someone on Craigslist saying they had a room ready for me in Queens. School started in about a week, so in the meantime, I roamed the City looking for a part-time job. Coming from sunny Southern California, it was quite a shock to the system wandering up and down the streets, in and out of high rises, in the middle of one of New York's coldest winters. I wasn't fashionable enough to work retail, but too arrogant to wait tables. Trawling through Craigslist (hey, it was 2004!) on a particularly bone-chilling afternoon, I came across an ad that immediately struck me as pure job-search gold. It went something like this:

> *Want to make the world a better place?*
> *Do you care deeply about the environment?*
> *Work with New York's largest environmental group!*

> *CLIMATE EMERGENCY! ACTIVISTS NEEDED!*

> *Climate change is the most urgent issue of our time. With climate deniers firmly in control of national policies, it will be up to the states to hold corporate polluters accountable. New York must lead the way.*

> *XXX (although I'd love to name and shame, the last thing I want is a lawsuit on my hands. Therefore, dear reader, you'll have to look up the names of these organizations yourself) is looking for motivated students seeking full-time, part-time, and permanent positions. Our training program is the best around. You'll learn from experts who have dozens of years of experience. We'll give you all the skills you need to succeed!*

We provide medical, dental, vision, paid vacation, sick days, holidays, and leave. Advancement and travel opportunities are available, too. Build your resume, make friends, earn up to $700 per week, and help build a movement to stop climate change and win a renewable energy future.

Wow! This was exactly the type of job I was looking for. I could really put my skills and passions to good use. Plus... look at all the benefits. Screw working at Nordstrom, I was going to start making a real difference for the future (and my wallet).

I should have started suspecting something when a recruiter called me within 20 minutes of submitting my CV. The recruiter seemed almost too happy to have me come on board. I thought to myself this was just enthusiasm. It turned out to be something more sinister. Before she hung up, I was reminded to bring a coat and report to work the next day.

The following afternoon, I ended up in some small suite at the Hotel Pennsylvania across from Madison Square Garden. There, I met up with a ragtag group of mostly younger college students. Our dear leader, the person in charge, couldn't have been more than 22 years old. As I came to quickly learn, seniority mattered. This guy just seemed to have outlasted all the others before him.

A quick tour of the 300 square foot office and a couple of signatures later, we were ready to begin our shift. Without a lick of training, the next thing I knew I was on the New Jersey Transit train headed for the upmarket communities of Orange and Montclair. You might recognize these picturesque towns as they featured prominently in the Emmy-award winning documentary series, *The Real Housewives of New Jersey*. That's right. We were headed straight for the belly of the money-laden beast.

Three days into my New York experience, though, I didn't know any of this. I was just excited to be seeing something different, with new friends, earning what I thought would be a steady paycheck.

The 45-minute train side served as the scene of my induction. Hardly the best training program around, I thought to myself. But this was New York City, center of the proverbial universe. These people must know what they're doing. This must just be how things are done in the big city.

On that short trip, I was given a script from which to read and a clipboard for signatures. My buddy told me how a typical shift worked and reassured me most learning would be done on the job. They regaled me with tales of their first day and how it all seemed a bit weird to them too. Nothing to worry about! This was going to be an amazing, impactful way to put my mark on the world. We were really at the forefront of change and rah, rah, rah.

Awwrange!!! (There was still a novelty to the brash New Jersey accent). Stepping off the train onto the platform, wind and sleet immediately slapped me in the face. It was a rude awakening, but I assumed we'd be back in an office campaigning soon enough. I was so wrong. We exited the station and walked about a half-mile to a row of exquisite stone mansions. The streets were covered in snow. Trees were bare. Wind was whistling. To my surprise, this was our office for the day. It was here my buddy (now a term not so endearing) told me about the organization's commission structure. I'd earn a portion of every check I collected that afternoon. That's right. We weren't collecting signatures from concerned citizens. No, we had to convince them to hand over their (I assume) legitimate, hard-earned money for a cause they couldn't be more removed from.

To make things just that much more stressful, I had a target. After a full 45 minutes of training and an October surprise, I was now going to be penalized if I couldn't do a good job.

And yet, I had convinced myself this was all part of doing my bit for the planet. If Buddhist monks could set themselves on fire for what they believed in, what was a little frostbite?

Almost every door I knocked on did open and, to their credit, most people welcomed me in. Can you imagine? Bringing a total stranger in off the streets in this day and age? Maybe I was lucky enough to find a street full of Jersey's best Christians. For this, I was thankful.

Shaking and nervous, I tried my best to ad-lib off the script I had been given. My passion for the environment certainly showed through. As with anything, the more passionate you are about something the more people tend to believe in you and your cause. Low and behold, people actually listened, signed my petition, and opened their wallets. Again, I was a total stranger. Checks for hundreds of dollars, bills in twenties and fifties, and plenty of hot chocolate started to flow my way. This organization seemed to know *The Secret* before it was a thing.

Meeting back up with my buddy later on that afternoon, he asked how everything had gone. I was so excited to report back my success and he seemed to echo this in his performance for the day. Frozen and tired, we made our way back to the train station for the journey home. I remember being over the moon with everything, unable to nod off. Crossing Eighth Avenue back to the Hotel Pennsylvania suite, we must have been the last group to return for the evening. With a perturbed look on his face, since we were clearly cutting into his evening routine, our dear leader greedily took the envelopes of checks and cash from us. He shoo-ed us away, letting us know we did a great job for the world. One of the most memorable things about him was his strange habit of encouraging us to go out and celebrate with a warm shawarma. This was the first time

I heard him utter that ridiculous statement, but it wouldn't be the last.

Over the next several months, I continued to give my time and effort to the cause. Whether it was going door-to-door in upmarket areas of Jersey or Long Island or canvassing the streets of Soho and the Upper East Side, I felt like a warrior for the Earth. What I didn't feel was a sense of remuneration for my service in her majesty's army. While my first day on the job certainly was a windfall, most days weren't so great. Sometimes, we'd struggle to get a single donation. It was then I truly understood the meaning of the term "up to" when talking about salary. I could certainly earn "up to" $1,000 a week. I could also certainly earn "less than" anywhere close to that much. If memory serves, I was bringing in just a couple hundred dollars per week consistently. According to *Independent Sector*, though, the estimated value of a volunteer is US$25.43 an hour.[1] That means I should have been making close to $1,000 a week as the advertisement promised. Maybe that's how they were fudging their numbers.

On days where we would miss our target, the dear leader would go into a tirade about how the Earth needed us more than ever and we had let her down. He didn't seem to fancy shawarma on these days. I came to discover his outward care for the Earth had a more intrinsic motivation. His salary was directly correlated to how much each of us brought in. Ponder that for a second. For every check a concerned citizen wrote, thinking the money was going to save the trees or the polar bears, most of it was spent on overheads like salaries, train reimbursements, and middle eastern cuisine. That's right. Your money was going to fund the organization itself, not to save the world as you thought.

And this is how most, if not all, NGOs work. They are money-hungry animals, ever on the search for their next feed. NGOs can only be successful if they have the funding to "make a difference." It has probably been this way from the beginning of time. That pre-historic canvasser with a stone tablet, the ancient Egyptian trying to get signatures on their papyrus scroll, or the Mandarin elicit-ing cowrie donations for a new protective wall would have experi-enced the same issues with funding. There is so much to do, but not enough money to go around.

Take Africa, as an example. A heartland of donated time and money, Sub-Saharan Africa receives approximately US$56 billion in official development assistance each year, down from a 2014 peak of US$135 billion annually in loans, foreign investment, and devel-opment aid.[2] How far has that money gone to help the region "lift itself out of poverty" as I'm sure many slick campaign brochures ad-vertise? While the money might make it to bank accounts of aid or-ganizations, it probably doesn't go much further.

That makes even the best of us greedy and tribal. There are more non-profit groups today than you can shake a stick at. According to the US State Department, there are approximately 1.5 million reg-istered NGOs in the United States alone. Non-Profit Action places this number at 10 million worldwide.[3] These don't even count gov-ernmental, intergovernmental, and private-sector agencies trying to do their part as well. Since we're on a roll, why don't we look at a few other interesting stats about NGOs?

- In India, there is one NGO for every 400 people.
- Individuals donate over US$1.5 billion to charities every year.
- Three out of four employees in the NGO sector are female, but the majority of leadership positions are held by men.
- The average Canadian donates close to US$500 per year to charities.

- 80 percent of citizens worldwide believe NGOs are an easy way to get involved.[4]

Yet, for some reason budgets seem to constantly run thin. That means every time some donor opens up their coffers, all hell breaks loose. Clamoring and clawing for this new round of funding, NGOs become as cutthroat as a hooker working the piers. In this struggle for survival, there's no room for feelings.

They've become dicks to each other. These groups find any little fault to undercut reputations of competitors when they should be supporting the great work each says they do. I mean, these folks are all supposed to be on the same team, right? Why, then, do they need to operate in little fiefdoms? What benefit is there in dividing up pieces of a puzzle by starting another organization that's just going to have to fight for funding? What's worse, there are real impacts on non-financial areas like, you know, actual people. Stephen Browne, founder of the Future United National Development System, often recalls an anecdote of what happens when there are too many cooks and not enough chefs. The story comes from Kenya, where "…18 different types of water pump had been provided by 18 different donors. Each required a different instruction manual and set of spare parts."[5] Way to go NGOs! That's real change in the making.

In a perfect world, people with shared interests would come together to form a singular organization. This would not only help alleviate some of the funding issues we see in the space, but also create a stronger force for change. Instead of hundreds of five-person NGOs vying for limited airtime, you'd have smaller numbers of groups with exponentially larger numbers of people starting conversations with the powers that be. There is power in numbers. Unfortunately, this fact is something the NGO world still seems to not understand.

And that's why they put such a preference on bringing in the young and altruistic. In Kenya, for example, 80 percent of NGO workers are under the age of 24.[6] These segments not only have the energy, drive, and resilience required in non-profit jobs, but also the naiveté to work long hours for little (or no) pay. It's a win-win situation, at least for the organization. You have people who can be the loudest, but who might feel inauthentic asking to be compensated fairly for their voices. There will always be a new group of students ready to do their part when the current group ages out, gets tired, or starts to catch on to the game.

That's exactly what happens, too. For me, it took about three months before I finally gave in. Maybe I would have lasted a bit longer if I had joined in the warmer months of spring. As it was, there weren't enough layers of clothing to stand outside in the cold for hours on end without starting to resent your choices in life. This was New York City and I was spending it bundled up like that kid in *A Christmas Story*, trying to convince jaded people to part with their cash. It was thankless but enlightening.

Life in the Ivory Tower

In the Netflix show, *Altered Carbon* (2018),[7] a very Asian-looking, dystopian future is split (unsurprisingly) between the haves and the have nots. Nearly 400 years from now, humanity has finally been able to conquer death using technology. We have developed cortical stacks; small devices placed in the vertebrae to collect and store our consciousness. When the outmoded physical body—the sleeve—dies, one can have their stack removed and placed inside a new sleeve. Billed as the ultimate solution over death, mankind quickly found a way to commodify. It's amazing that even in such an advanced future, we still refuse to embrace equality. However, I digress.

On one side of the spectrum, you have the everyday plebs going about their business pretty much the same way we do today. They have the same problems, concerns, and dramas as us, except they're getting around in flying cars and have a lot more digital advertising to contend with. Sure, the thought of everlasting life is appealing. The execution, however, leaves a lot to be desired. Although sleeves are available for most of the rank and file given bodies still die in the future, there's no guarantee you're going to want the body you're given. Options are pretty much left up to chance. A petite grandmother in this life? You may very well end up in a 300-pound man's body in the next. Olympian today. Bedridden tomorrow.

Quite literally sitting over this side of humanity are the Meths. No, this isn't a reference to the copious amounts of drugs they'd invariably do given that they don't have to worry about money or physical decay. It's a nod to the Biblical Methuselah from the Book of Genesis. Contrary to all manner of scientific evidence or common sense, people believe the old Methuselah lived to be 969 years old.[8] That would make him (at least up until the future invention of stacks) the oldest human to have ever lived. The Meths in *Altered Carbon* are the upper class, able to afford the best sleeves on the market. They can also have their memories and consciousness uploaded to the cloud, or whatever they're calling it in this futuristic depiction. This final point is important. Although mankind has been able to overcome physical death, the destruction of one's stack cannot be reversed. One is only considered totally deceased once their stack is gone. They even call it "real death."

As with vampires, Meths are able to accumulate quite a bit of wealth given their retirement age is, well, non-existent. And, like the rich and famous today, the first thing most Meths decide to do with all that money is get the hell out of dodge. Except for Meths, it's not a home in the suburbs, a condo near the sea, or a villa in the mountains they're after. In this futuristic world, Meths head to the sky. They build homes which float miles above the fray of normal life. Sun pours through floor-to-ceiling windows, perfectly manicured lawns allow for plenty of space to play, and you're always just a stone's throw from the best schools Bay City has to offer. Clad in blinding white and gold, Meths have managed to build for themselves ivory towers.

Why talk about a futuristic world which, in all likelihood as things stand today, we're not on a trajectory to even reach? Because it relates quite well to the next group of dicks I want to talk about: academics. Like the Meths, modern-day academics sit in their figurative ivory towers. From this vantage point, they can pass down judgment on others while remaining at an arm's length from the problems they purport to solve. This has the added benefit of ensuring they don't get the oversized sleeves of their academic robes dirty.

To be clear, I'm not talking about all academics. There are plenty of academics all over the world who have done amazing things at furthering the cause of a sustainable future. I'm talking more about the quintessential form of academic thinking. That means we shouldn't just be looking for culprits hidden amongst co-eds in the quad. We can find these people in all manner of places, from the halls of power to the board room and everywhere in between. They certainly like to talk a lot, and this is likely the only exercise they get. That's because with all the jaw flapping there's very little time left to get out and take action.

These people, somewhere along the line, have lost their heart.

Of course, many of us begin to take a different approach as we get older. We might replace a Greenpeace-type attack on whaling ships with talking our way to a brighter future. Whether it's a gray-bearded intellectual or a smartly dressed diplomat, people seem to think these are the folks making a difference.

They're not.

How can you make a difference if you really don't know what's going on?

How can you make a difference if you're not really making anything at all?

Academics and their ilk sit around air-conditioned conference rooms talking about the state of the world. Many take private jets to get to such destitute places as Aspen or Davos. Like the Meths, they sup on sumptuous meals and drink only the finest wines. Sitting on panels and giving keynote presentations to audiences more concerned with business deals than mass extinction, these imposters may have the money to solve our issues but lack the guts to do anything about it. How do I know this? Well... I used to be one.

My professional career started at the United Nations. It had been my dream to work at this rarified organization, something I had wanted all through high school, university, and grad school. Luckily, I was able to be at the proverbial right place at the right time and landed a job at the Secretariat. Over time I was promoted, eventually landing in the non-descript Department of General Assembly and Conference Management. My role was to work with other UN staff, ambassadors, and delegates to set agendas, work on resolutions, and represent the interests of the UN. My favorite job, though, was passing notes between delegations. It was like high school, except there was no teacher to call you out.

Late one summer, my boss called me into his office to chat. He was sending me to Istanbul to work with the United Nations Convention to Combat Desertification, part of the United Nations Convention on Climate Change (you know, the same meetings which passed the Kyoto Protocol and Paris Agreement). It would be my first overseas posting and I couldn't be more excited. I had grown tired of my day-to-day work with the delegates in New York. Their continuous squabbling over the same issues, year in and year out without resolution, was starting to wear me down. Istanbul seemed like the perfect place to shake this up.

I imagined a room full of scientists, politicians, and civil society actors working in tandem towards a common goal. Hurricane Katrina, Al Gore's *Inconvenient Truth*, and air pollution concerns from the Beijing Olympics were still fresh in the minds of people everywhere. Surely, coming together to do our part to change things would be easy.

Day one of the week-long conference was packed to the brim with all the people I had imagined. Heads of state, cabinet officials, and other high-level policymakers were everywhere. There was even a good mix of scientists floating around. Activists from concerned NGOs mixed with ambassadors. The conversations were lively. Speeches inspired.

Then came day two. The roar of the previous day began to die down as the reality of the work ahead set in. How would we get 192 countries to agree on a common goal around desertification? Never mind that. How could you get 192 countries to agree on the color of the sky? Irrefutable scientific evidence, given by scientists present at the conference, was refuted. Pleas for aid from impassioned civilians, some with their societies on the brink of extinction, largely ignored. I swore there were even people asleep when case studies of success were shown on the big screen.

The issue, as with all academic exercises regardless of the form they take, was one of proximity. Those people sitting in front of me fell into one of two camps—either they were being impacted by desertification, or they weren't. For those in the latter camp, there was no real impetus for them to do anything. Those experiencing desertification in their countries had the imperative. In a cruel twist of cosmic irony, they also lacked the funding to do anything. Getting the two sides to meet in the middle—where one would have to recognize an intangible threat while the other would have to compromise on a life-or-death issue—wouldn't be easy. Luckily, these were the days where politics were still somewhat civil. By the end of the week, everyone had played nice and passed our resolution. What became of it, and the impact the resolution had, is anyone's guess.

For academics, their world has to be on fire before they'll move faster than a glacier (the jury's still out on whether this is a result of complacency or over thinking). Modern events are not much different from Istanbul. I attend a lot (a lot!) of conferences on sustainability. Most are in some five-star hotel conference facility, freezing but with bright lights. Rows of tables stretched out as far as the eye can see, the fortunate will snag a seat close to the front (but never, ever, the front row as these are reserved for speakers). Sitting on top of the white tablecloth is your standard-issue embossed hotel stationery, plastic bottle of water, and a box of mints. With the boom of some ridiculously peppy song (my all-time favorite is the Olympic theme), your emcees command attention. The conference is ready to start.

Most conferences follow the same format: high-level speaker; keynote presenter; networking break; a panel discussion; lunch; another panel discussion; networking break; final address; drinks. You can pretty much guarantee the high-level speaker will give a glowing report of what their government or organization is doing to further whatever topic the conference is about. I can imagine a template with spaces for [conference name], [conference theme], and [generalized examples of how we're helping address the conference theme]. Someone just fills in the blanks and hands the speech to the official. It's then the official's job to present it, likely in the most mind-numbing way possible.

The keynote speaker is usually a little better, but they often play things safe. You've heard of writing at an eighth-grade reading level. These speakers present the same way. They fall back on basics, facts, and stats folks in the audience would probably already know. A conference on climate change? They'll explain what the two-degree threshold is. Human rights? Twenty minutes explaining every international convention on the subject. Maritime law? Well, you get the picture.

The real impact of the conference comes down to this next moment: the panel discussion. It's the first time that audience will be able to hear from true experts on the subject at hand. Many delegates will come armed with burning questions that, if answered, could change the world. Others are ready with their notebooks to write down pages and pages of new information. Microphones on, the panelists take their seats. Invariably, the moderator first asks them to introduce themselves. What happens? They each spend what seems like an eternity spouting their CV.

I could have read that in the conference packet.

Now, a quarter of the way through a one-hour panel, we finally get to what will hopefully be the meat-and-potatoes of the conversation. If you're lucky, questions from the moderator will be thoughtful and engaging. Some may even hit at the heart of critical issues that need to be solved or confrontational matters to be addressed. Most of the time, though, panelists are asked to recall outdated case studies or come up with solutions to hypotheticals. You'll usually have someone who doesn't understand the concept of time and decides to suck in all the airplay. Before you know it, there are five minutes left. These "ample" 300 seconds are given to the audience for Q&A.

What could we possibly accomplish in this short amount of time? In a room of 100, 200, 500 people, how is anyone going to solve anything? Your brilliant question is relegated to the pile of lost opportunities as you, frustrated, pack up to leave for lunch.

The problem here, just as it was in Istanbul, is proximity. You'll rarely see a panel with anything but educated (typically white) professionals. These types of panels even have a nickname: "pale, male, and stale." Sure, some run successful businesses. Others have a high rank. Academics, subject-matter experts, and PR hounds round out the list. What you don't often find are people directly impacted by whatever your conference is about. And that's what defines these conferences as academic exercises.

In the past, this may have been fine. But people it's time to wake up! After decades of conferences on every subject known to man, our world is still burning. In fact, it's worse than ever before. This shows just how little a panel of experts are actually accomplishing and why the conference-industrial complex is simply a way to take your money and waste your time.

Here's a question for you: Who is most disproportionately impacted by climate change?

If it was the make-up of conferences on the subject of climate change as our indicator, you'd think the educated elite living in first-world cities were most at risk. As we've seen, however, the countries with the least ability for resilience are being impacted the most. These are also the ones least represented at these conferences. While cities like Shanghai, New York, and Rio may be inundated with rising sea levels over the next hundred years, so too are places like Dhaka. The former, given their access to infrastructure and capital, will likely be able to rebuild. Even though this is, of course, an unfortunate scenario, these places will survive. Dhaka, on the other hand, won't be so lucky.

The capital of Bangladesh, Dhaka proper is one of the most densely populated places on Earth. The greater metro area, low-lying and awash with river systems, houses over 21 million people.[9]

Relatively poor, and with a lax regulatory environment, it has grown in recent years as a popular source of cheap labor, particularly for the fast-fashion industry. Bangladeshis from all over the country are streaming into the capital looking for employment opportunities. This is placing strain on systems already stretched thin.

One of these weak systems is the aqueduct network, which helps to alleviate the annual flooding of the city's rivers. In the rainy season, it's not uncommon for one-fifth of the country to flood. Climate change is dramatically changing weather patterns at the exact time the country can least handle them. Nearly one million people in Bangladesh have been displaced every year over the past decade due to climate-related catastrophes. Experts estimate this will rise to 13 million annually by 2050. Women and girls are particularly vulnerable to these, and other changes.[10]

Yet, when's the last time you saw a female factory worker from Bangladesh take the mainstage at Davos? Or better yet, a high-level conference of "experts" meeting in Dhaka? The so-called solutions for these parts of the world are being made in and developed by other countries. Never mind the fact these developed countries are a principle cause of the problems under discussion. Those with an academic mindset can hide behind this academic exercise to pass blame and shun doing the heavy lifting. And believe me, they are passing blame. They may not say it outright, but there is a sense of superiority often coming off the panelists. How come people in the developing world still live in such conditions? Why won't their governments do anything about the issues at hand? Where is the push for better working conditions and living standards? The algorithm says it should be a simple fix. Our trajectories show change should have happened by now.

I'd bet if you had someone from the developing country in question on that same panel, the discussion would be very different.

Unfortunately, the fight for a better future has become a blame game pitting us versus them. Some have forgotten, or never knew in the first place, that we're all in this together. You can blame the Government of Bangladesh all you want, but what about the influencer in Las Vegas who needs that pair of cheap jeans for their video? Both are to blame because both are part of the problem. There is no us and them.

Nothing demonstrates both the "us-versus-them" mentality and holistic nature of sustainability better than the state of recycling today. Growing up in Southern California, I knew very early on about separating all my trash. Cans in one bucket. Plastic in another. Paper in another still. Then the trash man would come and collect the waste. Did I ever question where it went? Of course not! I assumed it was going down the road to my local trash yard, where machines would keep holy the separation job I had done at home. Little did I know, it was being shipped much further away than my local junkyard. In fact, most of our trash ends up finding its way to Asia.

Fellow Shanghai ex-pat, Adam Minter, has done a great job at summarizing just how much trash ends up this side of the Pacific. His book, *Junkyard Planet*, is part exposé, part environmental call to action.[11] Published in 2013, Minter makes his way across Asia, following the trash trade to see where it goes. He starts with the humble Coca-Cola can, but eventually finds his way into everything from electronics, to cars, to all manner of scrap metal.

Most of the stuff you throw away, recycling or not, is probably loaded up onto a cargo ship and sent across to Chinese cities you've never even heard of. Experts estimate in "…the U.S. alone, nearly 4,000 shipping containers full of plastic recyclables a day had been shipped to Chinese recycling plants."[12] A full 70 percent of the world's plastic waste ended up somewhere in China as of 2017.[13] We're talking millions of tons a year. The Chinese were more than happy to buy these recyclables as they could cheaply take them apart and reuse the materials.

This approach to recycling has had an adverse impact on both the environment and the people living within trash sorting hot spots. The stuff you so diligently (or, maybe, not so diligently) separate in your suburban model home will eventually get separated further by the hands of a scrap sorter somewhere in Asia. Minter recalls his first trip to Foshan, one of China's centers for the scrap trade.

> *Meanwhile, over in the farthest corner of the yard, the flicker of flames might send black smoke into the not-quite-as-dark night. The smell would be noxious (and, depending on the wire, dioxin-laced), but the goal would be anything but: profit. Wires too small to run through the stripping machines were a favorite item to burn, but anything would do if copper demand was strong; in the morning, the copper could be swept out of the ashes. One night, I recall clearly, I saw a row of a half dozen electrical transformers—the big cylinders that hang on power lines and regulate the power—smoking into the night. When I realized what they were, I backed off: older transformers contain highly toxic PCBs. But nobody seemed to mention that to the workers who, through the evening, poked at the flames. I didn't like it, but there's not much to be said when you're standing in the middle of a scrapyard in a village you've never heard of in a province you've just barely heard of, as the guest of somebody you've just met.[14]*

This was the status quo for many years, a US$200 billion boat that nobody would dream of rocking. China produces stuff the west thinks it needs. People in the west consume these goods, usually disposing of them well before their use-by date. Then, the bits and bobs of these goods were loaded up and sent back to China on the same ships which brought them over. Far out of sight, people at the bottom of the economic pyramid would take your trash, risk their lives handling it, in the hopes of making enough to buy dinner. Yet, most people scrolling comfortably through their iPhone would have no idea any of this was going on.

Well, China certainly did, and it finally felt it was time to rock that boat.

In 2018, the Government put into effect a national ban on the import of foreign trash including recyclables. That meant, overnight, all the trash usually shipped out of places like the United States had nowhere to go. Many communities then turned to other, less developed, countries in the region like Malaysia. Following China's lead, Malaysia then closed the door. Now, all of a sudden, this us-versus-them mentality really started to bare its teeth. Headlines around the developed world vilified China for daring to do such a thing. Commentaries lamented the collapse of recycling programs throughout the US. The University of Georgia went as far as putting a number to China's dastardly deed. By 2030, 111 million metric tons of trash from around the world would have nowhere to go, all thanks to China.[15]

But wait. I thought we wanted China to clean up its act. Wasn't the global west of the view that the world's biggest polluter wasn't doing its fair share for the planet? Now that China finally put its hand up to be a better global citizen, in one of the biggest ways possible, why were we raking them over the coals?

Oh, I get it. It's all very well and good when someone else is cleaning up our messes. But when we're forced to take a hard look in the mirror, we don't actually like what we see. From our us-versus-them mentality, we're finally made to see, as I said before, it's really just us. This big planet of ours is pretty small when you think about it. Everything exists in an ecosystem of cause and effect, balance and imbalance. Not knowing what's going on on the other side of the world doesn't excuse you from repercussions to your actions. Eventually, the scales will even out.

And that brings us back to the Meths from *Altered Carbon*. For what must have been generations, these futuristic people quite literally lived the high life. Their sky-high mansions and access to infinite sources of sleeves, as well as not having to worry about the destruction of their stacks, gave them an abject sense of superiority over the rabble below. Politicians and the well-heeled of this society made laws reflecting their reality, but ultimately impacting the rest of humanity. The disconnect between the haves and have nots is as glaring as Marie Antoinette's infamous declaration centuries ago.

Spoiler alert! Eventually, the Meths push their luck just a little too far. As could be expected by anyone watching (except the people in the show, of course), the citizenry rose and declared war on their overlords. I'll spare you the details in case you want to watch the show yourself. Suffice to say things don't end well.

This is the same path we now find ourselves on. Those on one side of society sit about and elicit truths that don't apply to the other side. Except in this world, the real world, we're all living on the same rock. Unless some alien species comes down tomorrow and give us the cure for what ails us, we've got to get off our pedestals and work together.

The more we turn to academics and intellectuals to handle the issues surrounding sustainability, the more we will become embedded in our own echo chambers. This isn't to say academic solutions aren't good solutions: they certainly are. But they have their place. When it comes to the negative impact of things like climate change on real people, it's going to take a lot more than a UN resolution, talking head, or another conference to help them.

Vilified or Vaulted?

There's one more group of dicks I want to talk about, and this shouldn't really come as a shocker. For years, the environmental do-gooders have campaigned hard to get us to hate this group. Many have grown to become poster children for all that's wrong in the world. That's right, we're talking about the evil, polluting, greedy businesses in the corporate sector whose only desire is to turn the world into a shriveled mess. They've certainly done a hell of a lot to make things a lot worse for all of us. You have colossal disasters like the BP Deepwater Horizon oil spill which continues to negatively impact life in the Gulf of Mexico a decade after it occurred. Then there's the tobacco industry which accounts for one in five deaths in the United States each year, not to mention over 7 million annual deaths worldwide. Goldman Sachs, The Gap, Nestle, Koch Industries, Wellpoint, and others all find the ire of many an environmental organization for their mistreatment of our natural resources, human labor, and humanity.[16]

Up until recently, these private-sector corporations had been given carte blanche to do pretty much whatever they wanted in the name of progress. Yet, over the past decade or so there have been much stronger regulations in place to foster an environment of transparency. Sustainability reports, some the size of the Bible itself, are the new way to show you're a good corporate citizen. Never mind most of these are full of confusing statistics that don't add up to too much. You'll drown in data before you're ever able to decipher what the hell it all means. This is what we call greenwashing—making it look like you're doing your part for the Earth when, in reality, you're probably not as good as you say you are. This free reign is still alive and well in the developing world where old habits die hard. Corporations in places like India, China, and Brazil are likely not doing as much as they could to be good citizens.

What might really create some cognitive dissonance for you, though, is something I've essentially banked my entire career on. For all the bad apples out there (and, believe me, they're a dime a dozen), there are an equal number of companies we should look to as exemplars of good. Instead of vilifying all these corporate actors, we should instead be saluting and working with these good ones to make the world a better place. Rather than putting them on watch lists, we need to come together, hand-in-hand, towards a brighter tomorrow. I can already hear the groans now. But, wait! Before you throw this book across the room and start yelling at me for wasting your time and money, hear me out.

On the surface, those in the private sector have seemingly done a terrible job of being stewards of the environment and humanity. It seems like we've never evolved out of the Industrial Revolution. You'd imagine the inside of a factory at, say, Walmart to look like something from a Jacob Riis novel.[17] And I wouldn't blame you. The only side of the story most people have ever been exposed to is the bad one. Terrible treatment of workers—to the point of suicide—happening at Foxconn factories across China. The 2013 Rana Plaza disaster, where a garment factory used by such high fashion labels such as The Gap, Gucci, and Mango collapsed in Dhaka and killed over 1,110 workers. Drill baby drill would be a more appropriate slogan for the Adani corporation, which is currently digging the largest coal mine in Australia's history. The Carmichael Mine will, among a host of other things, annually allow 520 more coal ships to travel through the Great Barrier Reef, gain access to 270 billion liters of groundwater in the country's arid north, and add 4.7 billion tons of carbon pollution to the atmosphere.[18] Of course, I'm not trying to excuse any of these terrible truths. They've happened, and continue to happen, all over the globe.

There are thousands of corporations, though, making up for what these other companies lack. According to the 2010 US Census data, 18,500 American companies were operating with 500 or more people.[19]In other words, companies large enough to have an impact one way or the other at scale. Surely all of these companies can't be bad. On a scale from reforesting the Amazon to clubbing baby seals, I'd guess most fall somewhere towards the Brazilian side of the spectrum.

What I am advocating for is a deeper understanding of not just the operations of the private sector, but the depth and scope of what they can bring to the conversation. That's because the private sector, more than any other group of actors, has the capacity, resources, and economies-of-scale to tackle some of our most pressing issues. When used for bad they can do serious damage. But when put in the right hands and for the right purposes, amazing things can happen.

One of my favorite examples comes from the company most people, at least in the United States, pretend to hate the most. That company? Walmart. For years, do-gooders have fought against Walmart and its hegemonic family for their treatment of workers both Stateside and overseas. They cite Walmart's propensity to purposely squash mom-and-pop stores worldwide in their quest for dominance. The company also has a track record of employing people who are undereducated and therefore supposedly only entitled to extremely low wages, no healthcare, and certainly no job security. This is all meant to keep prices low and profits high. I'm sure you know, though, making cheap products doesn't come cheap at all.

If you want those rock-bottom prices you've got to watch your bottom line. While grinding down wages of American employees might do a bit to keep their costs low, it's really on the production side where things happen. Although Walmart has long prided itself on American-made goods, it's an open secret most of their products are produced outside the United States. A lot of this happens in China, where factories buzz along at breakneck speed to produce those products you think you need to have. Nobody in Omaha or Dallas wants to question how Walmart's able to produce so much, so cheaply. They just go about their daily business as if it all makes perfect economic sense.

Again, there is plenty of blame to pass around. Walmart, as a corporate operator and top of the Fortune rankings, certainly doesn't have its hands clean. We already mentioned their use of the Rana garment factory, underpayment of wages, and piss-poor store working conditions. But, let's take a trip to the southern Chinese city of Shenzhen, just across the border with Hong Kong. It's here that Walmart's China headquarters is based, and where most of the operations for its nearly 100 China mainland factories happens. It's quite the operation, too. There are thousands of staff making sure things are streamlined, but more importantly there are no hiccoughs. If something goes wrong with operations here, you might not get that treasured Barbie Doll in time for Christmas.

This isn't a story about how good Walmart's operations are. Obviously, they know what they're doing or they wouldn't be the largest company in the world. This is a story about the conditions their factory workers live under, in their tens of thousands. Take a minute and close your eyes. When I mention factory conditions in China, what do you imagine? Tired workers huddled in cold rooms, at risk of a missing hand if they doze off next to a machine? Dormitories with no air conditioning in the middle of summer, disease rampant, and food inedible? Automated machines buzzing quietly while specialized technicians keep things rolling along in near hospital-like conditions?

Wait, what?

One of these things is certainly not like the other. If you had to guess which the correct scenario is, you'd best place your money on option three. The level of automation going on in China is astounding. Each time I go into a factory I'm always amazed at how safe and technologically advanced the conditions are. Most of the time people are only used to program instructions into machines. Of course, there are still plenty of things done by hand but these are hardly the black market labor conditions you'd be likely to think of. Factories are safe, clean, and monitored or audited ad nauseam.

A big, evil company like Walmart would probably just lay off thousands of factory workers and put machines in their place, right? Wrong. Companies like Walmart are taking this once-in-a-lifetime opportunity not to replace workers with machines but to upskill workers for future employment opportunities. They are looking far into the future where China is no longer the world's factory, but instead the world's premier service provider. To get a sense of the scale of this undertaking, let's look at one of Walmart China's signature programs—the Women in Factories Program. As a consultant with BSR, I had the opportunity to work on this project, one which had great impact on workers.

The basic premise of the program was to help upskill female workers across Walmart's China-based factories. It would cover topics such as on-the-job training, business and management skills, communications, and the like. The program would also cover more of the soft skills needed to be a good worker: family planning; personal finance; health, and wellness. These were all areas most women in China just didn't learn in school. Over the eight or nine years of compulsory education in China, there is little time to teach things like personal hygiene. In a country where abortion is still considered a legitimate form of birth control, teachers don't help students understand why this is a bad idea. Touchy cultural taboo subjects such as these are hardly ever talked about by people, much less by the government.

And, that's where Walmart and other corporations fit in. They aren't under the guise of the government so have much more leeway when it comes to defining what business skills employees need.

That keeps the government off their backs and the programs rolling along.

From a business perspective, what's the rationale for all of this? How can a company justify helping out their workers, especially when it seems on the surface to be a huge expenditure? Sure, it might make Walmart executives feel (and look) good to be helping out. As with anything related to sustainability and business, though, there has to be an economic imperative for change to happen. In short, how can we still make money?

Take the abortion topic, for example. When workers get abortions, they are often out sick for several days afterward. If a worker comes to realize there are other forms of contraception, and in turn get fewer abortions, then they are going to show up to work more often. This leads to lower absenteeism, especially when calculated across an entire factory. Not only that, but these women are likely to be happier psychologically and thus less stressed. When you're happier, you're more productive. Lower absenteeism, higher productivity, and the bonus of greater appreciation for the company mean you are going to get more work out of each worker. This means more money for the factory and Walmart. A true win-win scenario. How much of a win-win?

If you're thinking it was small potatoes, think again. Over three-years, nearly 100,000 women across 60 major Chinese factories participated in the program. That's 100,000 lives changed directly and countless hundreds of thousands more indirectly. This is the type of scale most governments, and certainly most NGOs, just can't muster. That's the power of the private sector when used as a force for good. The impact on the participants is so much more than just learning hard skills. More than 70 percent of employees said the program helped them adapt better to, and solve problems in, their personal lives and at work. A full 80 percent of factory trainers said their self-confidence and communication skills improved.[20] That's real impact from a company that is supposed to be Satan incarnate.

It's not just Walmart, either. There are far more prolific programs in the fast-moving consumer goods sector positively impacting the lives of workers around the world. The Gap's P.A.C.E. program, The HER Project sponsored by corporations like Disney, HP, and Levi's, and Plan W from Diageo are all making a difference for millions of workers in the developing world. Some have been going on for a decade or more, operating seemingly under the radar from consumers where these products are sold. Few outside the circle of those impacted would even know such programs exist. Imagine how much more impactful these programs can be if more people knew about, and supported them? What would happen if you were able to make your purchase decision based on having this new information? How could things change? Nobody is asking you to spend more at the register to fund this stuff. It's already happening. But as long as certain groups keep vilifying the corporations doing good, how is the average consumer supposed to know any better? Even worse, how are we supposed to keep these impactful programs going if people are being put off by shopping at these places?

To bring all this together, let's think back through our three lacrosse-bro groups. We've talked about those in the non-governmental space who are as cutthroat as anyone in trying to survive, particularly when it comes to finances, regardless of the adverse impact this is having. Then, we have those who live life through an academic lens. Gray-bearded, holier-than-thou scholars, diplomats, and talking heads do a disservice to any cause because most of them are far removed from the causes themselves. Lastly, we looked at the corporate sector who are fighting a never-ending image battle between being the good guys but looking like the most despicable group of the bunch.

What these segments all have in common is they have created little fiefdoms from which they operate. We saw this a bit when we discussed the NGO world and how they've carved out nooks and crannies they work from. Greenies, especially the more militant of the group, gather in cliques and shun outsiders. They make the idea of saving the world a near-impossible task, only open to those who would reject modern life and live on a kibbutz.

The academics, too, do this by choice. They'd rather stay in their ivory tower than get their hands dirty doing the hard yards. Academics keep pushing their white papers, panel discussions, and recommendations in our face, even though most of us have stopped listening. We've stopped listening because very few of their so-called expert conclusions make any sense or are having much impact.

Corporations, on the other hand, operate in fiefdoms because they've been forced to by external parties, such as environmentalists. These are controlled operations that we're exposed to every day but have become blind to as well. While many are still colossal dicks, there's a campaign amongst a not-so-insignificant number to change this image. So, who's the bigger dick here: them for not doing more, or us for not paying attention?

It's not only these groups walking around in their own little siloed worlds. There are probably dozens of other groups out there as well. The reason it's easy to sparse them out is that they've done it to themselves. This process of self-ostracization immediately pits one group against another. It's become so rash some have even taken to guilt-tripping those on the outside. I'm sorry, but your viewpoint doesn't mean you get to be a dick to others.

For the sake of brevity, I'll introduce just a few examples. How about the vegans, organic mommies, and non-GMO campaigners who have turned eating into a balancing act from Cirque du Soleil? Have you ever actually tried to go out to dinner with them? What's worse is they want everything else to bend to their will, not a very inclusive mindset if you ask me. Oh... you don't want to live off the grid? Then you're just a corporate pawn and sell out. Ew... you drive an F150 and not a Prius? You can't sit with us. Instead of taking the time to explain, educate, and encourage, some would rather pit them-versus-us.

I'd like to remind you all: stop being dicks to each other. All this does is put a bad taste in peoples' mouths about the good work you're doing day in and day out. Instead, work together with inclusiveness. If someone doesn't understand what it means to be a vegan, the last thing you should do is roll your eyes. When they don't get why you refuse to wash your hair with shampoo or brush your teeth with toothpaste, explain why (from a distance). Work at a corporation and tired of having tomatoes thrown at you? Take a second to talk to the person through open and honest dialogue. Until we all come to the table as one, we're not going to do much more than what we've already accomplished.

It's not like I'm asking for the world here. History is full of examples where working together, even in the strangest or most dire of situations, led to results no one could have imagined. Think about the brave warriors during the ancient Battle of Thermopylae.[21] Glorified in the 2006 movie *300*,[22] this is a battle all students of military strategy or politics have to learn. In essence, Thermopylae is one of history's greatest last stands. The ancient Spartans, under King Leonidas, were waging battle against King Xerxes of Persia. If the historical accounts are to be believed, the Spartans were outnumbered 508 to 1. Not the best odds in the world. Still, they pulled a rabbit out of their little Greek hats harnessing ingenuity over brute strength. Thermopylae (in Greek, the Hot Gates) was a narrow coastal pass critical for the Persians to access and move through. Acting like a funnel, the pass essentially limited the number of Persians on the front lines at any one time. This gave the Spartans much better odds, balancing out the forces on both sides. We're not sure if the plan would have been entirely successful because a Greek traitor decided to tell the Persians what was up. As it stands, we do know the Spartans were able to hold off the pass for a good three days against one of the largest armies the ancient world had ever known. Sure, they lost. But they did an impressive job decimating what they could on the way out.

Okay, how about a more positive example? Consider the group of courageous soldiers during the siege at Dunkirk.[23] One of the first salvos of World War Two, Dunkirk is a good example of collaboration and humanity amid the hell of war. To make a long story short, we have the Germans advancing throughout France, the Netherlands, and Belgium. Allied forces are being pushed back to the sea as the Nazis use a spearhead-type formation relentlessly. Germany was able to easily overtake much of the region and ended up flanking the Allied troops. This is probably the worst position to be in militarily because it's just a hop, skip, and a jump away from being crushed. Retreating to the seaside town of Dunkirk, the British army became separated from the other Allied troops, setting up their defenses on the beaches of the English Channel. With German U-boats in the water, planes flying low overhead, and the docks destroyed, there was little chance the British could feasibly evacuate. They were stranded, sitting ducks waiting for German annihilation. Then, a miracle. Over ten days, a ragtag flotilla of 800 ships comprised of all manner of merchant and private vessel was used to ferry 338,226 soldiers across the Channel to Britain. While the city fell to the Germans, the incident inspired what came to be known as the Dunkirk Spirit. This Spirit would help galvanize the support, patriotism, and resolve which would eventually lead to Allied victory.

There are plenty of more recent examples too. The biggest one that pops immediately to mind is how humankind came together in the 1980s to fix the ozone layer.[24] In 1985, a group of British scientists began to notice a large "hole" in the Earth's ozone layer over the Antarctic. The ozone layer acts as a protective screen over the Earth, keeping out radiation from the sun. Without it, we'd burn up like toast as the sun's rays scorched everything on the planet. A massive hole opening up wasn't a good thing. Scientists soon linked the use of chlorofluorocarbons (CFCs) to ozone depletion. CFCs were found in most aerosol products at the time. As a shock to every global consumer, the cans of hairspray and shaving cream they so readily used were destroying the planet. The media immediately began to push the story, scaring the hell out of everyone, everywhere. In one *Newsweek* interview (which probably was a little on the nose at the time, as it certainly still is today) a terrified environmentalist said the threat was like "…AIDS from the sky."[25] The terror reached such a fever pitch the international community banded together to sign the Montreal Protocol, effectively banning the use of CFCs. In what is probably the biggest environmental victory of our time, we have been able to claw back and fill in the ozone hole in the Antarctic. While it still ebbs and flows with the seasons, scientists believe we will have entirely healed the ozone layer hole by 2050.

This is the power of collaboration. This is the power of working together, as one, to overcome our challenges. As the sage African proverb says, "if you want to go fast, go alone. If you want to go far, go together."

Let's go far, together.

| vi |

Point #4: Be a Pragmatic Altruist

It's 6:30 on a wet Friday evening and I'm running terribly late for a movie. Melbourne's traffic can be horrendous during rush hour, but the trams are a pretty safe bet to get you where you need to be on time. Not tonight apparently. We were making great time until we hit the central business district. Here, things just slowed to a crawl. The tram sat between stops for a good twelve minutes. Due to safety regulations, tram conductors can't let people off between official stops. After five minutes the grumbling started. After seven minutes, people started going up to the conductor and asking what in the world was happening. All the conductor knew was there were trams stopped in front of us and nowhere to go. Nothing was coming in off the radio, so she was running blind. By ten minutes, someone got so fed up they pushed open the doors on their own and let a good half of the tram off with them. Within another couple minutes, someone came onto the tram to say all services had been discontinued. We would have to walk the rest of the way. Mind you, it was pouring down rain at this point.

The second I stepped off the tram, I joined a sea of people headed up the main street of the CBD. I mingled amongst the typical tourists taking pictures, and business people on their way home for the weekend. It was certainly more crowded than usual. After about a block, I started to notice a third segment growing more populous by the foot. They grew in tandem with an overt police presence on the streets. Waiting at a traffic light, I turned to the woman next to me. She was soaked to the bone, mascara running down her face, wearing a garbage bag for a poncho. In her hand, she held a makeshift cardboard sign with the Shakespearean scrawling: "fuck the system, not the planet." Crap. It was a climate change protest march.

I could see, smell, and hear them now. Angry greenies, vocal university students, and weirdos of every ilk mingling around chanting in unison (kind of). "Hey hey! Ho ho! The government has got to go! Hey hey! Ho ho! Scott Morrison has got to go!" Those marching down Swanston Street were furious at Australia's federal government for its less-than-stellar response to the country's escalating bushfire crisis. While the stories of bushfire tragedy gripped international headlines, the Prime Minister vacationed in Hawaii.His deputies, beholden to the interests of the coal industry, refused to admit climate change had anything to do with the disaster. Images of blackened forests and walls of fire were made grimmer by the loss of human and animal life. Some estimates point to upwards of 1 billion animals losing their lives, with the emblematic koala added to the endangered species list.[1] The international outcry, and relief, was being met by political silence on the ground.

People had had enough and were demanding heads, and I have to say, I couldn't agree with them more.

But as I pushed my way up the street, narrowly avoiding that many umbrellas jamming into my eye, all I felt was frustration. Not frustration at the ineptitude of the federal government or the tram conductor sitting in her warm, dry seat blocks away. No, my frustration was with the protesters themselves. As they milled about, taking up four lanes of traffic and the entirety of both sidewalks, all I cared about was getting where I needed to be. In the busiest part of the city, at the busiest time of the week, these protesters weren't a force for good. They were just getting in the way.

This frustration only grew as the crowds began to morph from invested, well-intentioned activists to the parasitic hangers-on you often find at events like this. There was the fire dancer trying to get her torches going between downpours; the chanting of the Hari Krishna looking for converts; and, the inevitable Bible basher touting the end times. It was a mish-mash of characters diluting the message at the core of the march. For people on the outside, it was further confirmation that those fighting to save the world were just a bunch of freaks and geeks.

As I finally sat down for the movie, I started to think about all the frustrated people on the tram. Each was just trying to get where they needed to go. Maybe it was somewhere inconsequential, like a movie. Perhaps it was something more important, like a hospital visit or business meeting. Would they look at the protests as something meant to change the world positively? That's highly unlikely. They would remember the protests as a nuisance; something that forced them off the comfort of the tram and onto the cold, damp streets. It made them wet, late, and stressed.

For those with a keen eye, they'd also wonder what all this had accomplished. Weeks later the bushfires still raged, and the government still sat on their hands. There was so much time spent organizing and creating witty banners, tax money used for police patrols and security, and mental capacity thrown into the cause. While certainly coming from a place of passion and good intentions, a simple cost/benefit analysis would have put the protest squarely in the "unsound" column. Lots of cost, little benefit, and even less impact.

However, sometimes people need an outlet to air their grievances. They're raising awareness of an important issue and demonstrating people power! That's how things change…the will of the people.

Let's go with this idea of people power and imagination. Instead, all those thousands of people could have been doing something even more strategic and constructive. Maybe each could have donated a few dollars to relief efforts or supplies to emergency organizations on the front lines. Some could have corralled their passions to drive efforts at their places of work. Many of the university students, out on holiday break, were able-bodied enough to volunteer in fire-ravaged areas and could have availed themselves. Instead, they believed meandering a few blocks in the rain was going to make all the difference. What they forgot to do was to factor in the most important element to change. It's not people power. It's pragmatism.

I've said it earlier in this book, and I'll say it again: passion without pragmatism is just complaining.

As we've already seen time and time again, passionate individuals have certainly created impact when it comes to saving the world. We've also seen just how far their lack of pragmatism has gotten them (spoiler alert: not as far as they thought it would). A lack of pragmatism is the biggest barrier to further progress, yet it's also a barrier most passionate activists seem to continuously forget.

Whenever I discuss the need for pragmatism in the fight for a more sustainable future, I'm often met with sneers, daggered eyes, and tomatoes being thrown at me (luckily that's figurative… at least as of the time of writing). People hate to hear the message, mostly because they're not really hearing the message at all. I say, "passion without pragmatism equals complaining," and they hear "activists are worthless and John's a big corporate sell out." I know it doesn't make any sense. Yet, here we are.

Let's be clear, this is not at all what I'm talking about. I'm not discounting the need for passion. I, for one, understand that passion is the only thing that gets people like us out of bed in the morning. Passion is the driving force that helps us push the proverbial shit uphill. But, wouldn't it be so much easier to propel that shit around if there was an actual plan in place? To paraphrase a witty exchange between Alice and the Cheshire Cat in Lewis Carrol's *Alice in Wonderland*, if you don't know where you are going, any road will get you there.[2]Sometimes it certainly feels as if I'm gazing at all this through the looking glass.

In business, people often say "make a plan and work your plan." The sustainability community, too, must make a plan and stick to it. We're not talking about any old plan. The plan has to be strategic, executable, and most importantly, based on reality. As shown earlier in this book, reality isn't something people in the sustainability space like to embrace. From going off the grid to developing artificial moons, some of these ideas aren't the least bit sane. You wouldn't trust an architect to build a supertall skyscraper if they refused to take into account the law of gravity. You'd hope a pilot wouldn't push the engines to full throttle and take the plane up into the stratosphere just to get to your destination faster. No patient today would go to the hospital and ask for bloodletting to cure their ailments. That's because there are bounds to reality that we simply have to operate within.

Why, then, do we give folks in public good a pass when it comes to being realistic? Why do we let them propose plans, execute programs, or shut down city streets for fantastical dreams? When you think about it rationally, it just doesn't make sense.

Let's go back to my little Friday night misadventure and break it down a bit. You can't discount the passion of the crowds marching down the street. The guttural pangs of anger in their voices, painted with the tambour of ignored masses, stretched vocal cords to their limits. Tears and anguish on their faces revealed the fear of an uncertain future. But beyond passion, did they have an end game in mind? Sure, they wanted climate action and to upend a system of government culpable for the entire mess. How, though, were they going to get there? Systemic changes like the ones these protesters were fighting for do not happen overnight. It takes generations and generations. By demanding such an intangible outcome weren't they just setting themselves up for failure and disappointment?

Not only does failure breed frustration, but also lends itself to apathy, complacency, and despondency. Maybe this is what I saw on the faces of those protesters. After years and years of failed attempts at change—due to a focus on altruism over pragmatism—people were at their wit's end. Their ask was so big, though, the only possible answer was no. After hearing no enough times, even the most resilient of us would certainly give up.

A more pragmatic approach would harness the passion of those same people but have a realistic, shared goal in mind. What I noticed at the Melbourne protest described above was a lack of coherency. People were all there fighting for their own causes. What was seen on the surface appeared to be a march in support of climate activism. Actually, it was an effort to upend globalization and force out the current Liberal Government in Australia. Changing the global capitalist system in one fell swoop is not a realistic goal. Telling people that it's time to get rid of a political party that seems to base its entire strategy on negative political optics is not new news either. If the magic is in the message, these folks were cutting the beautiful assistant in a million different pieces.

Next, that shared goal should be meaty but bite-sized. The journey of a thousand miles begins with a single step, not with one giant leap. As this was a political protest at the heart of things, they should have started hyper-local. Although Melbourne is probably the most politically left place I've ever lived, there is still plenty of room for action. Politics is always local, so enlisting the help of Melbourne city councilors or federal representatives in the area would perhaps be a better starting point. The bushfire crisis was also a key component of the protest. Why not, then, get local businesses involved in donating time, money, or goods to the cause? How about looking into the impact on local stakeholders and how to prepare for future disruption? Hell, even walking up and down the street with donation buckets would have gone a long way at helping.

Lastly, the goal should be something we can all get behind. In essence, it should be sharable outside the group of passionate individuals driving it. The bushfire crisis (in the words of a PR pro) has mass appeal. That's possibly how the organizers were able to get so many people to come out in the rain on a Friday night. Who doesn't want to protest imbecilic policies destroying vast parts of the country? Who doesn't want to help their fellow citizens in times of crisis? Who doesn't want to show their support for firefighters putting their lives in harm's way? Unfortunately, protesters squandered all this great capital because the message became an unwieldy beast. Instead of an appeal for help in fire-ravaged communities, it became an angry litmus test on capitalism itself.

At no point in any of these recommendations would I ask anyone to give up their passion. Instead, I'm demanding they focus further in. This way, they can get what it is they're after. Passion is the car. Pragmatism is the road. It's a symbiotic relationship.

This symbiotic relationship is what I like to define as pragmatic altruism. At its core, pragmatic altruism is simply the act of doing good... passionately and strategically. Over time, pragmatism has become quite a loaded term. As the *Cambridge Dictionary* defines it:

solving problems in a sensible way that suits the conditions that really exist now, rather than obeying fixed theories, ideas, or rules:

In business, the pragmatic approach to problems is often more successful than an idealistic one.[3]

The most important part of being a pragmatic altruist is that you have to keep the big picture in mind. Our goal is to create a more sustainable future for everyone: ourselves; our children; and those adorable little kids in the graduating class of 3044. All too often we get caught up in our day-to-day and forget this simple mission. It makes sense. We're only human. Those who are passionate tend to lose the forest for the trees. They get bogged down in the details, which can often derail them from the task at hand. Instead of considering the impact of the plastics industry on global pollution, for example, passionate people might instead focus on getting their neighbors to separate their trash. It doesn't address the root problem, which is the use of plastics overall. A more pragmatic approach would be to reduce or eliminate plastics from the supply chain.

But a pragmatic altruist makes sure to remind themselves there is more at stake than just a deadline, new form to fill out, or disgruntled client. It's not easy to do, especially in our modern society. There are far too many distractions not just in our work, but in our personal lives as well. While this may be one of the most important characteristics of the pragmatic altruist, it's also probably one of the most difficult to attain. It's a constant struggle, but pragmatic altruists do what it takes to make it a reality. Stickers on their laptops, reminders in their calendars, even mantras repeated over and over and over until they're ingrained in the brain. Nobody said it was going to be easy. Pragmatic altruists are up for the challenge.

Keeping the big picture in mind can often seem impossible, though, especially with all the heart-wrenching causes we often embrace. That's why it's important to balance out what Mark Manson calls the Thinking and Feeling Brains.[4] The author of *The Subtle Art of Not Giving a F*ck* and *Everything is F*cked* explains our two brains using the analogy of a road trip. We like to think the brain behind the steering wheel is our thinking brain—which helps us make rational, measured decisions. We are the most advanced creatures on the planet, after all. Manson argues that, in reality, it's our feeling brain calling the shots. You can try your best to fight against it, but at the end of the day, your feeling brain is going to win. The more you resist, the more it gains the upper hand. This is even more pronounced in the important work of saving the world. We are constantly confronted with causes which not only grab our attention but also pull on our heartstrings. This is feeling-brain territory. As we've explored earlier, it's important to fight the impulse of trying to solve every one of the world's problems. The pragmatic altruist understands that when they spread themselves too thin by getting caught in the weeds, instead of looking at things from a 30,000-foot level, they aren't able to bring their best selves to the table. Don't be a cat distracted by shiny objects. Focus!

Pragmatic altruists also operate squarely in the realm of reality. They aren't going after pie-in-the-sky alternative universes like most hard-core environmentalists. Instead, they know today's society, not that of the 1700s, is our starting point. Nobody in their right mind is going to give up their mobile phone, cars, or trips to Ibiza. It's just not realistic. I mean, would you give any of these things up? I wouldn't! Now I understand that when you're passionate about something you tend to throw reason out the window. Even courts around the world take a lighter look at crimes of passion versus those that are premeditated. This isn't a contest. We're all passionate about saving the planet and making things better for the next generation. Just because you drive a Tesla, have a reusable coffee cup, or scorn bathing doesn't discount my daily work to make things better. Except for the ones who still think this is all a big joke, let's assume here everyone is equally passionate and that we're all on the same page. Now, we can get to work incorporating sense, reason, and realism into what we're doing.

If this is the starting line, where to from here? Perhaps instead of giving up mobile phones, pragmatic altruists would suggest phones equipped with more sustainably sourced materials that last longer than just 10 months. Is throwing red paint on a coat going to stop rich old ladies from buying furs? Nope. How about sitting down with fur traders themselves to discuss why alternatives make much more sustainable business sense. Cars? How about electric? While this has long been a pipedream for the automobile industry in the US, the rest of the world has advanced at lightning speed with the adoption and use of electric vehicles. Public transportation in the southern Chinese city of Shenzhen, for example, runs entirely on electric. That means the city's tens of thousands of buses, taxis, and motorbikes are all clean and green. Looks like someone there was thinking pragmatically. Oh, and international air travel. Instead of giving it up entirely, let's look at ways of offsetting it. Instead of flying, how about taking a train? Do you run an airline? What are the small things you can change that add up to having a big impact? The more we try to get people to give up their modern conveniences, the more we are going to see a backlash. All that's leading to are people simply tuning out. The pragmatic altruist understands this possibility and is doing their utmost to counter it.

Finally, pragmatic altruists are practical. By this I mean that they think like a marketer and not like an activist. Activists, and we've seen and will continue to explore throughout the rest of this book, love shock value. The eco-warrior unfurling a banner over a bridge.

PETA and their horrific videos. The poverty-stricken child in Latin America who, for just 20 cents a day, can have a new pair of shoes. These are all ways activists try to generate impressions and collect eyeballs (not literally, of course...that'd be a weird charity to work for).

A pragmatic altruist, on the other hand, thinks more strategically when it comes to getting their message out. They think like a professional marketer would: identifying their target segments, developing a message which resonates with those segments, and then offering people something they need. By the end, pragmatic altruists have people eating out of the palm of their hand. Only in this way will we get people to understand both where we're coming from and the imperative of saving the planet in a way that works for the individual.[5]

This is especially important when we consider the impact of the private sector on the future of the world. We've spent approximately 200 years, since the start of the Industrial Revolution, creating the environment we live in today. There's no way we can upend all of that overnight. It's going to take time and patience to change how business operates. We have to be practical and realistic about that. To expect H&M to become a sustainable fashion brand tomorrow is simply not going to happen. Taking measures, today, to improve their human rights, supply chain, and labor practices are a practical step in the right direction. Having oil and gas companies just shut down will only cause more problems. Bringing together stakeholders from the consumer, political, and scientific worlds to innovate future solutions (that aren't going to take fifty years to execute) is a better approach. Bring these companies along for the ride instead of ostracizing them. Then see how much progress they make. That's the thinking of the pragmatic altruist.

What's Really at Stake

Great. So, the organizers of the Melbourne protests really muffed things up in their planning. No harm, no foul, right? Perhaps in this instance, sure. Yet history is littered with examples of what happens when pragmatism and altruism move in very different directions. Aside from just a terrible way of running things, three major negative consequences arise. You'll quickly see how just having one's heart in the right place, or believing it's the thought that counts, isn't always the best way to look at things. This isn't some unwanted birthday present that you're planning to re-gift. With the future of the world, there's so much more at stake.

A Man and His Wall

The first negative comes as unintended consequences. While an idea might *seem* like the right thing to do, without strategic planning it can have many undesirable effects. Anyone who has ever worked for a startup will understand this point. Consider the founder or CEO of a new company. They're so very passionate about their product and have great hopes for the growth of their business. Often, this means they want to try everything under the sun to make money, sometimes without a real plan in place. Any idea that pops into their head is the task *du jour*. One day it might be a new marketing plan. The next is a great source of funding. Then, it's a seemingly novel idea for a product extension. For every 100 new ideas, only a small portion will ever actually make a noticeable impact. Even worse, time is spent fighting fires instead of fleshing out any one thing. With all passion and no strategy, great ideas end up getting stuck before they even get out the gate.

One of history's greatest leaders had a singular ambition: to build a wall around his nation. The purposes for this wall were many but ultimately it came down to protectionism. You see, this leader lived in a very uncertain time. Foreign incursion along the country's long porous border threatened to topple his society's way of life. Military action was only getting so far. This leader wanted a more permanent solution.

Over 200 years, this vision slowly became a reality and formed the Ming Great Wall of China as we know it today. Iterations of the Wall go back to the founding emperors of China, but what exists now is largely from the 1300s and onward. Hongwu, the first emperor of the Ming Dynasty, set up these fortifications to keep out Mongol invaders from the north. Over centuries, the Wall extended its serpent-like slither across the north of the empire, from the sands of the Gobi Desert to the golden yellow waters of the Bohai Sea.

This physical wall—used to keep Chinese safe—also had an intangible manifestation. Not only did it keep invaders out, it eventually kept ideas in. James C. Davis, in his monumental work *The Human Story* (2005), notes how the Wall changed the psychological blueprint of both the country's rulers and its people.[6] He discusses the great seafaring voyages of Zheng He's 317-strong fleet across the Malay Peninsula, Indian Ocean, Persian Gulf, Arabia, and East Africa. His 30,000 men were able to accomplish what would take Europeans another 200 years. But, after Zheng He's seventh voyage everything stopped. Davis claims in his book that emperors and advisors began to question why, if China was protected and at the center of the world, should they bother with these distant barbarians? This had a lasting impact. In the author's words:

Halting the expeditions was a fateful move. If the journeys had continued, they might, first, have made Ming China a major naval power. Then its merchants might have followed up with trading voyages of their own, making China a colossus in the world economy. China might have spread around the Earth its inventiveness, its energy, its taste in art, and the teaching of Confucius that, 'If one leads [people] with virtue…they will have a sense of shame and will come up to expectations.[7]

Instead China, similar to its neighbor Japan in the forthcoming centuries, walled itself off from influencing and being influenced by foreign ideas. This stymied growth. Although China was still one of the world's superpowers for centuries to come, it's interesting to imagine how much greater it could have been. With the trade of ideas, especially those as advanced as the Chinese had while Europeans were still coming out of the Dark Ages, could China have remained the world's dominant superpower? When Hongwu resuscitated the idea of a great northern wall, did he ever think it would severely hurt his people in the long-term? As China looked inward, the western world leapfrogged ahead. Done in a Eurocentric way, it was without much influence, partnership, or collaboration with the Chinese. This all came to bear with what the Chinese call the Century of Humiliation. From the forced opening up of its borders after the Opium War through to the disgraceful acts committed against Chinese people in the Second World War, the Wall proved to hold a fair share of negative and unintended consequences.

As we know, history has a pesky way of repeating itself. Fast forward to today and we're struggling with a rise in global nationalism, misinformation, and so-called fake news in the media. People refute commonly held facts, not least of which deal with the cause of global warming, and are retreating behind their figurative, and in some places literal, walls. Compared to 700 years ago, however, today's problems are only exacerbated by our interconnected, globalized world. When one person, idea, or country hides behind a wall they're not only hurting themselves. Now, it harms us all. I'm writing this during the height of the coronavirus pandemic, an excellent example of what happens when parties are resistant to collaboration. From China's failings at notifying the world of a potential problem early on, to failed attempts around the world at reopening leading to a second wave, through to the politicization of the disease, it's clear our walls are doing us no favors.

Oh, and if you're looking for a bit of extra credit, there's no shortage of more contemporary examples of unintended consequences resulting from well-intentioned ideas. Australia seems to have gone through a period in the early twentieth century where unintended consequences were something of a national policy. Farmers at the turn of the century brought over and bred non-native species as a form of pest control, assuming what worked in other parts of the world would work in Australia, too. Rabbits, foxes, and cane toads were just a few of those introduced. Unfortunately, without natural predators these non-native animals began to proliferate and become pests in their own right. All of this had catastrophic agricultural implications.[8] You've also got the not-so-successful War on Drugs in the United States. Although well-intentioned, Nixon's original program, as well as Nancy Reagan's Just Say No campaign, did more to increase drug use across the country. It also led to a massive increase in non-violent incarceration, particularly among non-white Americans, and is generally considered a massive policy failure.[9] The policies have also been a large contributor to America's strong-armed police culture and racial divide, two of the key reasons for this year's massive Black Lives Matter protests.

A Man and His Jet

The second negative consequence I would like to highlight when separating pragmatism from altruism is a loss of capital. In this sense, I'm talking about the capital needed to keep people engaged with your message, actions, or causes. Remember, a pragmatic altruist thinks like a marketer and not an activist. As a marketer, we know our audience is spoilt for choice. We have to find a way to hook them in and keep them coming back for more. This is especially important with a fraught subject like sustainability or climate change. People have more than enough reasons to tune us out. Therefore, we have to work even harder to hold their attention. One wrong step and you lose all credibility. Unfortunately, when it comes to planning and marketing, one hand often doesn't know what the other one is doing.

I'm sitting in a café in London, struggling with a bit of writer's block. When you're setting the foundation for a writing project such as a book, there are many ideas to consider. Sometimes these ideas stick, and other times they fall by the wayside. When it comes to sustainability, and what to do to save the Earth, there are endless things to talk about. I began with a laundry list of close to thirty big ideas I wanted to explore, and decided to focus on five that I believe are the most vital.

The only idea which made it in its entirety is my thinking around being a pragmatic altruist. It's central to how I position my work, my life, and my discussions on the practice of sustainability. I've spoken on sustainability at length in my work, but needed to think deeply around how to reformat my thinking for the page. Then—BAM—it happened. I looked over at the morning newspaper laid out next to me and saw just how I would start to explain the loss of capital to you. Big props go to the news of the day: Prince Harry, Google, and Sir Elton John.

Heir Heads. That was the headline sprawled out across the front page of British tabloid *The Scottish Sun*. Sitting happily, with toothy ear-to-ear grins, was a photo of Prince Harry and Meghan Markle. The royal couple, (well, at least they were royals when I saw that newspaper) were crowned by the quippy tagline, "Their Royal Hypocrites." It was clear to me that Emily Andrews and Chloe Kerr, the authors of the piece, had a pretty serious problem with the royals.[10]

Her problem stemmed from what she viewed as ultimate hypocrisy on the part of the duo, particularly Prince Harry. An outspoken environmentalist, the Prince has a track record of pushing climate initiatives on behalf of all Commonwealth nations. Markle has also got on board with this, going front-and-center in promoting a more sustainable future. According to Madeline Kearns of the *National Review*,

> *...Markle guest-edited a special edition of British Vogue. The cover of which featured Greta Thunberg, a teen girl with Asperger's, who has become the poster girl of European climate change activism. Prince Harry told Vogue that he and Markle would only be having two children on account of the 'terrifying' implications of climate change. Later, at a 'green summit' in Sicily, organized by Google, he delivered a speech barefoot — also, to 'raise awareness.'[11]*

Harry has spoken at several conferences or events on climate change over the past few years. His presentations have often referred to the dangers of pollution and the need for a change in how we approach modern life. Like many other people in positions of power or influence, the buck doesn't actually stop with them. As described in Kearns' article, celebrities at Google's Sicilian green summit, the same one attended by Harry, arrived in an armada of 114 private jets and a "flotilla of superyachts." Not exactly the most sustainable mode of transportation.

With *The Scottish Sun* and *National Review* articles being the tip of the iceberg, it was an easy job to find more and more media high-lighting the contradictions around the Prince's actions. Newspapers across the UK found that during this same period, the Prince took four journeys by private jet in less than two weeks. It's not unusual for celebrities and other leaders to fly private, but the implications for environmental impact are dire. Private flights, because they do carry far fewer people than commercial airlines, significantly im-pact the environment in terms of carbon emissions per passenger. What complicates this further is that there are no prohibitions on royals flying commercial. Flying private is usually done for reasons of security and comfort (never mind the impact on the individual taxpayer who's footing the bill). If you're one such royal, known for speaking out about environmental sustainability, it seems there's an obvious mismatch between words and deeds here.

As if this wasn't bad enough, the public was soon made aware that these trips weren't exactly for official business but rather per-sonal luxury holidays to places like Ibiza and Nice. It was a dramatic example of "do as I say, not as I do." For all the good work the Prince had done, using his position to bring environmental issues to the fore, people began to view Harry's words as empty. His related ac-tions started to seem like public relations stunts.

This is where the idea of pragmatic altruism comes into play. While we can assume Harry meant well, his massive errors in judg-ment cost him any capital he had previously built up. The first cardinal sin was in the Prince's lack of transparency. Most people become quite suspicious when they hear about the wealthy touring around in private jets under the cover of darkness. I mean, how many sinister spy movies have this as a premise? Harry, whether he meant to or not, fell right into the plot of a James Bond film. I get there are security issues at play here. Fine. But once he arrived at what I can only imagine to be a luxurious seaside villa, he should have come clean somehow. This was exactly the right occasion to employ those pesky governmental transparency rules. It could have saved him a lot of embarrassment had he done so.

The second fault can be found in his timing. The big song and dance associated with the launch of the Prince's new climate change initiative meant that media, civil society, and also the general public had it at the top of their awareness. This was the point. Yet, paint on the figurative walls of his new initiative wasn't even dry by the time he hopped on a private jet. In his bad timing, Harry did quite a disservice to the authenticity of his initiative. If the person leading the charge isn't going to follow through, why should anyone else?

Finally, you have to take into account the actors within this British tragedy. You've got the Duke and Duchess of Sussex, members of the House of Windsor, former royals of the United Kingdom (I think I got their current titles right). I'm going to go out on a limb right now and say that these folks aren't exactly relatable to the majority of the British public. They're not just at the upper echelon of society. They're somewhere in the stratosphere above that measly designation. Meanwhile, the rest of us are crammed into the hot, musty underground trying to make it to work on time. Instead of seeming like an initiative we can collaborate on and all get behind, having someone in such a high position of power lead this ends up smacking of an edict from on high.

When considering this example, it's easy to see how Prince Harry, and others involved in this event, were not practicing pragmatic altruism. To practice it, you have to embrace both elements. One cannot work without the other, so his efforts just became a lot of hot air. Harry was truly altruistic. Nothing can discount his life-long work in philanthropy for many causes. From disabled veterans, to HIV/AIDS, to climate change, Harry has been at the forefront of helping to impact the lives of millions. Unfortunately, at least in this case, he wasn't very pragmatic. The consequences of his actions and how these would influence the capital granted him by the general public were, simply put, not considered.

(M)ad Men: An Interlude

I would have loved to have been in the room when whatever genius thought up modern-day sustainability messaging. The burned-out hell-scape of an Earth brought to its knees by humanity's misuse of natural resources. Desert vistas covered in the red dust of a nuclear winter. There are no signs of plants, trees, or oceans. Animals, at least the ones who have endured, scurry around looking for scraps. Humans, somehow clad in black leather jackets, race around on motorbikes to find what they can to survive.

Or, maybe it's the heart-wrenching animal advertisements. We're still wondering what happened to that emaciated polar bear mother, perched precariously on a melting iceberg. Was she able to swim to the next floating piece of ice, or did she drown while trying to find food for her cubs? We've seen animals skinned alive for furs, chickens fattened up for the slaughter in conditions akin to a concentration camp, and the guts of whales filled with all manner of plastics and other rubbish.

Better yet are the actions of groups like Greenpeace. They sail the open waters searching for Japanese whalers, eagerly accepting water cannon fire in the name of environmentalism. Sometimes they rappel from the sides of buildings to hang banners dissuading people from buying X company's product. Red paint on fur, performance art in cages, handcuffs on light posts all call attention to issues these groups want handled.

Now I'd like you to take a step back for a minute and think about the impact of these types of ads. At the end of the day, advertisements are meant to generate what is known as impressions—essentially the number of times someone has seen the ad. Marketers love to ask how many eyeballs have watched a particular campaign. In the days before having to announce whether viewer discretion was advised, these early sustainability marketers were the original users of shock-and-awe tactics in public advertising. I would take a guess their campaigns likely had a high number of impressions. People just weren't used to being confronted with such terrible images or fear-inducing situations. It was novel and caught attention.

People for the Ethical Treatment of Animals (PETA) is an organization notorious for this type of marketing. Their ads go beyond shock value, showing in all graphic detail just how your clothes are made and your food produced. Juxtaposing black-and-white images of crowded concentration camp barracks with colored pictures of industrial chicken coops, a tagline reads, *to animals, all people are Nazis.* From the comfort of his velvety pink sheets, porn star Ron Jeremy asks viewers to spay and neuter their pets. Scantily clad, or often fully nude, women are placed in provocative poses with props from crucifixes to bullfighting spears. One stunt even had naked women sitting in a bath outside a KFC, rebuking the fast-food giant's practice of "scalding chickens to death."[12]

But after 30 years of this marketing strategy, are any of these ads having the same effect? A study by the University of Queensland found that, at least in the case of PETA, the ads are having an adverse impact on the message.[13]The trio of researchers measured if using sexualized imagery, as is done in many PETA ads, actually sold the same way it does in traditional advertising. In their words, "…is it effective to advertise an ethical cause using unethical means?" They studied responses by college-aged males in the United States and Australia, two of PETA's key market segments, to sexualized and non-sexualized PETA imagery. They concluded:

> *Intentions to support the ethical organization were reduced for those exposed to the sexualized advertising, and this was explained by their dehumanization of the sexualized women, and not by increased arousal.*

In short, when it comes to ethical advertising sex doesn't sell.

Nowadays, we're seeing a move from shock-and-awe to what's been named "sadvertising." Major companies are engaging in meaningful marketing, taking trendy social issues and incorporating them into powerful product ads. Feminine care company Always addressed adolescent stereotypes in their #likeagirl hashtag campaign. Dove's "Real Beauty" adverts encouraged body positivity, while Nike asked consumers to Find Your Greatness and strive to be the best at what you do. Meaningful marketing tends to be long-form and emotional, perfect for online campaigns. Yet, as more and more companies start to jump on this bandwagon, are we going to witness a dilution of the messages? Will it all just become more noise to filter out, in much the same way as those touching World Vision ads of the 1980s?

Consider, for example, the impact of the 24-hour news cycle on sustainability messaging. There is certainly no shortage of information coming through our televisions and mobile phones heralding the end of the world. For all the meaningful marketing adverts out there, it seems that shock-and-awe tactics still reign supreme. Much of the recent spate of doom-and-gloom messaging could be seen as a result of the United Nations itself. Their reports since the Paris Agreement in 2016 have been increasingly dire, using such loaded phrases as tipping points and irreversible damage, while setting deadlines beyond which the end times will draw nigh.

While I most definitely do not debate the merit and validity of these reports, I certainly take issue with their presentation of the facts. Yes, we are totally screwing ourselves out of a home. Yes, we are probably already past the point of no return. Yes, if we don't change our behavior then we're heading into an increasingly dystopic future. This is the stuff of dreams for a newscast trying to get viewers. However, it's not necessarily the best thing to galvanize people to get the facts and change their behavior. The way these reports are presented continue to make us freeze on the OMG rather than act on the WTF do we do?

This argument is in no way an advocation for anyone trying to refute the science. To be clear: THIS IS NOT THE WAY! What we need to do, since it's not being done for us yet, is to take all the great information available to us and figure out a plan of attack. What sectors do we focus on? Who should lead this, whether private sector, public sector, or civil society actors? How do we fast track the solution rather than get bogged down in the shock factor? If we only remain focused on the "what," we'll inevitably forget about the "how." That means we'll become complacent because, well, if it's all going to hell in a handbasket what are we supposed to do about that?

Man and His Guilt

The third, and final, consequence of a divorce between pragmatism and altruism is the creation of what I like to define as *false idols*. These figurative golden calves take our focus away from where it should be. Today we have to contend with larger-than-life personalities who suck up all the media attention they can get. Some we may turn to as a form of escapism. Reality stars, Instagram models, and "influencers" allow us to live vicariously through them. Others we turn to because they validate our way of thinking, no matter how wild it may be. Partisan political groups and out-there societies like the Flat Earthers come to mind. Then, there are those we turn to because they're cloaked in the fabric of credibility. Unlike those partisan and out-there groups, most of which can be easily debunked, this last group is not so easy to discredit. Sometimes they are genuine and absolutely credible. Sometimes they are not credible but lie so well they convince us they are. And, sometimes, they develop such a fervent following it doesn't matter if they're credible or not. Nobody's checking below the fold since the headline is just so juicy.

We've already run into a few of these characters earlier in this book. You've got the proverbial greenies and eco-warriors who would snatch our phones, ground our planes, and send us back to the Dark Ages if they could. Politicians and business leaders, particularly those of a more conservative bent, use their positions of authority to muddy the waters on climate science. Even the scientists and intergovernmental bodies trying their best to curb a disastrous future throw indecipherable data sets, hefty reports, and fearful scenarios at us. While it's hard to discount the passion with which these characters carry out their work (even if you don't agree with them), there's a huge amount of fault in their approaches. They don't become false idols because their pragmatism has gone out the window, however. They become false idols because people worship them regardless.

It's one thing to make your personal choices out of an abundance of pragmatism or altruism. While I'd always advise you to strike a better balance, these decisions are unlikely to go beyond a limited sphere of influence (no offense). For those with major platforms, though, their decisions do hold massive sway. They need to be kept to a higher level of accountability. Unfortunately, people have a tendency to blindly listen to and follow false idols, rarely questioning intent or approach.

Which begs the question: why? Why do people continue to prop up those among us not fit for the role? Beyond charisma or a meaningful platform, past celebrity or purpose, how can we still fall for these premeditated or naïvely created false realities? Psychologists call this phenomenon, not surprisingly, idealization. The idealization of someone exaggerates their positive attributes, and minimizes, ignores, or qualifies any faults they may have. The term originated with Freud. Psychologists associate idealization with the need to manage anxiety, like a defense mechanism.[14]

I believe that when it comes to sustainability, our idealization of particular characters goes beyond the Freudian need to manage anxiety and into the realm of absolution. Absolution can be understood as the absorption of something by another. For religions, it's usually sin. Like most young Americans, I was raised going to church on Sunday and often on days between. I grew to become quite familiar with the good book and therefore this notion of absolution. With just a thought, prayer, and a bit of repentance, Jesus would take away all my sins and usher me into heaven. In the Catholic faith, absolution is often achieved by a priest taking confession. For Muslims, absolution comes through prayer and sacrifice. Buddhists don't believe in a god that can absolve their sin, instead focusing on repentance as a means of purification.

Why all this talk of a higher power and absolution of sin? Because we're not only guilty of sins against our god. We're also guilty of sins against the Earth. These false idols in the world of sustainability absolve us of the guilt we feel by not doing enough. We idealize them because they can take our stresses away from us. Let's be honest for a moment: humans are essentially lazy creatures. We don't even get up to go to the grocery store anymore. Some of us can't even be bothered to type. Instead we just scream at our phones.

When it comes to something like saving the Earth, who's got the time or energy? False idols do! We look to them and assume since they're doing the lion's share of the work already, that more than makes up for the fuck all I'm doing. Never mind that what they're doing might not be the best solution, or even the right solution (are all those grocery tote bags you keep buying and stockpiling really a better solution than a single plastic bag?). As long as they've been "vetted" by the media or my close circle of friends, as long as they have the platform I can attach myself to, that's good enough for me. I've been absolved and can now go back to watching Love Island.

But that's not how reality works, is it? Just because someone, rightly or wrongly, is doing their utmost doesn't mean you get a pass. Even if you've jumped on the bandwagon of the most pragmatically altruistic person in the world, you've still got to do your part. While false idols may certainly move things in the wrong direction, they are absolutely not there to assuage your guilt or absolve your sins.

The worship of false idols is all very dangerous. Why? Because putting anyone, or anything for that matter, on a pedestal poses several risks. Firstly, how can you know that they belong on that pedestal in the first place? Some will certainly come with the right credentials, passion, or ideas. But, doesn't that just make them first among many? At the end of the day, they're only human. This leads to the second risk in placing people on pedestals. When we look at our idols through rose-colored glasses, we very often miss the glaring faults right in front of us. Instead of questioning their motives or actions, we take things at face value. Even worse still, we defend our false idols against those who see through the charade. Eventually, and inevitably, you run into the third issue being the spectacular fall from grace. With this fall they not only take themselves down. They also impact their followers, often putting them off of whatever cause they once supported. People become disillusioned, apathetic, or even counter-productive. This is also the point in time where their friends cue the old "I told you so!" We see this happen again and again. Yet, history continues to repeat itself.

Over the past year, there has been a move away from pacifist means of dealing with sustainability and towards hardline, often confrontational, tactics. This has led to the rise of a number of false idols. Obviously, my gripe isn't with the passion of these idols, but rather in their approach. Modern movements like Extinction Rebellion are taking a divisive, hardline approach to climate activism. Using mass arrest as a tactic to achieve their aims, the group has brought business centers like London, New York, and Sydney to a grinding halt. Much like the Melbourne protests I was caught up in, they've become more nuisance than savior. Andrew Montesi of Apiro Media has said shock-and-awe tactics risk "...marginalising and pushing away the very people they're trying to win over. While shock and awe may make some people think, others are simply trying to get on with their already complex, stressful lives."[15] All Extinction Rebellion seems to have gotten for their efforts, at least from governments, is being labeled an extremist group.

One of the more recent hardliners to gain a tremendous platform is Swedish environmental activist Greta Thunberg. I'd imagine many of you reading this book are fans of her work. I, for one, am awed by the passion she brings to the conversation, the following she has amassed, and her unique take on activism. Greta rose to notoriety with her School Strike for the Climate campaign. At 15, she began skipping school to sit outside the Swedish Parliament with the hopes of raising awareness around climate change. This campaign caught on in nearby communities and eventually grew to become a global phenomenon called Fridays for Future. Throughout 2019, news of students taking Fridays off school to demand climate action became the norm. In September 2019, the first Global Week for Future was held in line with the United Nations General Assembly in New York. What was likely the largest climate protest in history saw over 4 million participants across 163 countries.[16] Greta has also been recognized as Time's 2019 Person of the Year, was a Nobel Prize nominee, and ranked as one of the 100 most influential people in the world. She continues to be the spokesperson for a generation of climate activists addressing international audiences at the United Nations and other major forums.

While her passion is certainly indelible, her approach has made her a divisive figure. Greta believes in what can only be described as an in-your-face style. Not one to shy away from speaking her mind, she often delivers her addresses with an equal mix of impassioned pleading and admonishment of global leaders. Attacking your audience, especially when they are the very people who are the agents of change you seek to court, is not a very sound stakeholder engagement strategy. Yet the very phrase "how dare you" is now universally synonymous with Greta's addresses to the United Nations. While memorable, it made the false assumption that everyone in the room was sitting on their hands. French President, Emanuel Macron, summed up this sentiment best in saying "...such radical positions (as held by Thunberg) antagonise our societies...But they must now focus on those who are furthest away, those who are trying to block [sustainable initiatives]."[17] While everyone's ears perked up, some didn't stay that way for long.

Some might argue it's a refreshing take on galvanizing action on climate. Others might say she is making more enemies than friends. I classify her as a false idol because I believe she needs to evolve her approach in order to keep momentum, relevance, and attract new followers. What's she's done to date has been nothing short of amazing. The passion of young people has led to new ways of tackling our shared problems. What she does in the future will be telling. We need leaders who can unite rather than divide, who can think like marketers and not like activists, and who can be spokespeople for our shared responsibility to develop a better tomorrow.

A Pragmatically Altruistic Vision

With pragmatic altruists at the helm, what does this better tomorrow look like?

For starters, I think there would be a lot more progress because we'd stop pandering to those acting as roadblocks. Instead of tiptoeing around critical issues, worried we're going to offend sensibilities, we'd call a spade a spade. Like Greta, this future would be in-your-face. The only ones who would have to worry, though, are those on the wrong side of history. Instead of attacking everyone, we'd gather all our supporters together to face off against the true enemies. This army of pragmatic altruists would tell you to cut the shit when it comes to doing little but pretending to do much. There would be no room for armchair environmentalists in this world. Pragmatic altruists would be happy to name-and-shame companies who greenwash, instead of worrying about a potential lawsuit, because the law would be on their side.

It wouldn't all be about the environment, either. What about public health? A pragmatic altruist would happily go up to a smoker, grab their cigarette, and put it out. It's 2020. Nobody wants to die from second-hand smoke anymore. We'd live in a world without idiot politicians more in the pocket of special interests than concerned about the good of their constituents. No more hand wringing. No more frustration. No more "you can't say that!" "you can't do that!" "you can't propose that!" In short, it would be a refreshing alternate universe to the one we're living in now.

A world run by pragmatic altruists would also have a lot more money to go around. That's because, instead of wasting critical dollars on superfluous things, this money would actually go to the causes and purposes it was designed for. We've come to see there is a ton of waste in the world of doing good. Or, rather, funds that are misappropriated when they could easily be put to better use. Pragmatic altruists wouldn't let this happen. Instead, they'd make sure to watch their dollars and cents. If something wasn't working, they'd cut it or find another solution. Attacking whaling ships not stopping the Japanese whaling industry? Maybe find a different approach. Putting up a table at your local eco-fair not generating the impact you thought it would? Try something else. Today, we continue to operate in this Sisyphean world instead of thinking pragmatically about how to make it more functional. Like Einstein's famous definition of insanity, or Bill Murray's character in *Groundhog Day*, we're stuck doing the same things regardless of the outcome. Pragmatic altruists would audit, streamline, and make efficient those things that have grown out of control.

The private sector, if it was run by a bunch of pragmatic altruists instead of a cabal of greedy tycoons, would also look very different. We've come to learn that sustainability, in all its manifestations, has a positive impact on business. The case for this has become clear over the past decade, yet a plethora of companies today still refuse to look at the facts. Whether it's supply chain and logistics, worker welfare or water use, being a more sustainable business means you'll have a better business overall. With pragmatic altruists in the corner offices, embedding sustainable practices that not only benefit the Earth but the business itself, operations are going to be much smoother, products will get from A to B faster, consumers won't have to worry about whether or not the product they buy was made in a sweatshop, and prices will stabilize while profits increase. What's not to love?

Individuals, too, would feel the positive impact of a world run by pragmatic altruists. That's because the workload of saving the world is likely to be a bit more balanced. As it stands, some do more than their fair share to further the cause of sustainability. Meanwhile, some folks do less than nothing and are happy with that (remember when we talked about assuaging guilt?). This is a dynamic that won't last over the long run. Those doing too much will look at those doing too little and say "screw this, I'm done!" They'll burn out, and we'll be left with nobody to do much of anything. Although there's no guarantee it will be totally equal, striking a better balance will help ensure the longevity of the fight for a brighter future. Pushing hard for this balance, pragmatic altruists will help create a virtuous cycle where people are inspired, rather than discouraged, to do more.

My Ask of You

If there's only one grain of wisdom you get out of these 200 or so pages, please let it be this. *We need more pragmatic altruists in this world.* The way I see it, every other point I've made in this book rests squarely on their shoulders. Pragmatic altruism is the foundation on which the future will be built, assuming the lack thereof isn't the final nail in our collective coffin. If you want to be the change, you have to be pragmatic about it.

So, then, how does one incorporate pragmatic altruism into their everyday lives?

First, approach saving the planet the same way you would a business. For a long time, we've kept these two worlds at arm's length, but there is much we can learn from each other. Just like private corporations having more sustainable operations, healthier employees, and better transparency can all help the bottom line, pragmatic altruists know strategic planning, market analysis, and financial responsibility make for greater positive impact. There's a reason businesses are able to have the capital they do. Watch what they're doing and emulate the good stuff.

Second, and in the same vein, it's vitally important to think like a marketer and not like an activist. Don't use shock-and-awe tactics. We've seen the studies showing all these do is drive away the very people you're trying to reach. Instead, find your target segments and figure out what makes them tick. Then build your platform, catch those impressions, and get the word out there. Every single one of you, by virtue of just picking up this book, is part of the sustainability army. Whether you're trying to build a small following on your Instagram page, or are going out to the halls of Congress to enact change, pragmatic thinking is the foundation for success.

Third, and finally, keep the big picture in mind. What's your end goal and how are you going to get there? Instead of chasing those shiny objects which pop up and distract, remember why you started. Rather than get disheartened by negative blips on the radar, look at the long-term trends and see that they are moving in a positive direction. When you go out and do your work, make sure to operate within the realm of reality. Passionate people often forget the confines, limits, and scope of the real world. When it comes time to try and execute their visions, they very quickly learn all the passion in the world is no match versus the limits of what's possible. That's totally fine, but it's going to be up to you to make the incremental changes that will push back against those limits. All of this is going to require you to think before you act. Consider all possible consequences for your actions, talk to all necessary stakeholders, and question how your motivations match up with your actions. Remember the example of Prince Harry and try to practice what you preach.

For those still on the fence with what positivity pragmatic altruism can bring, look no further than Boyan Slat. The 25-year-old from the Netherlands began his climate activism at the age of 13. With a particular interest in ocean plastics, Slat is the founder and CEO of The Ocean Cleanup, a group with the mission of developing advanced technologies to rid our waterways of pollutants.[18] Since its founding in 2013, the group has raised over US$31.5 million dollars towards developing these technologies. Rather than just go out on a wing and a prayer, The Ocean Cleanup produced an extensive 528-page feasibility study before development began. Over time, they have iterated, refined, and launched proofs-of-concept for their ocean cleanup technologies. What he and his team have devised is pretty genius. It's basically a huge vacuum cleaner—ominously named The Interceptor—built to attack the Great Pacific Garbage Patch.In 2019, after several tests, the device finally went into operation. The group has since looked at ways to diversify services for further reach. Slat is a great example of how a pragmatic approach to one's passion can create large-scale, lasting change.

| vii |

Point #5: Don't Try. Do.

For generations, Adamu's family had been farming the land outside the Kenyan capital of Nairobi. It was a proud history, one steeped in the culture of his people. That's because Kenya is an agricultural land. Over three-quarters of the working-age population make a living by farming. It is, by far, the most important economic sector of the country and one Adamu worked hard to support.

Although farming was very important to both Adamu and his country, he wasn't out to become a billionaire by tilling the soil. No, he spent just enough time harvesting what he needed to provide for his family and sell at the local markets. It had been this way as far back as he could remember, and it worked well. Why try to rock the boat if there was nothing wrong with the system? From sweet potatoes to black tea, he really had everything he needed.

Things started to change in the early 1990s. It was then that Kenyan agriculture began to shift towards exports, especially to European countries. Adamu heard stories of people hitting the big time with this. Places like the United Kingdom, France, and the Netherlands were all willing to pay top shilling for Kenyan goods. They were even buying up all our fresh-cut flowers!

When Nairobi figured out it was sitting on a gold mine, things started to get a bit difficult. Rather than being able to grow our own goods freely, the Government implemented a series of regulations that got stricter and stricter. Adamu understood they were trying to be helpful, but it was just so hard to keep up. Rather than give up, though, he kept his family's business alive. Adamu began following these stricter regulations, partnering with the right people in the right places to make export a real possibility.

That's why he was very excited to learn about a new program designed exclusively for Kenyan farmers looking to get a leg up in the export market. DrumNet, a program sponsored by Pride Africa, was designed to connect smallholder farmers, like himself, with financial, retail, transport, and logistical services.[1] The program aimed to overcome some of the biggest gaps between the Kenyan farmer and global markets, including a dearth of reliable partnerships with exporters, price gouging, and little knowledge of export. It promised to upskill farmers and bring their goods to the international stage.

Wow! This was really the opportunity Adamu had been waiting for. He signed up, paid the required 1,000 shillings, and began to attend the program's seminars, workshops, and trainings. After his four-week orientation course, where he learned all about good agricultural practices, transparency, and safety, he was ready to start. DrumNet staff would get his products to exporters. They would even handle all the financial aspects of the deals. It was so simple.

After a bit of time, the folks at DrumNet toyed with different crops they felt would have even better chances of success overseas. Adamu started to grow passion fruit, baby corn, and green beans. These weren't the easiest things to farm in Kenya's climate. He didn't care for them but knew those Europeans would gobble them up.

He was right. After only a year in the program, Adamu's income had gone up by over 30 percent. Although he had to change a few things around with his farm to accommodate some of those new crops, he wasn't spending any more than he had before DrumNet. That 30 percent was pure profit. Not only that, but he had better approaches to farming, safer products, as well as new marketing and export knowledge. The world was his oyster and the sky the limit. Things were looking great for Adamu and his family.

Eventually, the program was in such a good place the organizers felt it was time to move on to other projects in other countries. The infrastructure was there, and the machine was running. The only thing to do was keep it chugging along. The DrumNet program had been such an unexpectedly wild success the farmers were more than confident to take up the mantle themselves.

Unfortunately, global markets depend on much more than just confidence.

A year after the end of the formal project, the export firm that had been buying Kenyan agricultural products for DrumNet suddenly stopped purchasing. The firm cited a lack of compliance on the part of Kenyan farmers with the new European export requirement EurepGap.[2] Yes, bureaucracy started to rear its ugly head. Instead of recognizing DrumNet's positive societal impact, farmers were getting bogged down in paperwork. The Good Agricultural Practices regulations were in response to a rise in lawsuits from European consumers concerned with food safety. Exporters would have to be able to trace the entire value chain of a product back to its original farm. This way consumers could track handling, hygiene, and pesticide use.

To get there, Adamu would have to conduct several infrastructure improvements to reach compliance. These included new sheds, toilets, and waste-disposal facilities. He would also have to be certified through a central Government ministry, keep two years of written records on his farming activities, and buy protective gear for all his farmers. Needless to say, this was going to cost a bit of money. Analysts put this cost at 34,600 shillings (US$333) for initial infrastructure improvements and 10,400 shillings (US$100) annually for certification applications. With an annual household income average of $1,200, these kinds of costs were simply out of the question.

So, the inevitable happened. Adamu and the other Kenyan farmers stopped participating in the DrumNet program. They just couldn't afford to keep up with European legislation. DrumNet lost money on its loans and collapsed. Adamu then had to find other ways to sell his crops. It pained him to go through middlemen because he would have to sell produce at a highly discounted rate. Even worse, he was forced to leave some of his harvests to rot.

Ultimately, Adamu returned to harvesting the traditional way. After just a couple of years, he was back to doing what he had done before. Sure, he made a few extra shillings in the process but the grand dream of exporting to the world had been a lie. Frustrated as he was with the program, there was nothing he could do. Now, he would have to figure out how to feed his growing family and keep his farm in business. It wouldn't be easy, but if generations before him could do it, so could he.

Throughout the developing world, this sort of story is played out over and over again. Aid groups enter with the best of intentions, but many ultimately fail the very people they were supposed to help. Some, like the DrumNet program, fall victim to unforeseen circumstances largely out of their control. Others are victims of their own ignorance, pushing programs that have no real viability or make a lick of sense. Still more are what author Robert D. Lupton likes to call "mission trips."[3] These are usually sponsored by some type of religious organization and involve going for a week into an impoverished community to help rebuild it. Lupton argues that these do little in the way of long-term assistance and cost organizations close to $15 billion annually. This money could certainly be better spent elsewhere.

To get a sense of just how difficult it is to run a successful aid program, take a look at the World Bank. Even with all the support of the international community, and the best and brightest minds on the planet working there, their philanthropic arm still has trouble. The International Finance Corporation noted in 2007[4] that only about half of its projects in Africa succeed. This isn't a "well if they can't do it, what hope do we have" kind of argument. I'm just trying to show the gravity with which we need to treat philanthropy and charity. It's not as simple as flying in, signing a check, and having a press conference.

Yet, these things have become just another piece of what trends.

Sustainability has become very trendy. Sure, it's always been trendy among a small group of people. From the hippies to the eco-warriors, we've always had some who were willing to give it all up to save humanity. Now, though, it's gone mainstream. Everywhere you look, sustainability, green, LOHAS is being shoved down your throat. In many ways, this is a good thing. Change is finally happening, even though it's at the barrel of a proverbial gun. We've even got the private sector on board. Good luck finding a plastic straw at your favorite fast-food restaurant. Whereas before we hoped people would make a change in their behaviors, we now realize that is a big ask. So, through mounting pressure from all sides, we're forcing it. Awesome.

Unfortunately, because it's become so fashionable it also falls prey to the whims of what's hot. Things trend, like a hashtag, only to crest and wane. What's hot today may not be tomorrow and it's on you to keep up. Today, pulling out a plastic bottle in a place where everyone else brings their paraben-free cups would be a huge faux pas. Tomorrow, you may have to boycott your local coffee shop altogether. Oh, your profile picture has a blue background?

Tsk, tsk. It's supposed to be pink! Stop worrying so much about the whales. We've got to save the pangolins.

The big problem with all of this is that causes last far longer than fads.

The worst part about our 24-hour-news-cycle society is just how much it's screwed with our sense of priority. We quickly move on to the next thing no matter how important it might be. Gun deaths are now just as critical as Rere's red carpet dress. Starving children in Darfur on par with what super berry will help you get that sexy summer body. Collusion with a Christmas wish list. When issues come and go like the wind, how realistic it is to care enough before the next big piece of news hits?

Oh...but I do care, John! I watch the news, read first-hand sources of information, and try to limit how often I take Buzzfeed quizzes. I swear!

Okay, okay. I believe you. But, let's run a little experiment.

Cast your mind back to the immediate past. What were you eating for lunch on the third Thursday of last month? I'm going to guess that most of you can't remember. I know I certainly can't. Which Middle Eastern country is embroiled in one of the worst humanitarian crises in modern history? Forgot? Try and name five celebrities who have died this year. Nothing coming to mind? These are people who were in our faces, on our screens, and in our hearts. Yet, you'd be hard-pressed to name them.

Why is this so difficult? It's difficult because unless it was an important meeting where you got a huge promotion, lunch was just another part of your day-to-day routine. Because unless you live in a war-torn country and are constantly worried about bombs dropping through your roof, you've got your own to-do list to get through. Because unless you knew the person directly, their passing had only a fleeting impact on your life.

The same is true when we think of how we process news today. Unless it has a direct impact on our lives (and I'm talking a truly linked, experiential impact), there is just too much going on to remember. That's how the mind works. It compartmentalizes and limits the scope of information it processes. There's not enough room to house all our memories, especially in the modern world, so most things get filtered out. The only things that remain are those with a direct impact on our wellbeing.

Getting back to the first problem with trendy sustainability, treating causes as temporary blips on a radar ignores the fact that these are often long-term, systemic issues. While there may be a big push to do a particular thing today, the problem will likely still be around for a long time to come. Although a bit of help may make a temporary difference, it does very little to change the problem you pretend to care so much about. Imagine you're in a military helicopter flying over some destitute village rife with warlords, starvation, and disease. You open the door, grab a bundle filled with money, or food, or clothes, and drop it to the ground. Then, you fly off. God, it feels great to do good! Don't look back, though, because you're likely to see those warlords taking off with all the money, food, or clothes. Just stay happy in the thought you've made a difference.

It may sound preposterous, but this is pretty much what happens when you pick a cause du jour. You go in with a big song and dance, only to leave just as quickly. Do you even know the nuts and bolts of what you're doing? What is the purpose of the cause? How did the need some about? Is the cause reputable? Why are you even involved? If you don't know what you're talking about, you can't begin to ask the right questions. And when you don't ask the right questions, you certainly can't get the right answers.

We witness this often, especially with humanitarian causes. The earthquake in Haiti? Host a one-off benefit show. Ethnic cleansing in South Sudan? Show disdain by changing your profile picture. Beyoncé says someone shouldn't be in prison? You better hashtag the shit out of that. But what happens when the show is over, or you've changed your profile pic filter? People still need your help, but the publicity has gone dark. Life goes on, but the initial moment of help has faded. You're already in the helicopter, off to tackle the next big issue of the day.

Because many of us have found ourselves caught in this endless cycle of helping the latest, trendiest cause, we've had little time to dig deep into what we're doing. In essence, we're blindly following a leader, without question, similar to that of a cult member. Granted, this particular cult is trying to make things better. But I'm pretty sure all cults start off with good intentions. It's in the execution where things start to go sideways. The same holds with saving the world.

Not convinced? Check out some of the trendiest causes and judge for yourself.

Let's start with one of the most well-known, the old TOMS shoes.[5] Are you wearing a pair right now? Have you worn them in the past? Then you probably know their infamous "buy one, give one" claim whereby for each shoe sold, one is given to a child in need. It's like your purchase triggers a mystical system that drops a pair to an underprivileged child in some other part of the world. You can almost imagine a pair of these canvas shoes falling from the sky and whacking some innocent kid in the head. They look up to the heavens and shout "thank you, Tom!" Since you're paying a day's wages for the privilege, you're glad the money is going to a good cause.

Yet, who says anyone wants a pair of shoes? Sure, you can assume children need shoes to protect their feet from pain and disease. But is the underlying problem a lack of Foot Lockers in developing countries? Of course not! The problem is a lack of money.

People can't buy shoes because they can't afford them. Which means they are likely having trouble making ends meet elsewhere as well. A lack of shoes is just one part of the larger, more systemic issue of poverty. Now a kid has shoes. But, they're still hungry.

There are many better alternative solutions to help alleviate poverty in the developing world. The most widely circulated when it comes to TOMS is changing where the shoes are made. If the company wants to make a difference, why not put their factories in the poor communities they are supposed to be serving? That way people can learn a skill, earn a decent living, and have a nice pair of shoes to prove it.

If shoes aren't of interest to you, how about we check out what 50 Cent's up to? This popular rapper partnered with the World Food Programme to raise awareness of food insecurity in Africa.[6] Traveling to the Dolow slums in Somalia, he sought to highlight an issue plaguing the region for decades. He must have been trying to succeed where Live Aid and that incessant *Feed the World* song weren't able to. Rather than just doing a photo op, 50 Cent decided to crank things up a notch.

Instead of simply donating money, setting up a giving program, or bringing much-needed food to Dolow, he did something entirely different. What quickly became apparent was that his intentions were not entirely altruistic. In addition to the collaboration with the WFP, he was in Somalia to promote his new Street King energy drink. As part of his launch campaign, he would donate a meal to a hungry child for every like you gave the drink on Facebook. You read that right. He tied food donations to social media marketing for his own product. Also, if he got a million likes within the week he would donate an additional million meals. How magnanimous! Richard Stupart of the Matador Network captures the idiocy of this campaign better than I ever could.

That, ladies and gentlemen, is called extortion. Dramatically photographed, concealed-as-humanitarian-activism, extortion. I can feed so very many meals to these starving children, but I won't unless you give me something.[7]

But, Tom and 50 pale in comparison to an example that's actually been given an international award for its work. Radi-Aid, the student-run Norwegian Students and Academics International Assistance Fund, gives out an annual award as an "up yours" to groups that traffic more in stereotypes than impact. The 2017 winner was none other than singer-songwriter Ed Sheeran for his role in Comic Relief's "Ed Sheeran Meets a Little Boy Who Lives on the Streets."[8] In the video, the megastar wanders the streets of Liberia offering to pay for hotel rooms for homeless children. Basically, he's channeling the privileged white savior narrative the Brits have been so good at for centuries. Sheeran also made himself the star of the video, in essence forgetting who this is all supposed to be about.

Radi-Aid was ruthless in their analysis of the video. The jury said the video bordered on poverty tourism and was devoid of dignity. It was a throwback to the outdated charity commercials of the 1980s, being more exploitative than elucidating. They questioned how in the world Sheeran was planning on paying for these hotel rooms in perpetuity, a fair question to be honest, regardless of how much money he might have. Even worse, he never addressed the core issues of poverty, corruption, or public welfare. Coming from such a renowned group as Comic Relief, the jury was especially disappointed. The video was deemed "poverty porn" with people just sitting around waiting to be saved.

When it comes to philanthropic blunders, my personal favorite, one which doesn't necessarily need an entire write up, comes to us courtesy of the US military.[9] During the height of the Afghan War in the early 2000s, some bright soul decided to wrap daily humanitarian food rations in canary yellow packets. Unfortunately, these were the same color as the packets containing cluster munitions capable of destroying anything within a 50-meter radius. With text in English, it was unlikely Afghan children on the steppes would be able to decipher between the two.

These are just a few of the examples we can look at and shake our heads. Kind of. That's because they haven't caused irreparable damage to anyone...well, except maybe that last one. They've just not been thought through by the brightest bulbs in the vanity. Things can certainly get worse, especially when governments are involved. In Chad, $4.2 billion earmarked for an international oil pipeline eventually found its way into the campaign coffers of the country's president. Further south in Lesotho, a $3.5 billion project to divert freshwater for electricity generation led to environmental and economic disaster. The project's chief executives found themselves thrown behind bars for corruption. Even projects run by multinational organizations sometimes can't get things right. The Roll Back Malaria campaign, started in 1998, has actually overseen an increase in malaria rates across the continent.[10]

I'm convinced all of this is because we're just not seeing the critical importance of planning, strategy, and understanding with these programs. When it comes to the time you devote as an individual, this is a critically important point. Rather than stepping in and out of caring, why not jump in with both feet? Do you want your legacy to be one attached to a failed project negatively impacting the lives of millions? Or, would you rather spend your time, resources, and expertise on something that's going to make a difference?

I thought so.

That's why, to paraphrase the words of the famous philosopher Yoda, don't try. Do.

But, But, But

Right about now, you're probably thinking a few choice things.

Isn't something better than nothing?

I can't just get up, leave my life, and move to Ouagadougou.

I'm just one piece in a bigger puzzle. Aren't there thousands of other people who can pick up the slack?

All of these are valid questions to have and you wouldn't be alone in having them. What needs better understanding, however, is that the school of thought around philanthropy and giving has changed considerably since the days of the 1980's TV ads. Today, we know that not all giving is created equal. It's taken a whole lot of false starts and missteps to bring us to this realization, but at least we've finally made it. What we've learned after several decades of programming is that long-term, sustained assistance always trumps a single trip to build a house. Or clean a cage. Or donate money. Yet, people are still looking at things through outdated lenses.

Those questions you're probably asking yourself are just part and parcel of this filter. Don't worry! I'm going to help you remove that filter off so you can see clearly. Let's take a look at each concern so you can gain a bit of an understanding of where I'm coming from, how things have evolved, and what you can do to make a true impact.

Isn't something better than nothing?

Well, if you're stranded in the Sahara Desert then a bit of food or water is going to be better than nothing. Unfortunately, when it comes to the world of giving, we've realized something isn't necessarily better than nothing. Oftentimes, it's this something that can cause a lot of unintended negative outcomes down the road. Now imagine that delicious piece of meat you miraculously found as you traversed the world's largest desert came from a sick camel. That bit of tainted meat is going to do you more harm than good. If it doesn't kill you then the diarrhea will. The same is true for a lot of efforts in giving, where the cure is much worse than the disease.

Previously, I provided a few examples of one way this can be the case: programs aren't always solving the real central issue. Like TOMS providing shoes to millions of children, instead of finding ways to address systemic poverty in those communities, it just puts a band-aid on a broken arm. This is often linked to another issue in giving, in that programs aren't always well thought out. The tech community is one of the biggest culprits in this regard. With lots of cash and cool new gadgets, many firms have their eyes set on saving the developing world. But rural Afghanistan certainly isn't the same as Silicon Valley. The infrastructure needed to fuel these pieces of machinery isn't there. All you end up with is a pile of plastic instead of improved communities. Eric Bellman summed up some of these blunders as tech firms targeted India.

> *A $40 tablet that was supposed to revolutionize education has not been getting the government orders it expected. The national networks of Internet kiosks that were supposed to empower farmers have largely shut down. The $2,000 Tata Nano minicar that was supposed to allow millions of people to upgrade from the dangerous family motorcycle was not popular and anti-rape apps which were supposed to use mapping and automatic SMS to protect women were never connected to the country's police force.[11]*

Therefore, not only have aid groups forgotten to look at the true issues faced by the disenfranchised but they're also neglecting to even consult with the stakeholders who know these communities best. What happens when aid groups return to their comfortable lives back home? We saw in the DrumNet program just how bad things can get without a sustainable, long-term outlook and plan. Of course, this isn't the only example of things going to hell in a handbasket without a plan in place. A World Bank program to improve water conditions in Tanzania fell apart because communities didn't have finances or know-how for upkeep of the systems after the Bank left. Eventually, 3.5 million fewer Tanzanians had access to clean water after the program than before it started.[12]

Even when a project is deemed a success, it can still have negative consequences. That's because it can upset, or kill, local economies. Let's go back to TOMS for a second and pretend one of the communities they send shoes to already has a small shoe-making business. Sure, this business won't be able to produce products at scale, but it's been good enough to provide for the local people for generations. The owners are happy, the locals are happy, and the business makes money and creates jobs. TOMS comes in and drops off a shipment of one million new shoes. People are like cats: we love shiny, new objects. The townspeople immediately pick up a dozen new pairs of TOMS shoes, forgetting all about the family-run shoemaker down the road. Those one million shoes are going to last a while, so that small business continues to become a distant memory. Eventually, they close shop. What's worse? When the TOMS shoes finally run out there's no more local shoemaker to take care of the community's needs. Now they've entered into a dependence loop where they not only want, but need, TOMS shoes to survive.

My old high school band director, Mr. Ewell, had a saying that has stuck with me all these years. "Practice doesn't make perfect. Perfect practice makes perfect." The same is true with charity. Giving doesn't lead to impact. Perfect giving leads to impact. Before even entertaining the idea of giving or volunteering your time and expertise, ask yourself a couple of important questions.

First, does the group have a realistic, sustainable, long-term plan? Has this plan been created in consultation with local stakeholders, or have a bunch of white millennials in Middle America devised the "next big thing"? Second, does the program make sense? Use your gut instinct to tell you whether or not it's going to work. Don't be scared to question the big kids on the block. As we've seen, even people at the World Bank and the IMF make huge mistakes. Lastly, is the programming addressing the heart of the issue? Keep peeling away those layers of onion until you reach the smelly center. This doesn't mean the program needs to solve world hunger or poverty outright, but it does need to understand how it fits into the grand scheme of things. If it doesn't, the program risks doing a lot more damage than good. So, when you ask whether something is always better than nothing, it's clear the answer is no.

I can't/won't/don't wanna give up my life here to help someone halfway across the world!

I took liberties with that second thought of yours. Really, though, isn't this what you're saying? You want to save the world, but you want to do it from the comfort of your own home? Lucky for you it's the digital age and the opportunity to do just that has become a reality. Why get your hands dirty putting up houses in some dusty Mexican village when you can point and click your way to a better world?

Hold on a second. Just because you can doesn't mean you should. There are a lot of highly problematic digital "solutions" available, mostly because they either fail to address a central issue or they create a problem that wasn't there before. It seems like these tech companies are going the same route as the aid groups before them. For example, there's the ag-tech startup, Iron Ox, which creates farms run entirely by robots.[13] They claim this improves productivity and reduces resource waste. They fail to talk about the impact they have on the actual people these robots are replacing.

The gold star of tech-for-not-so-good, though, has to go to AID:Tech.[14] In 2015, the cryptocurrency-based initiative provided digital cash vouchers to Syrian refugees in northern Lebanon. Where to begin with this one? I'm sure if you've been paying attention you can probably help me out. Firstly, they failed to address the central issue at hand: the ongoing Syrian war and refugee crisis. Nobody was expecting their execs to have a sit down with Bashar al-Assad, but cryptocurrency seems a little off the mark. Secondly, they forgot to ask stakeholders whether or not they wanted to have digital currency versus cold, hard cash. While I understand the issues inherent in having physical money as a refugee, digital may not have been the best solution. I'd also question whether AID:Tech understood enough about refugee populations and their access to the internet, mobile phones, and digital education (in case you're wondering, there's likely little to no access to any of these things). If people don't know how to use the internet, or have a way to securely go online, how are they supposed to access their money? And, speaking of money, where is ongoing funding for this project going to come from? Syria, Lebanon, AID:Tech donors? Without a stable source of funding, especially with a digital financial institution, the whole project risks collapse.

On the flip side, there is also no shortage of digital technologies and apps on the market that successfully improve the social, environmental, and economic state of the world. A couple of years ago I was fortunate enough to be part of a very special team. We were tasked with developing China's first mobile application for the country's 5 million blind and visually impaired. In China, populations with disabilities are often excluded from society. While things are getting better in terms of societal inclusion, the country still lacks the proper infrastructure to address many of their unique issues. This is true with the visually impaired, who suffer from higher rates of loneliness and depression, and lack access to the tools they need to lead successful, independent lives. Two of the biggest challenges facing the population are navigating unfamiliar environments and understanding information, particularly at a point of sale.

Working with one of the world's largest tech companies, we set out first to understand a population none of us had much experience dealing with. We adopted what we called an "inclusive-by-design" approach, meaning we took stakeholder viewpoints in from the start. These included the views of some of China's key players like the China Blind Association and the China Disabled Persons Foundation. Through a series of iterative refinements, made in collaboration with these stakeholder advisors, we eventually created a product that was not only impactful but also addressed a large societal gap.

A major component of the app helped the visually impaired navigate unfamiliar situations. This could range from taking a bus ride to a new neighborhood to understanding the label on a prescription at the pharmacy. How the app did this was through the use of sighted volunteers. When someone needed assistance, they would log onto the app and be connected with a volunteer who could help. Using the phone's camera, the volunteer could guide them, read labels, or assist in other ways. On a deeper level, though, the app served as an educational platform. Sighted people, who may have never even met a visually impaired person in their life, were now interacting with and learning from them. All of this could be done without having to staff a phone bank, go to a certain location, or uproot one's life.

Around the world, many great products just like this are making a huge positive impact. Again, you have to ask yourself the same set of questions you would for the traditional "brick-and-mortar" giving programs. Also, make sure you're not distracted by the sleek new technology or app. Remember to judge it based on its merits, not simply its appearance.

Looking for a bit of direction? Recently I connected with Melbourne-based socialpreneur Matthew Boyd, who runs a website called Vollie.[15] Vollie aims to take advantage of Australia's invisible economy, the nearly $20 billion in unpaid volunteer labor. Instead of the traditional model, which is usually filled with time-consuming applications and then volunteering hours that don't always work with a busy professional schedule, Vollie takes a different approach. The website helps connect volunteers with opportunities around the world. The clincher? Everything is done online. From the job advert, to the application, to the volunteering work, you don't have to ever put on a pair of pants! After only a couple of years, Vollie users have already contributed over 12,000 volunteer hours and close to three-quarters of a million dollars in value. If you're serious about helping, check them out.

What difference am I really going to make?

Then there's your role in the grander scheme of things. You're absolutely right. The bigger NGOs certainly have lots of volunteers at the ready to fill gaps in their workforce. Groups like Habitat for Humanity, the World Wildlife Fund, and Save the Children rely on the generosity of others to stay afloat. This generosity often takes the form of either monetary donations or donations of time. If you give to these or similar groups, that's great!

On the surface, things might look like they're running smoothly. You see their big campaigns and names in the news. Underneath, though, there is a constant struggle going on. This often involves the organization's volunteers, and how to make sure there are enough of them. Volunteers come and volunteers go. Without a stable corps of volunteers, though, the fluctuation can have an adverse impact on an organization. What impact can just one little person have, you ask?

Firstly, there's the money. These cash-strapped organizations don't have the budget to be constantly going out and looking for volunteers. On average, non-profits spend between 5 and 15 percent of their budgets, totally, on the areas of marketing, communications, HR, and fundraising. Only a small sliver of that is going to be earmarked for volunteer recruitment, even though it's the lifeblood of most of these groups.[16] Every time one of these organizations has to post a job ad looking for volunteers, that takes money away from the mission.

Secondly, when faced with staffing shortages the leaders of these organizations have to turn their attention away from helping others and focus instead on operational firefighting. As we discussed earlier in the book, the privatization of sustainability has already forced many of these aid groups to become hyper-efficient. They are now run more like businesses than charities. That means staffing is likely a key KPI that needs to be met. Wouldn't it be better if leaders could worry about more important metrics, like helping their target populations, than where they are going to poach talent? When leaders have to constantly think about how they're going to meet staffing needs, it's just another distraction from their mission. By you dipping one toe in and taking it out again, you're distracting from the cause you are trying to help.

Finally, take into consideration the impact on learning and development. With people coming and going, there isn't a stable bank of institutional knowledge spread across the organization. Often, you'll have one person (typically sitting at the top) holding the proverbial keys to the kingdom. If they leave, the whole house of cards could come crashing down. What's more, without a *stable* volunteer force there isn't going to be a *skilled* volunteer force. If volunteers help out once a year, how much skill could they possibly develop? That means these organizations are hemorrhaging money—donated by you very fine people—while at the same time only operating with the most rudimentary levels of skill.

These issues are even bigger in smaller organizations. Your local foodbank, hydroponics lab, or animal welfare league do so much on so little. The last thing they need is the added stress of trying to figure out how they're going to keep doing what they do. The lucky ones will be able to stay solvent through the generous support of their local communities. Some, though, will not be so lucky. The National Center on Charitable Statistics found 30 percent of nonprofit organizations in the United States failed within ten years. *Forbes* went further and noted, "...half of all nonprofits that are chartered are destined to fail or stall within a few years due to leadership issues and the lack of a strategic plan."[17]

So, think critically the next time you feel like going down to your local animal shelter to pet the puppies. Is what you're planning on doing, going once and never showing up again, really helping advance the mission of the organization? Maybe, it is. Maybe they need one-off people to fill in some gaps in volunteers. Go for it! Most, though, need something a bit more stable and predictable. It doesn't matter if you give locally or if you volunteer with one of the world's biggest organizations. Just do so consistently. That way, these groups can not only get closer to achieving their missions but also become the best versions of themselves.

What, then, am I supposed to do?

The way I see it, there are three big ways you can "do" instead of "try."

The first is to give of your time, freely and often. One of the biggest problems with saving the world is that there just isn't enough time to do it all. Time has become the greatest perceived commodity in today's society, something to be held onto at all costs. Ask anyone how they're doing and you're likely to hear them say they've just been soooooooo busy. In her research on the subject, Columbia Business School professor Silvia Bellezza talks about how this is vastly different than perceptions of busy-ness in the late 1800s. If you've seen an episode of *Downton Abbey*, you know that leisure time was a sign of the aristocracy. The richer you were, the less busy you were. Today, though, we are "…driven by the perceptions that a busy person possesses desired human capital characteristics (competence, ambition) and is scarce and in demand on the job market."[18] If you're busy, you're in demand.

Look, we're all busy. You don't have a monopoly on time. The way I look at it, if the President of the United States (the good one, not the current one) had time to run the free world and still play with his kids, then all of us can probably squeeze a bit more usefulness out of our day. It's not that you're soooooooooo busy. It's that your prioritization is soooooooooooo out of whack. We all have the same number of hours in the day. The difference is in how you allocate those hours between the various tasks you want to complete.

I'm not just saying this, either. I've actually challenged myself a bit to see where my prioritization wasn't really balancing the right way. In January 2019 I challenged myself to read an entire book each and every week of the year. That's 52 books in a year when 24 percent of Americans won't even read one.[19] I took my inspiration from those infuriating Facebook ads claiming "busy" professionals like Bill Gates can read two books a day. How? By listening to the condensed versions on audio. Hold up… this isn't even close to reading. Yet, it's what many are turning to because they feel they just don't have the time to sit down with a good book.

Low and behold, all it took were a few tweaks to my normal schedule and I was well on my way to a book a week. We're not talking about staying up till all hours to finish a novel or forsaking work. I did cut out a lot of brainless television, but that isn't much of a loss. By the end of the year, I had kept up my challenge with ease and have been better for it.

Turning back to giving time out of your busy schedule, ask yourself where you can make a few simple tweaks. I bet TV will be the first to go. Then, it'll be all that time on social media. Next, you'll have to face just how lazy you are (I mean... you honestly can't get up and go down the street to buy your lunch? You need it delivered?). Now with all that extra time in your day, spend it in a more useful way. I'm going to pressure you to carve out just a little bit to give to that thing you want to do. Hell, carve out a lot of time to devote yourself to it. Do this freely and without guilt, because at the end of the day your goals, dreams, and wants are the most important thing in the world. If you want it bad enough, you'll find the time to do it.

The second way to take action is to give of your expertise where it's needed the most. Do you love cuddling puppies or reading to kids? Guess what? So do about 95 percent of people around the world. It's not really an expertise either, is it? As long as you have hands and are literate, you'll be able to pretty much pull off these activities no worries. If you're heading to the dog shelter or the orphanage, that's probably just adding to an already overflowing kettle of fish. Instead, take a deep look at what your true expertise is. This, again, is that thing very few people can do. Then, look at where that very unique skill would be best suited. I can guarantee there are groups out there looking for that very expertise and are finding themselves up against a wall trying to find it. Why not make yourself really useful and loved by sharing your special skills with the world?

Stop it! I know what you're thinking.

"I don't really have any special skills. Even if I did, there's probably someone out there who's better than me."

Oh, how I hate that we've gotten ourselves to this point. We're constantly comparing ourselves to others instead of realizing all the great things we're capable of. Where does this come from and why has it become such a big problem? Maybe it's because we're constantly looking at images of lifestyles photoshopped into perfection. We're inundated with images of lives that are no longer things we can even try and aspire to. All of that is taking a big hit on our psyche. The Social Comparison Theory tries to address this very unique issue to modern society. It states that we determine our self-worth based on how we compare ourselves to others around us. In a small social circle, this can be manageable. Expand this out to the millions of people we see on social media and there's a big problem.

In their research, scientists at the University of Michigan measured the impact of Facebook on self-esteem. They found that

> ... *people who used Facebook more often tended to compare themselves to other people more, and to objectify themselves more. Social comparison and self-objectification, in turn, had a whole range of ugly effects. People who engaged in these behaviors more also had worse mental health, lower self-esteem and greater body shame on average.*[20]

This has made its way into the professional world and how we view our talents. I'm here to tell you there is definitely a skill you have which few, if any, others possess.

If you're having trouble identifying your expertise, go through a mini-personal branding exercise. Find your strengths by looking at the most successful project you ever tackled and what made it so. Or, look at your go-to skill for overcoming obstacles. You can also think about what strengths others acknowledge in you, what you enjoy doing, and which strengths or skills of yours will be more important as the business world evolves.

Still stuck? Consider what makes you most excited to get up in the morning, when you've felt the most accomplished, or the types of people you gravitate towards. When you turn on the news, what grabs your attention? And the big question: if money weren't a concern, how would you spend your day?

These should help you narrow down that special skill, or skills, locked deep inside you. Again, share these with the world. There's no use keeping them to yourself when so many people can benefit.

The third way you can "do" instead of just "try" is to give of your funds. Did some of you cringe reading that? Don't worry! Doing good and talking about money do not have to be mutually exclusive. Money makes the world go 'round, after all. Without it, we're not going to get very far so it's important for those people fortunate enough to have a fat bank account to give, give, give. (By the way…that ten-cent donation to the Salvation Army might make you feel good, but it isn't doing a bit of difference. Sorry to break it to you. Why not focus on giving your time and expertise first?)

In her analysis on different philanthropic views, Jane Arsenault takes a look at how authors Robert D. Lupton and Anand Giridharadas would boil down impact projects. Earlier, I mentioned how Lupton vilifies "mission trips" as being wasteful and arrogant. Giridharadas, too, takes aim at philanthropic capitalists who think their knowledge in one field gives them purview over helping disadvantaged populations. In sum, Arsenault notes that, from the perspective of the authors mentioned here,

...philanthropy is toxic if it does not promote or provide a path to independence and participation in society. Prolonging dependence can be disempowering and disabling...some philanthropic efforts that simply give people stuff without effort on their part actually do harm.[21]

The ultimate goal of any person or organization doing impact work, whether through consulting, volunteerism, or some other novel approach, should be singular. We should be working to empower others and put ourselves out of business. Only then will we know that we've realized the missions we've set for ourselves. To get there, we have to stop simply trying and get busy doing.

| viii |

Agree to Disagree?

M ind blown? Feelings validated? Still confused?

Good! At least I've got you thinking.

If you've managed to reach this far then there's been plenty to chew on. I've thrown a whole lot of ideas, information, stories, and cringeworthy jokes your way. Remember back at the beginning of the book when I said some of this wouldn't necessarily sit too well with everyone? That we were going to go against the status quo, the commonly held notions curated over four-plus decades? They certainly aren't part of the conventional train of thought. Nor are they things some people would feel comfortable talking about in mixed company. Hopefully, though, you've come to embrace some of these. At the least, you're now more inquisitive than before.

It used to be one would listen to alternative viewpoints as part of a balanced discussion and understanding of the world. Sometimes you might be persuaded to change your mind. Other times, you would stick to your guns and hold fast to your opinions. Even then, you would simply agree to disagree.

Unfortunately, we're living in a highly polarized time in history. Appreciating views different from your own has become quite a rare commodity. This polarization of our global society is something you hear about quite often. We have become more extreme in our viewpoints, with fewer and fewer moderates holding down the center. This is as true in the United States as it is in Europe and Asia-Pacific. Ipsos data guru Bobby Duffy breaks this polarization down in his highly recommendable book *The Perils of Perception*. In talking about polarization in the US political system, for example, it's beneficial to quote him at length.

> *There is significant evidence of this polarization across societies, suggesting we're fragmenting into 'tribes' with highly divergent views. For example, evidence from the Pew Research Center for the US is compelling. This outlines how the partisan gap in political values in the US has widened dramatically in the past twenty years, and particularly since the early 2000s. In 2004, there was only a 17 percentage point gap between the average Democrat and average Republican supporters on ten political values, such as whether the government should do more to help the needy, or whether racial discrimination is the main reason why Black people can't get ahead these days. By 2017 this gap had more than doubled to 36 percentage points.*

> *Between 1994 and 2017, we moved from a position where 65 per cent of Republicans were more 'conservative' in their attitudes than the average Democrat, to almost entirely distinct tribes where 95 per cent of Republicans have more conservative views than the average Democrat.[1]*

Ultimately, Duffy posits this leads to a "...fracturing of a shared sense of what the world is really like, where the risks lie, and why our misperceptions really matter." In other words, civil debate has become civil war.

Today, it seems like we've gone from an agree-to-disagree mentality to the less-than-courteous disagree-to-disagree thinking. It's as if we've forgotten that just because someone has a different opinion doesn't make them our enemy. It doesn't mean we have to hate them. Now we enter the safety of our information bubbles where we don't even have to hear opposing viewpoints. We're encouraged by similar opinions, research, and newscasts that reflect our thinking. God forbid we have to step out of this bubble and hear from the other side. If we do, we do so with a heavy touch of suspicion. Most times, we only listen to other views because we want to validate our own, not necessarily listen or learn something new.

How the hell did we get here? Even twenty years ago you could have a civil conversation with people you didn't agree with. Debate and discourse have been part of societies the world over for centuries. I'll pose the question to you: what's different in our society today versus twenty years ago? What has been so monumentally impactful it's changed the very nature of how we live our daily lives? It's not a difficult question. Of course, I'm talking here about the internet.

I remember when we got our first dial-up AOL service at home. I must have been a freshman in high school. The internet was a new and wild land, full of possibilities and with a bright future. Now we had the world at our fingertips. We had access to information, people, and ideas like never before. This was an uncorrupted internet. It was an internet—at least for a fleeting moment—free of porn, violence, and extremism.

Then the bad crept in. You started to hear stories of men luring young girls to meet through seemingly innocuous chat room conversations. They pretended to be people they weren't, an unsettling foreshadowing of the troll factories evident in today's world. Kids at school began to talk about the sites they were looking at and where to find the best celebrity nudes. The alt-right movement would be born in the dark corners of this young internet. Extremists shared information that would soon force the whole world to wake up.

To counter all of this, we started to experiment with ways to make the internet a safe space. Sitting in my room at the Kappa Sigma fraternity house, one of the guys came in one night and told me about this new site being rolled out. Some geniuses at Harvard designed it and called it TheFacebook (yes, THEFacebook). At that time, only certain universities around the country had permission to use TheFacebook. Our university would come online in the next month. Everyone was so excited by the idea of a site just for university students to share with and learn from each other. I remember thinking how cool it would be to exchange ideas with students in the Ivy League. It seemed like a real democratization of the university system, a system that had always been about the haves and have nots. As a hungry young professional, I saw it as a way to get a leg up on the competition.

And you know what? In those early days of TheFacebook it worked out quite well. It allowed me to connect with lots of fraternity brothers, other Greeks and political science nerds, as well as learn of potential internship opportunities across the country. TheFacebook also helped me network my way into grad school and eventually the United Nations. By that point, it was still a semi-closed system. But not for long.

By 2008 or so, TheFacebook began to evolve and morph into what we're used to seeing today. Now it's not just catering to select university students. Anyone who's had their grandma or dad comment on a post knows it's become a free-for-all. What was once a closed system is now open to everyone—bots, porn stars, spam-flinging Nigerian princes. Facebook houses the best and worst of humanity, from cute kitten videos to Neo-Nazi propaganda. That's a far cry from what Facebook's founders originally marketed it to be.

This evolution is simply a mirror for how we've evolved as a society, especially in the way we argue and debate with one another. Social media platforms like Facebook and Twitter allow anonymity for those who want it. At the least, they put a barrier between you and whoever you might be talking to. This has led to an increased sense of protection for those who would otherwise keep their mouths shut in a public forum. Saying some of the things you find in the comment section of a website out loud would get you punched in the face. Behind a computer screen, though, the worst you'll suffer is a bit of online vitriol. Besides, if things get really bad all you have to do is click delete.

Yet even though you know trolls are out there, how often do you click into the comment section of a salacious or controversial story just to see what they wrote? You know it's just going to make you angry. But, you can't help yourself. That's because compounding the anonymity of the internet are the machinations of social media which keep you coming back for more. Scientists have discovered the impact of such sites on dopamine levels in the body. With each like, comment, or share, you're getting validation from the community. When you read those troll comments and find people who agree with your viewpoints fighting back, you feel justified. This gives you a bump of dopamine, the happy chemical. According to Harvard University researcher Trevor Haynes, "…when you get a social media notification, your brain sends a chemical messenger called dopamine along a reward pathway, which makes you feel good. Dopamine is associated with food, exercise, love, sex, gambling, drugs … and now, social media."[2]

Those geeks in Silicon Valley quickly realized this. They became less like tech gurus and more like drug kingpins. Now, social media sites aim to give us our hits of dopamine as often as possible. To do so, they feed us more of what we like. Have you ever been scrolling through Instagram before bed, just to check in on what your friends are up to? Maybe you thought it'd take just a couple extra minutes of your time. Then, you see a cute video of a dog playing catch. Then, you see another one. Then another one. All of a sudden, you're facing a barrage of similar videos that keep you scrolling all night long. The next thing you know it's two in the morning and you've got to be up early for work. Damn you Instagram!!!

You don't think this just happens by accident, do you? It's the way the site is programmed. Facebook is the same. Instead of similar pictures and videos, though, it gives us a curated newsfeed of information we would tend to agree with. That includes not only posts from your friends, but also recommended sites, people, and news pieces supporting your view of the world.

It could be argued that social media platforms give us tunnel vision, throwing us down a never-ending rabbit hole of self-validating information. Google does this by giving you the most popular search results over what might be the most verified ones. As the seduction continued, more misinformation started to creep in. But by the time most of us realized this, it was too late. We were so far gone, these misleading sources of information started to look reputable. Many have even gone mainstream, calling into question journalistic ethics and reputation.

Don't believe me? Consider Rupert Murdoch and his empire of conservative news. By most estimates, his News Corp organization circulates nearly three-quarters of all daily metropolitan newspapers in Australia.[3] That's a lot of power given to one man who, by the way, is known to have made offers to influence federal elections by publishing glowing commentary on Australia's Liberal Party. His stance on climate change became apparent in false and misleading information published during Australia's bushfire crisis as well. Headlines blaming arsonists, green legislation, and even the United Nations were all pushed to the public. Mentions of climate science were nowhere to be found.[4] When people started to question the corporation's motives and links to conservative politics, they simply pushed the story off the front page. Incidentally, the Murdoch family also owns Fox news. Are you beginning to see the pattern?

I can imagine some of you nodding your heads thinking about all those right-wing news sites, friends, and family who live in their little misinformed bubbles. Well, don't get too far up onto your high horse just yet. Maybe it's time to take a long hard look in the mirror as well. That's because it's not just conservatives operating inside their echo chambers. Liberals are just as bad. I'd argue that there are just as many extremists on both sides of the political spectrum. Check out these media bites.

I was able to go and buy an automatic weapon. Most people can go out and buy an automatic weapon.

ISIS lures women with kittens and Nutella.

One percent of candidates that the NRA endorsed in 2012 won.

All of these were stories or opinions pushed by CNN.[5] All of them have been proven false (although extra credit for kittens and Nutella). The Atlanta-based news giant is a darling of the left and almost exclusively promotes left-leaning ideas, stories, and commentary. They are often critical of the right, such as in their coverage of the 2016 US Presidential election. All Sides Media Bias Ratings even placed CNN in the far left of their ratings.[6] While they aren't exactly as bad as the *fake news* moniker the Trump Nation would bestow on them, CNN certainly isn't living up to being impartial. Although they may not overtly falsify stories, theirs is a sin of omission. Their audiences simply don't get the whole picture.

You see, we've become so accustomed to these echo chambers we don't even realize we're in them. They're comfortable, supportive, and most importantly predictable. There's no risk of a shock (or need for critical thinking) when you know what's coming. Thus, it's become next to impossible to discuss something with someone who has opposing views. Most of the time we just refuse to listen to each other. Our arrogance and certitude have gotten the best of us, only compounding the divide. There's no need for me to drone on about it because I can guarantee each and every one of you reading has experienced this first hand.

But how do we break out of these echo chambers? My favorite author, Paulo Coelho, is known for inspirational books like *The Alchemist, Warrior of the Light,* and *The Pilgrimage.* In these, he often discusses how to interact with those who might not agree with you. While you'd expect this type of metaphysical author to take a measured approach, Coelho does nothing of the sort. He says to "...be arrogant with arrogant people, this is the only language they respect—as they confound kindness with weakness."[7] Unlike ancient Chinese philosopher Lao Tzu, who recommends saying little in times of conflict, Coelho encourages us to face conflict head-on.

Make no mistake. We are certainly in a time of conflict. Now is not the time for retreating and ignoring others. Enough with niceties and politeness. It is not the time to let the mud settle or to shut our mouths. No. At this stage of the game, if someone doesn't even want to consider the very basic science behind things like climate change, your job is to call them out on their bullshit. It's also incumbent on you to bring those with lofty, unrealistic ideas back down to Earth. Yes, yes, yes. You have a job in all this. You didn't think just reading a book was going to change the world, did you? I didn't think so.

An ambassador for change doesn't have to go out and develop a vacuum to suck up ocean plastic or start a movement of millions. No, ambassadors for change typically start first with themselves. At the heart of it, that's what this book is all about. It's about changing how you view the very real threat we've brought upon ourselves. Then, it's about changing how you react to the threat and bring others on board with you. Ultimately, this is going to be a team effort. Unfortunately, some still think there's an "I" in team.

It's these folks I'm worried about. Even with all the irrefutable information available, they continue to have their heads so far up their asses it's now nearly impossible to pry them free. We often hear about the 97 percent of scientists who agree climate change is real. This makes us believe the 3 percent of scientists/politicians/ crazy radio personalities who don't are a very minuscule minority. Don't be fooled. In case you were wondering, there are still a mind-bogglingly large number of them. Americans, by example, are the biggest climate change doubters in the developed world. A full 30 percent of Americans still don't believe man-made climate change is a thing, while 17 percent think "...the idea of manmade global warming is a hoax that was invented to deceive people." Only 1 in 10 have ever contacted their government representatives on the issue and only a quarter speak about it with family and friends.[8]

The rest of the world isn't much better. Only 38 percent of Israelis view climate change as a major threat, while an average 20 percent of people globally consider it a minor threat. Across Asia-Pacific, less than 40 percent of people believe climate change is something to worry about, even though it is this region that will experience the most suffering from it. In China, the world's largest economy and polluter, a mere 15 percent of citizens felt climate change has a personal impact.[9] Having lived in China and suffered through more smog-ridden days than I'd care to remember, this stat was especially concerning. Environmental pollution is very much in your face in China. If people come up against it day in and day out, yet still don't see an impact, that's a huge red flag.

These are the people we are up against. It's all of those who would have seen this book and walked right by it. The shock value of the title alone should have gotten them to pick it up! It's your climate-denying uncle screaming at the Thanksgiving dinner table. It's the heckler at a rally with some really stupid sign. Most likely, it's hate from random trolls on social media. Don't forget the internet personalities, politicians, and loonies who would deny what's right in front of them. They add less than nothing to the conversation—a very critical conversation, mind you—by acting like spoiled, immature brats.

It's not that I'm opposed to listening to different viewpoints. My anger comes when these viewpoints have no basis in reality or critical thinking. Hell...most don't even have a basis in the most elementary of thinking (insert third Flat Earthers reference here). They are rife with conspiracy and built on lies that even Nancy Drew would be able to topple. I have to wonder whether these folks actually do believe the crazy things they're saying, or if they just get off on standing out.

Yet we've been walking on eggshells to avoid offending these folks. It's time to be arrogant because we're being trampled on. To be clear: they're taking advantage of your kindness. In turn, they've been able to drive us closer and closer to extinction.

By now I'm sure you recognize I don't like to use hyperbole. What's at stake, though, is our very existence. Instead of trying to crystal ball the future, let's just look at the damage we've already caused. Two dozen animal species went extinct in 2019 alone. Scientists believe the global extinction rates are up to 10,000 times higher than natural extinction rates.[10] The World Health Organization estimates 90 percent of us breathe air with high levels of pollutants. Global sea levels have already risen 8 inches since 1920, with the ice caps melting at 9 percent per decade.[11] All of this comes along with warmer average global temperatures and crazy weather patterns making events more extreme. This isn't a distant dystopian future we're talking about. Like the frog in a pot of boiling water, we don't seem to realize the clear-and-present danger surrounding us right now.

It's high time each and every one of us gets off our asses and put on our armor. Lucky for you, you're now equipped with what I consider the five best ways to prepare yourself for battle. Before we go any further, let's make sure you've got everything straight. Any mistakes on the battlefield are only fodder for the enemy, so pay attention.

First, you've got to know what you're talking about.

One must have a basic understanding of the ins and outs of saving the world. This will require you to get rid of some commonly held misconceptions and establish a solid foundation. From here, you can build up your arsenal. How do you do all that?

- **Know your fundamentals**. You have to learn to walk before you can run. That means gather all the information you need to make an informed choice. This doesn't mean you have to learn everything about everything. Pick those areas which interest you most to start. Learn about them and hopefully you'll begin to open a Pandora's Box of information which will lead to further exploration.

- **Don't believe the hype.** Once you're armed with information, it's much more difficult to be fooled by the misdirection of others. Before you fall prey to the latest scare tactic (from either the left or the right), be a bit skeptical and look things up yourself. You're the owner of your choices, so don't get led around like a sheep.

- **Identify your mentors.** As with anything, many have come before you. Tap into their knowledge. These could be close friends or professional associates. Most likely they are going to be those who have books or articles under their names. Look through their pieces and feed your appetite to learn.

- **Stay up to date.** We're in uncharted territory here. Because of that things are likely to change over and over again. You've got to stay up to date with all that's going on. Relying on outdated information, which could even be as recent as last year, might lead you in the wrong direction. Nothing is gospel. Okay, maybe a few things are. By and large, there is plenty of wiggle room in what we're doing. Don't agree with something? Change it! Change not happening fast enough? Move it along in your special way. Believing everything is sacred will only keep us marching in place.

Second, remember you can do anything, but you can't do everything.

You've got to focus and contribute, but not get to the point of burning out. There will be pressure from all sides trying to get you to give here, there, and everywhere. Your job is to quiet the noise, focus your attention, and ruthlessly stay the course. So, what's it going to take for you to focus?

- **Embrace and reclaim the power of no.** There's nothing more liberating than saying no to things. A bit of great advice: don't let today's you say yes to something tomorrow's you will regret. Once you've reclaimed the power of no, you'll be able to focus yourself on what you actually should be doing, instead of what others want you to do.

- **Find your passion.** With so much space freed up now that you're saying no all the time, you'll be able to search for and discover your true passion. This is usually hidden deep inside your childhood dreams. What was it you always wanted to do? What is it you naturally gravitate towards? Your passion is probably somewhere around there.

- **Stay laser-focused on what it is you want**. Once you've found your passion points, keep at them. It's going to take a laser focus because, as we all know, today's society is full of distractions. Put those blinders on and keep moving forward.

- **Get over the "you're heartless" naysayers**. This is probably the most complicated thing to achieve. With the six principle negotiating tactics, though, it should be a breeze. When you've decided to say yes to certain things, and no to others, you'll start to have people questioning your decisions. "How could you not want to help stray dogs? Do you hate animals?" "Big pharma's evil. Why don't you want to help us bring them down?" And on and on it goes. Remember, there are enough of us to accomplish everything.

You fit into your part of the puzzle and let everyone else fit where they do.

Don't force it. If it's not working, switch things up. Thought you found your passion, but maybe you were wrong? Been working with focus on one thing for many years, but now it's becoming routine? There's no shame in changing direction. Passions are passions because you're passionate about them. If you've lost that spark, that flare, find something that reignites it. Keep the fire burning bright!

Third, don't be a dick.

As we've seen, the world's full of dicks. They come in all shapes and sizes. Unfortunately, they're not going anywhere anytime soon. So in the meantime, what can you do instead of constantly fighting against them?

- **Identify the dicks around you**. Who are those dicks in your life right now? Is it your boss (probably), your neighbor (maybe), or your partner (hopefully not)? Who are the dicks of your past? Your future? Find out where they're hiding so you can be prepared when they strike.
- **Stop being a dick**. Oh, it's you who's the dick? Well, then, knock it off! Easier said than done, I'm sure. What you need to do is figure out what makes you a dick. When you've come to that realization, you can start to be constructive instead of destructive.
- **Ignore or get rid of them**. Once you've identified all the dicks in your life, figure out how to downsize them. Maybe you can get rid of them entirely, which is great. Perhaps

you can only ignore them. Like buzzing gnats they'll keep pestering you. But you'll be so calm, cool, and collected you won't even notice.

- **Name and shame**. Sometimes, you have to get aggressive with those dicks. That's where this little tactic comes in. Even dicks hate being embarrassed and will often change their behavior when called out. That's why I'm a big fan of naming and shaming. Whether it's a person, organization, or company, call them out on their bullshit and see the miraculous happen.

- **Embrace a dick-free life**. Wow. How does that feel? You've identified the dicks, cleared them out of your life, and even got a few to change their tune. Now, keep that dick-free life moving forward. Keep those energy vampires at bay and focus on what's actually going to make a difference.

Dicks want it all and they want to do it all themselves. Perhaps it's a vanity thing. Maybe they just want all the credit. Regardless, there is only so far that an individual can go. If you really want to get somewhere, you have to rely on the help of others. Only when you stand on the shoulders of giants can you see the path ahead.

Next, don't forget passion without pragmatism is just complaining.

For too long we've been going about our altruistic work without a pragmatic view of why, how, or what we're doing. That's idled us for decades. Before you join that protest or stage that sit-in, think about the overall impact of what you're doing. And, make sure to watch out for the three big trappings that come to those who forget to marry pragmatism with altruism.

- **The first are unintended consequences**. Remember what happened when the Ming emperors built that itsy-bitsy wall around their empire? While they were successful in keeping the Mongols out, they were even more successful in keeping out a critical exchange of information. Eventually, other countries leapfrogged ahead of China. Only now has the Middle Kingdom been able to catch up.
- **The second trapping is the loss of capital**. Your words and actions must match. When Prince Harry talked up climate protection and then hopped on his private jet to Ibiza, people saw right through the mismatch. The result was a loss of credibility for the endeavors he surely felt passionate about.
- **Finally, watch out for false idols**. Just like you might do with a new romantic interest, do a little research and stalking before getting into bed with every sustainability warrior out there. Do you like them because they are reputable to the cause? Or, are you just propping them up to assuage some sort of guilt you have for not doing enough?

We need more pragmatic altruists in this world. Every other point I've made in this book rests squarely on this. Pragmatic altruism is the foundation for a brighter future. If you want to be the change, you have to be pragmatic about it.

Finally, remember that it's more important to "do" than "try."

Dipping your toe in and out of the water doesn't do anyone any favors. In fact, it often does more harm than good. That's why you've got to figure things out quickly and dive right in. Before you head off to that eco-resort in the forest, or to build a house in a slum, remember these five points to make you a better doer.

- **Take stock of all the things you're already doing**. Your passion is in there somewhere. What is it you naturally gravitate to in your free time? There is usually an underlying (or sometimes very overt) meaning that might indicate what it is you're truly passionate about.
- **Be critical**. Is what you're doing making a positive impact, negative impact, or no impact at all? Sometimes we do things just for the simple fact we've always done them. Don't do that! Take a real good look at how you're spending your time. Is it truly, truly, truly making a difference? What kind of difference? If it's positive, keep it up. If it's negative or a wash, figure out how to make things better or switch it out.
- **Jump in with both feet**. Once you know what it is you want to do, and can do, then go out and do it with all the gusto you can muster. Don't half-ass anything. There is no room or time left for trying things out. Get ready to give for the long term, because short-term bursts aren't doing any good.
- **Act now...tomorrow is certainly not guaranteed**. We're really up against the clock here. If you want to make

a difference, don't wait for the right time. You'll always find an excuse as to why it isn't. Do it now.

- **Use it or lose it**. Capitalize on your strengths. If you're a tech genius, offer your time to a group that could benefit from that knowledge. Love crunching numbers? I'm sure there are more than a few charities who would need a good part-time accountant. Rich? The doors are going to be swung wide open for you. Whatever it is you can do, do it and do it well.

Don't fall into the trap of thinking all good is created equal. As I've stressed before, do your homework if you really want to make a difference. Philanthropy should not be vain or self-serving. Your donations should stretch far, not just act as a stop-gap. Social-good organizations should have a singular mission: to do such a good job they put themselves out of business. How are you helping them reach that goal?

Executing this five-point plan to save the world isn't going to be for the faint of heart. You'll be mocked, ostracized, and constantly told you're wrong. That is, until you find your tribe. Then all the suffering will have been worth it.

While I often come up against the pesky naysayers telling me I'm approaching this all wrong, every so often I'll meet folks who whole-heartedly agree with me. It gives me no greater pleasure in life than to have someone tell me "John…I've always thought the same thing but was too afraid to say it. Thank you!" Some of you might think I'm nuts, but there is a silent majority out there who believe much of what I say (hopefully all of what I say) is right. Search them out and charge into battle together.

All good books are supposed to end with a call to action. Think about those old infomercials on the Home Shopping Network and the part where they urge you to "call now." Maybe they even threw in something extra...a limited time offer. Calls to action are meant to galvanize the viewer/employee/soldier to do something. Books are the same. But, hasn't this entire book been a call to action?

My hope, though, is that you are inspired and ready for more. You've stopped and searched for more information. You set the book down and had a long think about how you approach things. Maybe you've already put some of these words into action. For some, my words might be a breath of fresh air. For others, an aggravation. Either way, I've succeeded.

The only thing I can do at this stage is continue to challenge you. How are you going to use what you've read to do more, better? Who are you going to challenge first? Is it yourself, a family member, friend, or total stranger? What are you going to do to make this a better world for yourself, your children, and the rest of humanity?

When are you going to cut the bullshit and get to work?

| ix |

Afterword: Sustainability in the Time of the Coronavirus

When I began writing this book a little over a year ago, the world was a very different place. How could any of us have ever known just how much things would change? We would have never thought the era of globalization would end with xenophobic fear. The idea that any one country would close its borders, let alone the majority of nations around the globe, was preposterous. Lockdown in democratic societies? Supermarket shelves empty? Economic collapse? No way.

Yet, I'm sitting here at my computer under a two-week quarantine in a hotel near Gimpo Airport in Seoul. Down below I can see people wearing medical masks, face shields, and in some cases full hazmat suits. My three meals a day are being delivered by army personnel, who also do spot checks to make sure I'm sticking to my isolation. All of this thanks to the coronavirus, COVID-19. At this point, we're up to nearly 10 million cases globally and many places are already undergoing a second wave of the disease. With no vaccine in sight, it looks like a long road ahead.

As the coronavirus will be the defining point for a generation, and since we're still in the midst of it (with minute-by-minute reporting ongoing), there's no sense dredging up all the gory details about how it started, where it's spread, which celebrities and royals have fallen ill, and all the negative impacts of the disease. Hopefully, by the time you read this, there will be a cure and we'll be over the worst of it.

But in case we're not, I'm here to tell you there's at least one silver lining in all of this despair. No matter how many people may eventually die from COVID-19, or how many businesses will fail, there is one clear winner: the environment. That's because with all of humanity locked in their homes, the Earth has been able to catch its breath. While it might sound terrible, COVID-19 has been able to do what the Paris Agreement could not. Without cars on the road, planes in the sky, or factories running at full steam, the environment is starting to balance itself out.

Let's take China as an example. They've made it through the worst of the virus (at least at the time of this writing), so serve as a good case study of COVID-19's impact on the environment. Looking first at China's manufacturing sector, Government-mandated shutdowns early in the outbreak reduced emissions in the short-term. The Central Government extended the Chinese New Year period initially. We typically see factories close their doors for the holiday mid-January and return to full steam by early March. By April, though, things were still not quite back up and running. While it's difficult to get exact figures on factory emissions, an extra day, week, or even month of closures is only going to have a positive impact.

Going further into the future, understand that global epidemics have a direct impact on economies. Some estimate this to be close to US$570 billion annually.[1] These, though, are unprecedented times. With countries on lockdown, and businesses shuttered, global consumer spending is next to nothing. That means factory production is, too. No production means no emissions, another win for the Earth.

A huge environmental impact came from the inbound and outbound tourism industry as well. British Airways, Cathay Pacific, and Lion Air were among the first airlines to cancel flights to and from China due to the coronavirus. Chinese account for over 150 million international tourists and about 20 percent all global tourism spend.[2] About 32 million international tourists visit China each year, too.[3] That's close to 850,000 planes coming in and out of China in a given year. British Airways alone operates at least 80 flights a week to and from London and the Chinese mainland. As an example, each roundtrip BA flight to Shanghai accounts for at least 484.75 metric tons of CO_2 emissions. That's the equivalent of 533,302 pounds of coal burned.[4] Airline shutdowns have grown exponentially since the start of the virus, with over 95 percent of all flights around the world grounded. If you just do the math, that's a lot of junk taken out of the atmosphere.

We're already seeing what these shifts are doing to the environmental numbers. According to the Center for Research on Energy and Clean Air (CREA), emissions in China are down a quarter over last year. They point out this is equal to 200 million tons of carbon dioxide, roughly the same CO_2 emitted during Australia's bushfires or half the annual output of Great Britain.[4] There's also been a nearly 40 percent drop in coal consumption, China's major source of fuel. China's Ministry of Ecology and Environment note this all contributed to a 21.5 percent increase in the number of "good quality air days" the country had in February.[5]

The same thing is now happening around the world as economies endure a temporary hiatus. The famed canals of Venice are clearing up, smog-ridden cities in the Middle East and South Asia are seeing blue skies for the first time in a long time, and major metropolitan areas of the United States are reaching historically low levels of particulate matter. Even my own native Los Angeles, the smoggiest city in the country, has had a record number of days without pollution.

Of course, we're not just going to feel the impact of the coronavirus in industrial emissions and travel. Broadening out to sustainability writ large, health, wellness, sanitation, and hygiene will all improve. It worries me there have been so many public service announcements teaching people to wash their hands. What were they doing before? Regardless, expect COVID-19 to fast track sanitation and hygiene practice improvements around the world.

Why tack this on to the end of an already long book you may be asking? Because I don't want people to become disillusioned or distracted by the coronavirus. The virus doesn't change anything. I actually see it as a bit of a hard reboot and inspiration to push even more for change. Not to wax poetic, but we've got the chance to rebuild a better, greener post-coronavirus world. The five strategies I've harped on throughout this book will serve as a strong foundation for that.

Whether you're stuck at home with loved ones, in some quarantine center with strangers, or alone overseas without a way to get back, don't give up the fight. The Earth needs you now more than ever.

ABOUT THE AUTHOR

A life-long pragmatic altruist, John Pabon's work has focused on the fields of sustainability, geopolitics, and strategic communications. For the past 15 years, he has advised governments, corporations, and organizations of all sizes. The result is a portfolio of leading programs, campaigns, and strategies across all industries.

John's global career has taken him from Los Angeles to New York, Shanghai to Melbourne. He's had the privilege of working with the United Nations, McKinsey, A.C. Nielsen, and as a consultant with BSR, the world's largest sustainability-focused business network. A decade of experience living and working in Asia inspired him to found Fulcrum Strategic Advisors with a mission to help companies, governments, and individuals understand, adapt, and capitalize on the seismic shifts happening in the world today.

He is a regular contributor to major publications, and speaks to an array of global audiences on issues of sustainability, geopolitics, communications, and societal change. John is a member of the United Nations Association of Australia and also serves on the board of advisors to the U.S. Green Chamber of Commerce.

When he's not working or writing, John is an avid dragon boater, out-of-shape Muay Thai fighter, reiki healer, and proud dad to the world's best Shiba Inu. He currently lives with his partner in Melbourne, Australia.

ACKNOWLEDGEMENTS

Even though most of you won't read this part, I still want to say thank you for making it through this labor of love. It's so cathartic to be able to get words down on paper and out to the world. More than that, tough, I hope it's been cathartic for you. With all the crazy happening in the world today, making sense of our own little plot of land is more important than ever. Please, take what you've learned and share it with the world. Now is not the time for fiefdoms. Our future is on the line.

While my name might be on the cover, there are so many others who have had a hand in making this book a reality. Andrew, thank you for pushing me to be a better version of myself and for your passive-aggressive reminders to keep me writing. Your unwavering support, through struggle and triumph, may go unacknowledged but never goes unnoticed. Klare Lanson, you challenged me in just the right way to ensure the arguments in this book were sound and not just rants. You tightened everything up better than a personal trainer at the gym. For everyone who took the time to read and comment on the advanced copies of the book, a huge thank you. That includes: Raul Alcala, Jennifer Baugher, Henry Boyter, Jr., UB Chiu, Thom Cullen, Shaun Deverson, Selena Ferguson, Sean Khaligh, Yulia Khisamova, Gauravi Saini, Drew Schneider, Maggie Wang, and Christian Wiegele. All of us are so time-poor, making it that much more meaningful you'd take the time out of your busy schedules to support this project and make it the best it could be. Although you might think you're all "behind the scenes," without your guidance this probably would have never seen the light of day. To the folks at BSR, particularly Jeremy Prepscius and Aron Cramer, thank you for throwing me in the deep end. That murky body of water not only provided some of the best case studies in this book, but also helped shape my perspectives as a sustainability professional. Also, a big thank you goes to Margarita Felix for working on the design of the book and all those amazing social media images driving sales.

Last, but not least, I want to thank all those present and future generations who will ensure the survival of our planet. Many of you will not have seen my book, but I hope the ripple-effect from it leads us all to bigger and brighter things.

NOTES

Your Survival Guide for the Anthropocene

1 Thomas Hale and David Held, "Why is the Anti-Global Backlash Happening Now?" The World Economic Forum, November 29, 2017, https://www.weforum.org/agenda/2017/11/anti-globalization-brexit-backlash-nationalism-control/.

2 If you're particularly interested in the case of Jeffrey Epstein, I'd highly recommend the 2020 Netflix docuseries *Filthy Rich*.

3 Ben Stiller, director. *Zoolander*. Paramount Pictures, Village Roadshow Pictures, and VH1 Television, 2001.

4 For a history of the Paris Agreement, please refer to https://www.nrdc.org/stories/paris-climate-agreement-everything-you-need-know.

5 "PwC: Not a Single Country On Track to Meet Paris Agreement Emissions Reduction Targets," Simply Switch, accessed June 2, 2019, https://www.simplyswitch.com/pwc-not-single-country-track-meet-paris-agreement-emissions-reduction-targets/.

6 Jonathan Cribb, "Intergenerational Differences in Income and Wealth: Evidence from Britain," Fiscal Studies, vol. 40, issue 3 (2019): 275-299, https://doi.org/10.1111/1475-5890.12202.

7 "The History of American Income," Bizfluent, accessed June 3, 2019, https://bizfluent.com/info-7769323-history-american-income.html.

8 "Average Salary in New York, New York," Payscale, accessed June 3, 2019, https://www.payscale.com/research/US/Location=New-York-NY/Salary.

9 **On Chinese literacy**: Ted Plafker, "China's Long - but Uneven - March to Literacy," *The New York Times,* February 12, 2001, https://www.nytimes.com/2001/02/12/news/chinas-long-but-uneven-march-to-liter-

acy.html; "'The Single Greatest Educational Effort in Human History,'" Language Magazine, accessed June 3, 2019, https://www.languagemagazine.com/the-single-greatest-educational-effort-in-human-history/; "Literacy Rate, Adult Total (% of People Ages 15 and Above)," The World Bank, accessed June 3, 2019, https://data.worldbank.org/indicator/SE.ADT.LITR.ZS.

10 "Internet Usage Worldwide - Statistics & Facts," Statista, accessed June 3, 2019, https://www.statista.com/topics/1145/internet-usage-worldwide/.

11 Gaia Vince, "Cities: How Crowded Life is Changing Us," *BBC*, May 17, 2013, https://www.bbc.com/future/article/20130516-how-city-life-is-changing-us.

The Sustainability Industrial Complex

1 "4 Charts Explain Greenhouse Gas Emissions by Countries and Sectors," World Resources Institute, accessed March 1, 2020, https://www.wri.org/blog/2020/02/greenhouse-gas-emissions-by-country-sector.

2 "Dreadlocks in Rastafarianism," Religion Facts, accessed July 1, 2019, http://www.religionfacts.com/rastafarianism/dreadlocks.

3 **Examples of extreme measures taken by Greenpeace**: John Vidal, "Greenpeace Fights Sea Battle With Rival Anti-Whaling Ship," *The Guardian*, January 2, 2006, https://www.theguardian.com/environment/2006/jan/02/whaling.activists; Shaun Walker, "Greenpeace Activists Could Be Charged With Terrorism After Ship Stormed," *The Guardian*, September 20, 2013, https://www.theguardian.com/environment/2013/sep/20/greenpeace-ship-stormed-russian-coastguard; Dan Collyns, "Greenpeace Apologises to People of Peru Over Nazca Lines Stunt," *The Guardian*, December 11, 2014, https://www.theguardian.com/environment/2014/dec/10/peru-press-charges-greenpeace-nazca-lines-stunt.

4 "25 Giant Companies That Are Bigger Than Entire Countries," Business Insider, accessed August 1, 2019, https://www.businessinsider.com/25-giant-companies-that-earn-more-than-entire-countries-2018-7.

5 "Informal Waste Management in China," Collective Responsibility, accessed August 1, 2019, https://www.coresponsibility.com/china-informal-waste-management/.

6 "Amount of Disposed Garbage in China From 1990 to 2018," Statista, accessed September 19, 2019, https://www.statista.com/statistics/279117/amount-of-disposed-garbage-in-china/.

7 Aldo Leopold, *A Sand County Almanac* (Oxford: Oxford University Press, 1949); Rachel Carson, *Silent Spring* (Boston: Houghton Mifflin, 1962).

8 Ibid., Leopold.

9 "Rachel Louise Carson," Pennsylvania Conservation Heritage Project, accessed November 19, 2019, https://paconservationheritage.org/stories/rachel-louise-carson-3/.

10 "Torrey Canyon and the Changes in International Maritime Regulations," MTI Network, accessed December 1, 2019, https://www.mtinetwork.com/torrey-canyon-changes-international-maritime-regulations/.

11 Ibid.

12 David Leonhardt, "The Charts That Show Big Business is Winning," *The New York Times,* June 17, 2018, https://www.nytimes.com/2018/06/17/opinion/big-business-mergers.html.

13 **Corporate mergers**: "History of the RJR Nasisco Takeover," *The New York Times Archive,* December 2, 1988, https://www.nytimes.com/1988/12/02/business/history-of-the-rjr-nabisco-takeover.html; Klaus Ulrich, "Mannesmann: The Mother of All Takeovers," *Deutsche Welle,* February 3, 2010, https://www.dw.com/en/mannesmann-the-mother-of-all-takeovers/a-5206028.

14 Harry Bradford, "These 10 Companies Control Enormous Number Of Consumer Brands [GRAPHIC]," *The Huffington Post,* December 7, 2017, https://www.huffingtonpost.com.au/entry/consumer-brands-owned-ten-companies-graphic_n_1458812?ri18n=true.

15 "Cendant Corporation," CFA Institute, accessed August 28, 2019, https://www.econcrises.org/2016/11/29/cendant-corporation/.

16 Elliot Negin, "Why is ExxonMobil Still Funding Climate Science Denier Groups?" Union of Concerned Scientists, August 31, 2018, https://blog.ucsusa.org/elliott-negin/exxonmobil-still-funding-climate-science-denier-groups.

17 George Hunt, *Toward Self-Sufficiency: A Community for a Transition Period* (Indiana: iUniverse, 2018).

18 Ibid., Union of Concerned Scientists.

19 David Adam, "Exxon to Cut Funding to Climate Change Denial Groups," *The Guardian,* May 28, 2008, https://www.theguardian.com/environment/2008/may/28/climatechange.fossilfuels.

20 Sunil Babu Pant, "Why Grassroots Activists Should Resist Being Professionalised Into An NGO," *The Guardian,* July 7, 2017, https://www.theguardian.com/global-development-professionals-network/2017/jul/07/why-grassroots-activists-should-resist-being-professionalised-into-an-ngo.

21 United Nations Department of Economic and Social Affairs, "Multi-stakeholder Partnerships: Making Them Work for the Post-2015 Development Agenda," https://www.un.org/en/ecosoc/newfunct/pdf15/2015partnerships_background_note.pdf.

22 "Rio +10 and the Privatisation of Sustainable Development," Global Policy Forum, accessed November 1, 2019, https://www.globalpolicy.org/component/content/article/225-general/32234.html.

23 Maya Fehling, Brett D. Nelson, and Sridhar Venkatapuramd, "Limitations of the Millennium Development Goals: a Literature Review," *Global Public Health,* vol. 8, issue 10 (2013): 1109-1122, https://doi.org/10.1080/17441692.2013.845676.

24 Michael Hobbes, "The Millennium Goals Were Bullshit, and That's Okay," *The Huffington Post,* September 10, 2016, https://www.huffpost.com/entry/the-millennium-development-goals-were-bullshit_b_8114410.

25 **On sustainability reporting**: Curtis C. Verschoor, "Sustainability Reporting Increases," *Strategic Finance,* October 1, 2017, https://sfmagazine.com/post-entry/october-2017-sustainability-reporting-increases; "86% of S&P 500 Index® Companies Publish Sustainability / Responsibility Reports in 2018," Sustainability-Reports.com, accessed November 1, 2019, https://www.sustainability-reports.com/86-of-sp-500-index-companies-publish-sustainability-responsibility-reports-in-2018/

26 John Henley, "European Elections: Triumphant Greens Demand More Radical Climate Action," *The Guardian,* May 28, 2019, https://www.theguardian.com/environment/2019/may/28/greens-eu-election-mandate-leverage-climate-policy.

27 "Unpacking the Sustainability Landscape," A.C. Nielsen, accessed November 10, 2019, https://www.nielsen.com/us/en/insights/report/2018/unpacking-the-sustainability-landscape/.

28 "Top FMCGs in Race to Keep Up with Conscious Consumers," Carbon Disclosure Project, accessed December 1, 2019, https://www.cdp.net/en/articles/media/top-fmcgs-in-race-to-keep-up-with-conscious-consumers.

29 "Statistics: China Internet Users," China Internet Watch, accessed May 1, 2020, https://www.chinainternetwatch.com/statistics/china-internet-users/.

30 Ella Chochrek, "China Caught Up With the US on E-Commerce — Then Blew Past It," *Footwear News,* July 30, 2019, https://footwearnews.com/2019/business/retail/china-vs-us-e-commerce-digital-sales-1202809514/.

31 More information on IPE is available at http://wwwen.ipe.org.cn/.

32 "15 Interesting Mobike Statistics and Facts (2020) | By the Numbers," DMR, accessed May 25, 2020, https://expandedramblings.com/index.php/mobike-statistics-facts/.

33 Ben Bland, "China's Robot Revolution," *The Financial Times,* June 6, 2016, https://www.ft.com/content/1dbd8c60-0cc6-11e6-ad80-67655613c2d6.

34 "The Automation of China's Labor Force," China Briefing, accessed April 3, 2020, https://www.china-briefing.com/news/automation-chinas-labor-force.

35 An excellent write up on the history and impact of the 2008 China melamine scandal is available from: Echo Huang, "Ten Years After China's Infant Milk Tragedy, Parents Still Won't Trust Their Babies to Local Formula," Quartz, July 16, 2018, https://qz.com/1323471/ten-years-after-chinas-melamine-laced-infant-milk-tragedy-deep-distrust-remains/.

36 More information on Star Farms is available at https://www.metro.cn/en/metro-food-safety/traceability.

37 "The Wasteful Dragon: Food Loss and Waste in China," Future Directors International, accessed November 10, 2019, http://www.futuredirections.org.au/publication/wasteful-dragon-food-loss-waste-china/.

38 "Look East Instead of West for the Future Global Middle Class," OECD Development Matters, accessed March 1, 2020, https://oecd-development-matters.org/2019/05/07/look-east-instead-of-west-for-the-future-global-middle-class/.

39 Carole-Anne Sénit, "Leaving No One Behind? The Influence of Civil Society Participation on the Sustainable Development Goals," *Politics and Space,* vol. 38, issue 4 (2019): 693-712, https://doi.org/10.1177/2399654419884330.

Point #1: Know What You're Talking About

1 "Why Titanic's First Call for Help Wasn't an SOS Signal," National Geographic, accessed September 10, 2019, https://www.nationalgeographic.com/history/reference/modern-history/why-titanic-first-call-help-not-sos-signal/.

2 "Sustainable Development," OECD Glossary of Statistical Terms, accessed September 12, 2019, https://stats.oecd.org/glossary/detail.asp?ID=2626#.

3 "Corporate Social Responsibility," Investopedia, accessed September 12, 2019, https://www.investopedia.com/terms/c/corp-social-responsibility.asp.

4 "Environmentalism," Merriam-Webster Dictionary, accessed September 12, 2019, https://www.merriam-webster.com/dictionary/environmentalism.

5 "ESG Definition," Robeco, accessed September 12, 2019, https://www.robeco.com/en/key-strengths/sustainable-investing/glossary/esg-definition.html.

6 "What is Carrying Capacity?" GDRC, accessed September 12, 2019, https://www.gdrc.org/uem/footprints/carrying-capacity.html.

7 "World Population Prospects," United Nations Department of Economic and Social Affairs, accessed September 20, 2019, https://population.un.org/wpp/Graphs/Probabilistic/POP/TOT/.

8 "What are the Sustainable Development Goals?" United Nations Development Programme, accessed September 10, 2019, https://www.undp.org/content/undp/en/home/sustainable-development-goals.html.

9 **On passing the two degree Celsius mark**: "'Terrifying' New Climate Models Warn of 6-7°C of Warming by 2100 If Emissions Not Slashed," Common Dreams, accessed September 20, 2019, https://www.common-dreams.org/news/2019/09/17/terrifying-new-climate-models-warn-6-7degc-warming-2100-if-emissions-not-slashed#; "Earth Likely to Warm More Than Two Degrees This Century," University of Washington, accessed September 20, 2019, https://www.washington.edu/news/2017/07/31/earth-likely-to-warm-more-than-2-degrees-this-century/.

10 **On international protocols**: For more information, including lengthy analyses of each protocol, refer to https://sustainabledevelopment.un.org/frameworks.

11 "History of UN Climate Talks," Center for Climate and Energy Solutions, accessed September 20, 2019, https://www.c2es.org/content/history-of-un-climate-talks/.

12 **The global scientific consensus on climate change**: "Scientific Consensus: Earth's Climate is Warming," NASA, accessed September 20, 2019, https://climate.nasa.gov/scientific-consensus/; "The 97% Consensus on Global Warming," Skeptical Science, accessed September 20, 2019, https://skepticalscience.com/global-warming-scientific-consensus.htm.

13 **On global temperature rise**: "The Last Five Years Were the Hottest Ever Recorded," National Geographic, accessed August 1, 2019, https://www.nationalgeographic.com/environment/2019/02/2018-fourth-warmest-year-ever-noaa-nasa-reports/; Graham Redfearn, Australia Records Its Hottest Day Ever – One Day After Previous Record, *The Guardian,* December 19, 2019, https://www.theguardian.com/australia-news/2019/dec/19/419c-australia-records-hottest-ever-day-one-day-after-previous-record.

14 **On recyclables not making it where you think they do**: There's an oft-cited waste ratio of 3 percent household to 97 percent industrial that's been promoted as a general guideline for several decades. While it's not perfect, it does begin to show the disparity between the two segments. For a full analysis on this, please refer to Samantha MacBride, *Recycling Reconsidered: The Present Failure and Future Promise of Environmental Action in the United States* (Boston: The MIT Press, 2014).

15 For more information on the Basel convention, please refer to http://www.basel.int/.

16 "Veolia Environnement," Fortune Global 500, accessed January 3, 2020, https://fortune.com/global500/2019/veolia-environnement/.

17 "A Whopping 91% of Plastic Isn't Recycled," National Geographic, accessed September 20, 2019, https://www.nationalgeographic.com/news/2017/07/plastic-produced-recycling-waste-ocean-trash-debris-environment/.

18 Jeff Sparrow, "Recycling: How Corporate Australia Played Us for Mugs," *The Guardian,* July 18, 2018, https://www.theguardian.com/environment/commentisfree/2018/jul/19/its-not-recycling-its-collecting-how-australians-were-sucked-into-the-crisis.

19 "World Population Growth," Our World in Data, accessed August 3, 2019, https://ourworldindata.org/world-population-growth.

20 The Wachowski Brothers, directors. *The Matrix.* Warner Bros. and Village Roadshow Pictures, 1999.

21 **On having fewer children**: Seth Wynes and Kimberly A. Nicholas, "The Climate Mitigation Gap: Education and Government Recommendations Miss the Most Effective Individual Actions," *IOP Publishing* (2017), https://doi.org/10.1088/1748-9326/aa7541.

22 Water and textiles: "How Many Gallons of Water Does it Take to Make a Single Pair of Jeans?" The Fashion Law, accessed August 1, 2019, https://www.thefashionlaw.com/how-many-gallons-of-water-does-it-take-to-make-a-single-pair-of-jeans/; Kathleen Webber, "How Fast Fashion Is Killing Rivers Worldwide," *EcoWatch,* May 22, 2017, https://www.ecowatch.com/fast-fashion-riverblue-2318389169.html.

23 **On China's sustainability achievements**: Liam Kelly, "China to Invest $360 billion in Green Energy by 2020 to Reduce Pollution," *Newsweek,* January 5, 2017, https://www.newsweek.com/china-invest-360-billion-green-energy-2020-reduce-pollution-538844; Charlie Campbell, "China Is Bankrolling Green Energy Projects Around the World," *Time,* November 1, 2019, https://time.com/5714267/china-green-energy/; Alfred Schipke, ed. *The*

Future of China's Bond Market (Washington D.C.: International Monetary Fund, 2019); "Shenzhen's Transition to the World's Largest Fully-Electric Fleet," Intelligent Transport, accessed January 2, 2020, https://www.intelligenttransport.com/transport-articles/96209/shenzhens-transition-to-the-worlds-largest-fully-electric-fleet/.

24 "Full Text of Xi Jinping Keynote at the World Economic Forum," *CGTN*, January 17, 2017, https://america.cgtn.com/2017/01/17/full-text-of-xi-jinping-keynote-at-the-world-economic-forum.

25 "Greenwashing," Investopedia, accessed September 1, 2019, https://www.investopedia.com/terms/g/greenwashing.asp.

26 **On water use in hotels**: "Hotel Water Use: Are You Flushing Money Down the Drain?" Environment and Energy Leader, accessed May 1, 2019, https://www.environmentalleader.com/2016/07/hotel-water-use-are-you-flushing-money-down-the-drain/; "A truly clean matter – Steps toward eco-friendly laundry in hotels," Green Pearls, accessed May 1, 2019, https://www.greenpearls.com/newsroom/a-truly-clean-matter-steps-toward-eco-friendly-laundry-in-hotels/.

27 "Implementing a Linen and Towel Reuse Program," Guest Supply, accessed May 1, 2019, http://thesolutionsdesk.com/implementing-a-linen-and-towel-reuse-program/.

28 **On corporate greenwashing**: Bruce Watson, "The Troubling Evolution of Corporate Greenwashing," *The Guardian*, August 20, 2016, https://www.theguardian.com/sustainable-business/2016/aug/20/greenwashing-environmentalism-lies-companies; "Greenwashing Costing Walmart $1 Million," Environment and Energy Leader, accessed May 1, 2019, https://www.environmentalleader.com/2017/02/greenwashing-costing-walmart-1-million/; "Everything You Need to Know About the VW Diesel-Emissions Scandal," Car and Driver, accessed May 1, 2019, https://www.caranddriver.com/news/a15339250/everything-you-need-to-know-about-the-vw-diesel-emissions-scandal/.

29 "More Than Values: The Value-Based Sustainability Reporting That Investors Want," McKinsey, accessed December 1, 2019, https://www.mckinsey.com/business-functions/sustainability/our-insights/more-than-values-the-value-based-sustainability-reporting-that-investors-want.

30 Ibid., "Greenwashing," Investopedia.

31 Emma Bowman and Sarah McCammon, "Can Fast Fashion And Sustainability Be Stitched Together?" *NPR*, July 27, 2019, https://www.npr.org/2019/07/27/745418569/can-fast-fashion-and-sustainability-be-stitched-together.

32 "Fast Fashion's 'Sustainability' Endeavors Need to be About More Than Fabrics, Recycling," The Fashion Law, accessed September 20, 2019, https://www.thefashionlaw.com/fast-fashion-sustainability-is-about-more-than-the-fabrics/.

33 "Zara Announces Sustainability Initiatives — But What About Its Factory Workers?" Refinery29, accessed September 20, 2019, https://www.refinery29.com/en-gb/zara-sustainable-initiatives.

34 Christina Caron, "Starbucks to Stop Using Disposable Plastic Straws by 2020," The New York Times, July 9, 2018, https://www.nytimes.com/2018/07/09/business/starbucks-plastic-straws.html.

35 Christian Britschgi, "Starbucks Bans Plastic Straws, Winds Up Using More Plastic," Reason, December 7, 2018, https://reason.com/2018/07/12/starbucks-straw-ban-will-see-the-company/.

36 "Reynolds American Deceives Consumers by Marketing American Spirit Cigarettes As 'Eco Friendly,'" Campaign for Tobacco-Free Kids, accessed September 30, 2019, https://www.tobaccofreekids.org/press-releases/2011_07_25_reynolds.

37 Ibid.

38 Futerra and BSR, "Selling Sustainability: Primer for Marketers," October 2015, https://www.wearefuterra.com/wp-content/uploads/2015/10/FuterraBSR_SellingSustainability2015.pdf.

Point #2: You Can Do Anything (But You Can't Do Everything)

1 "Nielsen Numbers for Television Viewing Time Since 1949 (Nielsen)," Joshua Spodek, accessed January 12, 2020, https://joshuaspodek.com/americans-disciplined-lot/americans_tv.

2 **On World Vision's donations**: "Our Work," World Vision International, accessed January 12, 2020, https://www.wvi.org/.

3 **Andrew Geoghegan and Foreign Correspondent**: "World Vision International," Wikipedia, accessed January 12, 2020, https://en.wikipedia.org/wiki/World_Vision_International.

4 **World Vision's response**: "World Vision Response to Foreign Correspondent Story From Ethiopia Broadcast on 25 November 2008," Foreign Correspondent, accessed January 13, 2020, https://web.archive.org/web/20081208114321/http://www.abc.net.au/foreign/World_Vision_Response.htm.

5 **On major contemporary appeal campaigns**: "Making a Smash," The Chicago Tribune, April 14, 2008, https://www.chicagotribune.com/news/ct-

xpm-2008-04-14-0804140385-story.html; David Daniel, "Celebrity Telethon to Raise Money for Haiti Efforts," *CNN,* January 15, 2010, https://edition.cnn.com/2010/WORLD/americas/01/14/haiti.quake.george.clooney/; Isabella Kwai, "Donations are Pouring Into Australia. Now What?" *The New York Times,* January 18, 2020, https://www.nytimes.com/2020/01/18/world/australia/fires-donations-help.html.

6 Jia Jiang, *Rejection Proof: How I Beat Fear and Became Invincible Through 100 Days of Rejection* (New York: Harmony, 2015).

7 William Leith "Say No and Change Your Life," *The Guardian,* March 18, 2018, https://www.theguardian.com/global/2018/mar/18/the-power-of-saying-no-change-your-life-psychology-william-leith.

8 James 2:10 KJV.

9 Drake Baer, "Dwight Eisenhower Nailed a Major Insight About Productivity," *Business Insider,* April 11, 2014, https://www.businessinsider.com/dwight-eisenhower-nailed-a-major-insight-about-productivity-2014-4.

10 Malcolm Gladwell, *Outliers: The Story of Success* (New York: Back Bay Books, 2011).

11 J. Philippe Rushton, Roland D. Chrisjohn, and G. Cynthia Fekken, "The Altruistic Personality and the Self-Report Altruism Scale," *Personality and Individual Differences,* vol. 2, issue 4 (1981): 293-302, https://doi.org/10.1016/0191-8869(81)90084-2.

12 Roger Fisher, William L. Ury, and Bruce Patton, *Getting to Yes: Negotiating Agreement Without Giving In* (London: Penguin Books, revised 1991).

13 Ibid., page 40.

Point #3: Don't Be a Dick

1 "Value of Volunteer Time," Independent Sector, accessed February 1, 2020, https://independentsector.org/value-of-volunteer-time-2018/.

2 **On development aid to Africa**: OECD, "Development Aid at a Glance: Africa," 2019, https://www.oecd.org/dac/financing-sustainable-development/development-finance-data/Africa-Development-Aid-at-a-Glance-2019.pdf; Mark Anderson, "Foreign Aid Close to Record Peak After Donors Spend $135bn in 2014," *The Guardian,* April 8, 2015, https://www.theguardian.com/global-development/2015/apr/08/foreign-aid-spending-2014-least-developed-countries.

3 **On NGO registration**: "Non-Governmental Organizations in the United States," U.S. Department of State," accessed February 3, 2020,

https://www.state.gov/non-governmental-organizations-ngos-in-the-united-states/; "Facts and Stats About NGOs Worldwide," Non-Profit Action, accessed February 3, 2020, http://nonprofitaction.org/2015/09/facts-and-stats-about-ngos-worldwide/.

4 Ibid., Non-Profit Action.

5 "Bad Aid: Should All NGOs Close Down?" Hominibus, accessed February 1, 2020, https://hominibus.asia/southeast-asia/transnational-issues/bad-aid-should-all-ngos-close-down/.

6 Fabiana Sciarelli and Azzurra Rinaldi, *Development Management of Transforming Economies: Theories, Approaches and Models for Overall Development* (New York: Springer, 2016), 151.

7 Laeta Kalogridis, creator. *Altered Carbon.* Mythology Entertainment and Skydance Television, 2018-present.

8 Genesis 5:21-27 New Revised Standard Version.

9 "Dhaka, Bangladesh Metro Area Population 1950-2020," Macrotrends, accessed February 3, 2020, https://www.macrotrends.net/cities/20119/dhaka/population.

10 Tim McDonnell, "Climate Change Creates a New Migration Crisis for Bangladesh," *National Geographic,* January 24, 2019, https://www.nationalgeographic.com/environment/2019/01/climate-change-drives-migration-crisis-in-bangladesh-from-dhaka-sundabans/.

11 Adam Minter, *Junkyard Planet: Travels in the Billion-Dollar Trash Trade* (London: Bloomsbury Press, 2013).

12 David Carrig, "The US Used To Ship 4,000 Recyclable Containers A Day To China. Where Will The Banned Trash Go Now?" *USA Today,* June 21, 2018, https://www.usatoday.com/story/news/nation-now/2018/06/21/china-ban-plastic-waste-recycling/721879002/.

13 Christopher Joyce, "Where Will Your Plastic Trash Go Now That China Doesn't Want It?" *NPR,* March 13, 2019, https://www.npr.org/sections/goatsandsoda/2019/03/13/702501726/where-will-your-plastic-trash-go-now-that-china-doesnt-want-it.

14 Adam Minter, "How China Profits from Our Junk," *The Atlantic,* November 1, 2013, https://www.theatlantic.com/china/archive/2013/11/how-china-profits-from-our-junk/281044/.

15 **On China's recycling ban**: James Hataway, "Scientists Calculate Impact of China's Ban on Plastic Waste Imports," *University of Georgia UGA Today,* June 20, 2018, https://news.uga.edu/scientists-calculate-impact-of-chinas-ban-on-plastic-waste-imports/.

16 **On corporations and the environment**: For more information on the history and current state of the BP Deepwater Horizon oil spill, read: Alejandra Borunda, "We Still Don't Know the Full Impacts of the BP Oil Spill, 10 Years Later," *National Geographic*, April 20, 2020, https://www.nationalgeo-graphic.com/science/2020/04/bp-oil-spill-still-dont-know-effects-decade-later/; more information on tobacco-related deaths is available from the Centers for Disease Control and Prevention Smoking & Tobacco Use Fast Facts as well as the World Health Organization's Tobacco Key Facts; finally, if you're looking for a list of the world's least sustainable companies, you're not going to find one. But, a quick browser search can definitely help you determine which companies are doing well, and which aren't.

17 Jacob Riis was a social reformer and muckraker working in the United States in the early 20th century. Much of his work focused on the plight of workers in the impoverished Lower East Side of Manhattan. He also used his photographic skills to document things like child labor, unsavory workplace conditions, and government corruption. His seminal work, *How the Other Half Lives: Studies Among the Tenements of New York*, brought to light many of the social issues of the day and began a period of national reform.

18 **Corporations as bad stewards of the environment**: Brian Merchant, "Life and Death in Apple's Forbidden City," *The Guardian*, June 18, 2017, https://www.theguardian.com/technology/2017/jun/18/foxconn-life-death-forbidden-city-longhua-suicide-apple-iphone-brian-merchant-one-device-ex-tract; "The Rana Plaza Accident and Its Aftermath," The International Labour Organization, accessed February 2, 2020, http://www.oit.org/global/topics/geip/WCMS_614394/lang--en/index.htm; "Adani's Carmichael Coal Mine and Health Fact Sheet," Doctors for the Environment, Australia, accessed March 3, 2020, file:///Users/la/Downloads/19_attach1.pdf.

19 "Frequently Asked Questions," U.S. Small Business Administration, accessed February 2, 2020, https://www.sba.gov/sites/default/files/FAQ_Sept_2012.pdf.

20 **Walmart's worker betterment programs**: For more information on the Women in Factories Program, including performance metrics, please refer to the Program's website at https://www.bsr.org/en/collaboration/groups/women-in-factories-china-program.

21 **Thermopylae**: A great synopsis is available by Mark Cartwright at "Battle of Thermopylae," Ancient History Encyclopedia, https://www.ancient.eu/thermopylae/.

22 Zack Snyder, director. *300*. Warner Bros., Legendary Entertainment, and Virtual Studios, 2007.

23 "Battle of Dunkirk," History, accessed December 12, 2019, https://www.history.com/topics/world-war-ii/dunkirk.

24 "The World's Decision to Fix the Ozone Hole is Paying Off 30 Years Later," The Verge, accessed December 14, 2019, https://www.theverge.com/2016/6/30/12067830/ozone-hole-antarctica-healing-study.

25 "Life Under the Ozone Hole," *Newsweek*, December 8, 1991, https://www.newsweek.com/life-under-ozone-hole-201054.

Point #4: Be a Pragmatic Altruist

1 **On the Australian bushfire crisis**: Amy Remeikis, "Where the Bloody Hell Was He? How Scott Morrison Spent the Past Week of the Bushfire Crisis," *The Guardian,* January 3, 2020, https://www.theguardian.com/australia-news/2020/jan/03/where-the-bloody-hell-was-he-how-scott-morrison-spent-the-past-week-of-the-bushfire-crisis; "Australian Climate Change 'Sceptics' Mislead the Public About Bushfires," London School of Economics, accessed February 2, 2020, http://www.lse.ac.uk/GranthamInstitute/news/australian-climate-change-sceptics-mislead-the-public-about-bushfires/; "1 Billion Animals Killed in Australian Bushfires," The Wildlife Society, accessed February 2, 2020, https://wildlife.org/1-billion-animals-killed-in-australian-bushfires/.

2 While many attribute these words directly to Carrol's writing, they don't appear as such in *Alice in Wonderland*. The actual exchange is a bit different. "'Would you tell me, please, which way I ought to go from here?' 'That depends a good deal on where you want to get to,' said the Cat. 'I don't much care where…' said Alice. 'Then it doesn't matter which way you go,' said the Cat. '…so long as I get SOMEWHERE,' Alice added as an explanation. 'Oh, you're sure to do that,' said the Cat, 'if you only walk long enough.'"

3 "Pragmatic," The Cambridge Dictionary, accessed June 1, 2020, https://dictionary.cambridge.org/dictionary/english/pragmatic.

4 Mark Manson, *Everything is F*cked: A Book About Hope* (New York: Harper, 2019).

5 **Cause marketing**: There are numerous examples of strong cause marketing campaigns, some of which we'll get to later in the book. If you're looking for extra credit, check out the following campaigns: "The Best Men Can Be" by Gillette; "Rang-Tan" by Iceland Supermarkets; and, "Don't Buy This Jacket" by Patagonia.

6   James C. Davis, *The Human Story* (New York: Harper, 2005).

7   Ibid., 70.

8   **Introduction of invasive species to Australia**: "Rabbits Introduced," National Museum of Australia, accessed December 20, 2020, https://www.nma.gov.au/defining-moments/resources/rabbits-introduced; Phil Mercer, "The Rapid Spread of Australia's Cane Toad Pests," *BBC*, March 22, 2017, https://www.bbc.com/news/world-australia-39348313.

9   Christopher J. Coyne and Abigail R. Hall, "Four Decades and Counting: The Continued Failure of the War on Drugs," Cato Institute, https://www.cato.org/publications/policy-analysis/four-decades-counting-continued-failure-war-drugs.

10 Emily Andrews and Chloe Kerr, "Heir Heads," *The Scottish Sun*, August 14, 2019, https://www.thescottishsun.co.uk/fabulous/4605992/eco-warrior-prince-harry-slammed-for-flying-meghan-markle-to-ibiza-in-private-jet-with-massive-carbon-footprint/.

11 Madeline Kearns, "Royals, Climate Change, and Private Jets," *National Review*, August 19, 2019, https://www.nationalreview.com/corner/royals-climate-change-and-private-jets/.

12 **On PETA's marketing campaigns**: "Peta Ad Accused of Violating Dignity of Holocaust Victims," Campaign, accessed September 12, 2019, https://www.campaignlive.co.uk/article/peta-ad-accused-violating-dignity-holocaust-victims/205616; Drake Baer and Ivan De Luce, "18 Times PETA Ads Have Used Nudity, Gore, and Sacrilege to Get Your Attention," *Business Insider*, July 25, 2019, https://www.businessinsider.com/17-shocking-peta-advertisements-2014-9.

13 Renata Bongiorno, Paul G. Bain, and Nick Haslam, "When Sex Doesn't Sell: Using Sexualized Images of Women Reduces Support for Ethical Campaigns," *Plos One*, December 18, 2013: https://doi.org/10.1371/journal.pone.0083311.

14 "Idealization," Oxford Reference, accessed September 15, 2019, https://www.oxfordreference.com/view/10.1093/oi/authority.20110803095956542.

15 Shannon Molloy, "Extinction Rebellion Climate Change Protests Doing 'More Harm Than Good,'" *news.com.au*, October 9, 2019, https://www.news.com.au/technology/environment/climate-change/extinction-rebellion-climate-change-protests-doing-more-harm-than-good/news-story/a07617ee3ba5b2f8ace3c9c910802df2.

16 Eliza Barclay and Brian Resnick, "How Big Was the Global Climate Strike? 4 Million People, Activists Estimate," *Vox*, September 22, 2019, https://www.vox.com/energy-and-environment/2019/9/20/20876143/climate-strike-2019-september-20-crowd-estimate.

17 Jenny Hughes, "Macron Criticizes "Radical Positions" of Greta Thunberg, and Also Poland," *Frenchly*, September 25, 2019, https://frenchly.us/macron-criticizes-radical-positions-of-greta-thunberg-and-also-poland/.

18 For more on Boyan Slat and The Ocean Cleanup, check out their website at https://theoceancleanup.com/.

Point #5: Don't Try. Do.

1 **On DrumNet and Kenyan agriculture**: For those interested, the full and tragic story of DrumNet is available from the World Bank. Nava Ashraf, Xavier Giné, and Dean Karlan, *Finding Missing Markets (and a Disturbing Epilogue): Evidence from an Export Crop Adoption and Intervention in Kenya* (The World Bank Development Research Group: Washington, D.C., 2008).

2 For more information on EurepGap, and its modern incarnation GLOBAL G.A.P., please see https://www.globalgap.org/uk_en/who-we-are/about-us/history/.

3 Robert D. Lupton, *Toxic Charity: How Churches and Charities Hurt Those They Help (And How to Reverse It)* (New York: Harper One, 2012).

4 Christophe N. Bredillet, Janice Thomas, and Jacob Musila, eds., *Managing Projects in Africa: Essentials from the Project Management Journal* (Hoboken: Wiley, 2013), 207.

5 **Tom's Shoes**: More information is available at https://www.toms.com/.

6 **50 Cent's campaign (and other philanthropy blunders)**: Richard Stupart, "7 Worst International Aid Ideas," *Matador Network*, February 20, 2012, https://matadornetwork.com/change/7-worst-international-aid-ideas/.

7 Ibid.

8 Karen McVeigh, "Ed Sheeran Comic Relief Film Branded 'Poverty Porn' by Aid Watchdog," *The Guardian*, December 4, 2017, https://www.theguardian.com/global-development/2017/dec/04/ed-sheeran-comic-relief-film-poverty-porn-aid-watchdog-tom-hardy-eddie-redmayne.

9 Ibid, *Matador Network*.

10 **On multinational/governmental failures**: Lydia Polgreen, "World Bank Ends Effort to Help Chad Ease Poverty," *The New York Times*, September 10, 2008, https://www.nytimes.com/2008/09/11/world/africa/11chad.html;

"SCA Issues Arrest Warrant for Former Exec of Lesotho Highlands Project," Eyewitness News, accessed January 14, 2020, https://ewn.co.za/2019/06/04/appeal-court-issues-warrant-for-former-exec-of-lesotho-highlands-project; "Reversing the failures of Roll Back Malaria," The Lancet, accessed January 14, 2020, https://www.thelancet.com/journals/lancet/article/PIIS0140-6736(05)66391-X/fulltext?code=lancet-site.

11 Eric Bellman, "Epic Fail: Tech Tricks Are No Fix for Developing-World Problems," *The Wall Street Journal*, September 4, 2015, https://blogs.wsj.com/indiarealtime/2015/09/04/epic-fail-tech-tricks-are-no-fix-for-developing-world-problems/.

12 Jacob Kushner and Tom Murphy, "The World Bank's Water Failure in Tanzania," *The World*, November 24, 2014, https://www.pri.org/stories/2014-11-24/world-banks-water-failure-tanzania.

13 More information is available at https://ironox.com/.

14 **AID:Tech**: The case studies available all point to the success of the project in being rolled out to about 100 Syrian refugee families in Lebanon. Each family received approximately US$100 in digital currency to use. Consider, though, that there are 1.5 million Syrian refugees in Lebanon, the highest per capita rate in the world. Clearly, the program is not scalable in its current state. More information is available at http://media.ifrc.org/innovation/2017/01/04/using-blockchain-technology-to-assist-refugees-in-lebanon/.

15 More information is available at https://www.vollie.com.au/.

16 "Seven Deadly Nonprofit Marketing Budget Sins: Part One," Prosper Strategies, accessed February 3, 2020, https://prosper-strategies.com/nonprofit-marketing-budget-part-one/.

17 "Nonprofits Fail – Here's Seven Reasons Why," NANOE, accessed February 3, 2020, https://nanoe.org/nonprofits-fail/.

18 Joe Pinsker, "'Ugh, I'm So Busy': A Status Symbol for Our Time," *The Atlantic*, March 1, 2017, https://www.theatlantic.com/business/archive/2017/03/busyness-status-symbol/518178/.

19 Abigail Hess, "24 Percent of American Adults Haven't Read A Book in the Past Year—Here's Why," *CNBC*, January 29, 2019, https://www.cnbc.com/2019/01/29/24-percent-of-american-adults-havent-read-a-book-in-the-past-year--heres-why-.html.

20 Jane Arsenault, "What Are Some Examples of 'Toxic Philanthropy'?" Quora, December 18, 2018, https://www.quora.com/What-are-some-examples-of-toxic-philanthropy.

21 "The Dangers of Comparing Yourself to Others on Social Media," AllPsych, accessed February 1, 2020, https://blog.allpsych.com/the-dangers-of-comparing-yourself-to-others-on-social-media/.

Agree to Disagree?

1 Bobby Duffy, *The Perils of Perception: Why We're Wrong About Nearly Everything* (London: Atlantic Books, 2018), vi-vii.

2 Kelly McSweeny, "This is Your Brain on Instagram: Effects of Social Media on the Brain," *Now*, March 17, 2019, https://now.northropgrumman.com/this-is-your-brain-on-instagram-effects-of-social-media-on-the-brain/.

3 Tim Dwyer, "FactCheck: Is Australia's Level of Media Ownership Concentration One of the Highest in the World?" *The Conversation*, December 12, 2016, https://theconversation.com/factcheck-is-australias-level-of-media-ownership-concentration-one-of-the-highest-in-the-world-68437.

4 **On NewsCorp climate headlines**: During the Australian bushfire crisis of late 2019/early 2020, NewsCorp-owned papers circulated various pieces which many deemed irresponsible reporting. For a full run-down of these, and other claims, read *Carbon Brief's* excellent January 7, 2020 analysis "Media Reaction: Australia's Bushfires and Climate Change."

5 **On CNN's questionable reporting**: John Greenberg, "CNN's Don Lemon Says Automatic Weapons Are Easy to Get," *Politifact*, August 26, 2014, https://www.politifact.com/factchecks/2014/aug/26/don-lemon/cnns-lemon-says-automatic-weapons-are-easy-get/. Colby Itkowitz, "CNN: Islamic State Uses Nutella and Kittens to Entice Female Recruits," *The Washington Post*, February 19, 2015, https://www.washingtonpost.com/blogs/in-the-loop/wp/2015/02/18/cnn-islamic-state-uses-nutella-and-kittens-to-entice-female-recruits/; Louis Jacobson, "Van Jones Says Just 1 Percent of NRA-Endorsed Candidates Won in 2012," *Politifact*, September 17, 2013, https://www.politifact.com/factchecks/2013/sep/17/van-jones/van-jones-says-just-1-percent-nra-endorsed-candida/.

6 "Media Bias Ratings," AllSides, accessed June 1, 2020, https://www.allsides.com/media-bias/media-bias-ratings.

7 Paulo Coelho (@paulocoelho), "be arrogant with arrogant people, this is the only language they respect—as they confound kindness with weakness," Twitter, January 18, 2015, https://twitter.com/paulocoelho/status/556797209623416833?lang=en.

8 **The American disbelief in climate change**: "Americans Underestimate How Many Others in the U.S. Think Global Warming is Happening,"

Yale Program on Climate Change Communication, accessed March 15, 2020, https://climatecommunication.yale.edu/publications/americans-underestimate-how-many-others-in-the-u-s-think-global-warming-is-happening/; Oliver Milman, "US is hotbed of climate change denial, major global survey finds," *The Guardian*, May 8, 2019; "Americans on Climate Change," Climate Chat, accessed March 15, 2020, http://www.theclimatechat.org/americans-on-climate-change.

9 **The global disbelief in climate change**: "A Look at How People Around the World View Climate Change," Pew Research Center, accessed March 15, 2020, https://www.pewresearch.org/fact-tank/2019/04/18/a-look-at-how-people-around-the-world-view-climate-change/; "Concern About Climate Change and its Consequences," Pew Research Center, accessed March 15, 2020, https://www.pewresearch.org/global/2015/11/05/1-concern-about-climate-change-and-its-consequences/.

10 **On species extinction**: "The Faces of Extinction: The Species We Lost in 2019," The Revelator, accessed March 15, 2020, https://therevelator.org/extinction-species-lost-2019/; "Extinction Over Time," The Smithsonian, accessed March 15, 2020, https://naturalhistory.si.edu/education/teaching-resources/paleontology/extinction-over-time.

11 **On the dystopian present**: "Air Pollution," World Health Organization, accessed March 15, 2020, https://www.who.int/health-topics/air-pollution; "Sea Level Change: Observations from Space," NASA, accessed March 15, 2020, https://sealevel.nasa.gov/faq/13/how-long-have-sea-levels-been-rising-how-does-recent-sea-level-rise-compare-to-that-over-the-previous/; "The Canary in the Coal Mine," The World Counts, accessed March 15, 2020, https://www.theworldcounts.com/stories/Ice-Cap-Melting-Facts.

Afterword

1 **$500 billion annually**: World Economic Forum, "Outbreak Readiness and Business Impact," January 2019, http://www3.weforum.org/docs/WEF%20HGHI_Outbreak_Readiness_Business_Impact.pdf.

2 **On Chinese tourism**: Kate Springer, "Tourism Industry Hit Hard as Chinese Tourists Stay Home," *CNN*, February 3, 2020, https://edition.cnn.com/travel/article/wuhan-coronavirus-tourism-impact/index.html.

3 **32 million international tourists**: "China Tourist Arrivals," Trading Economics, accessed June 1, 2020, https://tradingeconomics.com/china/tourist-arrivals.

4 **324,000 pounds of coal burned**: I did the calculations myself based on British Airways' official route schedule prior to the shutdown. Now, calculating total carbon emissions for individual flights can be tricky. You've got to take into account the total number of passengers as well as which cabin they're in. So, consider this a very rough estimate. Plugging the numbers into the handy Flight Carbon Footprint Calculator, a round-trip from London to Shanghai gives us approximately 2.77 metric tons of CO_2 per person. Multiply that by the average load of 175 passengers and you get 484.75 metric tons of CO_2 for the return flight. Using the EPA's Greenhouse Gas Equivalencies Calculator, you can see that's the same as 533,302 pounds of coal burned. It's also equal in CO_2 emissions to 54,462 gallons of gas consumed, 60 homes' energy use for a year, or 61,725,596 smartphones charging.

5 **CREA report**: Lauri Myllyvirta, "Analysis: Coronavirus Temporarily Reduced China's CO_2 Emissions by a Quarter," *Carbon Brief*, February 19, 2020, https://www.carbonbrief.org/analysis-coronavirus-has-temporarily-reduced-chinas-co2-emissions-by-a-quarter.

6 **"good quality air days"**: Rebecca Wright, "There's An Unlikely Beneficiary of Coronavirus: The Environment," *CNN*, March, 17, 2020, https://edition.cnn.com/2020/03/16/asia/china-pollution-coronavirus-hnk-intl/index.html.

If you enjoyed reading *Sustainability for the Rest of Us*, please take the time to show it some love on social media, your favorite online retailer or bookstore, and by spreading the word to family, friends, and especially those who we need to bring onside in our fight for a better tomorrow.

Thank you.

Lightning Source UK Ltd.
Milton Keynes UK
UKHW022206140621
385503UK00008B/1248